Understanding the Music Business:

A Comprehensive View

Fifth Edition

First Printing

Written and Edited by

Irwin Steinberg

and Harmon Greenblatt

Printing History
Fifth edition, first printing, July 2009
Fourth edition, second printing, June 2008
Third edition, first printing, August 2007
Third editions, fourth printing, September 2005
Third edition, September 2003
Second edition, September 2001
First edition, September 1997
Printed in the United States of America

ISBN 978-1-60801-004-2

http://unopress.uno.edu

TABLE OF CONTENTS

EDITOR'S NOTE TO THE 5th EDITION

Welcome to the 5th Edition of *Understanding the Music Business: A Comprehensive View.* In this edition we have tried to bring all of the many changes that are affecting the industry into the text. Of course, with any book that tries to stop time, this is an impossible task. But we hope that this edition makes it possible for anyone interested in the music industry to gain an increased knowledge of how the business works and the many opportunities and threats that are part of its everyday life.

This is a unique book, unlike other music business texts. We do not deal with only the legal aspects of the business, and we don't treat our book as "How to protect the artist from being mistreated by the recording industry," as so many other texts do. Instead, we break down the recording industry into its component parts and explain how each of them works. Like any other for-profit business, the goal of the music business is to make money. So when decisions in the music business are made to maximize profits, readers need understand the rationale for those decisions. That is the goal of this book.

In this 5th edition, we have incorporated several additions which we think will benefit the reader:
1. There is an updated chapter on the role of the technology manager.
2. At the end of many chapters is a section called "The Music Business in Action" that gives illustrations of current developments in the music business.
3. We will continue Music Business Updates (MBU's), designed to keep readers on new developments since the publishing of the book. When you purchase this book, you also get permission to access the MBU's. See the last page of this book for details.

Your comments on the book and the MBU's are always welcome.

The preparation of this book would not have been possible without the help of my graduate assistants, in particular, Ashley Chavis, who has been instrumental in putting the pieces of this book together. I also want to thank Fran Ruffalo for her help in proof reading and editing.

Enjoy *Understanding the Music Business.* We hope you find it entertaining, enlightening, and the best book on the subject ever.

Harmon Greenblatt, Editor
Director, Graduate Program in
Arts Administration
University of New Orleans
New Orleans, Louisiana

PREFACE TO THE 5th EDITION

In the process of teaching a graduate course entitled "Decision Making in the Music Business," in the Management Department at Columbia College Chicago, I came to believe that a more comprehensive text was needed for both learning and teaching. This became more evident with the sensational growth in music business courses at hundreds of colleges, the growth of which correlated with a global $40 billion recorded music industry.

This book is intended as a text for courses in this growing field and is written both by the editors and a selected group of writers, each writing out of their very current and active experience. Every chapter thus strives to be insightful and relevant, and promotes reflection and Socratic discussion. The chapter subjects and related authors combine teachability, clarity and thoughtful provocation in an adroit way. The chapter on recording contracts, for example, is arranged to reflect surrounding controversy and the strengths and weaknesses of alternative positions.

I have had the outline for this text for many years, and it might have remained in that form had not Harmon Greenblatt, who had been teaching in this subject area at the University of Hartford's Hartt School, joined me. Harmon is now the Director of the Graduate Program in Arts Administration at the University of New Orleans, and has worked with me again on this 4th edition. We have not addressed every important question in the music business nor have we presented every point of view. However, the essentials are here to be augmented by teacher and pupil alike.

As you might expect in an industry where change seems to have become part and parcel of the industry's fabric, events have not stood still since the publication of our last edition in 2007; there are many new developments that have occurred in that short time. With that in mind, you will find a digest of update notes and a new preface that we hope students and instructors alike will find useful.

Acknowledgements

My special appreciation is owed to the late president of Columbia College, Mirron Alexandroff; Dr. Lya Rosenblum; and Fred Fine, who in 1982 convinced me to take my years in the music business to the classroom, and arranged special scheduling so that I could continue my work while traveling between offices in New York and Chicago.

My thanks also to Columbia College Colleagues Dennis Rich, Carol Yamamoto, Phyllis Johnson, and Chuck Suber. And to Debra Hale who supervised our course-related in-house student-run record company, and who copyedited past editions of this book, my gratitude. My gratitude is additionally extended to the contributors to this book, whose names and backgrounds are separately listed preceding the index.

Finally, my appreciation to my wife, Dr. Dominique Moyse Steinberg, for her valuable counsel and inspiration.

Irwin H. Steinberg
June 2009

About the Authors/Editors

Irwin Steinberg is president of HIS Corporation and Domilin Films, vice-chairman of the Music Connection and former member of the faculty at Columbia College Chicago. He is a graduate of the University of Chicago Graduate School of Business and California State University. A founder and President of Mercury Records, he was Polygram's First U.S. Chairman and CEO. He is also a long-time director of the Record Industry Association of America.

Harmon Greenblatt is the Director of the Graduate Program in Arts Administration at the University of New Orleans, New Orleans, Louisiana. He was formerly Director of the Cultural Arts Division and the Arts Council of the City of Evanston, Illinois. In addition, he was Chairman of the Music and Performing Arts Management Department of the Hartt School, University of Hartford, Connecticut, and was the associate director of the Arts Management program at Columbia College Chicago. He holds degrees from Northwestern University and DePaul University.

Introduction to the Fifth Edition

The state of the recording industry today brings to mind a story about the automobile giant, Toyota. In an article by Jon Gertner in the New York Times magazine of 2/18/07 he writes about how Toyota constantly seeks to *prevision* the future and thus sustain and grow their position in the marketplace. Toyota does not think in terms of months or quarters but rather the long view. While designing new cars for the present, they are seriously thinking about where society will be in 20 years. Witness the Toyota Prius, first built in 1991 and now it makes up 10% of Toyota's sales for 2007. Pollution and availability of oil were considered in the long view.

Now consider the countervailing thinking in the music industry as the certainty of the digital music world became known. The operative word is *denial*. The digital CD, developed by Philips Lamp, became known in 1969, and was withheld from the market until 1982. The long view here was to subjugate the Digital CD because without encryption it was duplicable, morphable and streamable. The inevitable was denied and that philosophy continued until finally, in 1985, the CD was introduced to offset a music industry recession of the early 1980's – Pandora had opened the box.

The year 1999 marked the beginning of the piracy of music from CD's into MP3 files as well as the direct duplication of CD's through the burning process, since there was no defeating encryption. Napster brought ease of file sharing which was greatly enhanced as college students employed campus broadband networks. Between 2000 and 2003 the USA music industry lost 21% of its sales revenue, an immense technology driven loss.

Toyota both envisioned and embraced needed and inevitable new technology while the music industry did neither. The music industry was in denial, spending years suing everyone and anyone in the downloading chain of digital music. The company Musicmaker, founded and financed in 1996 and precedent to Apple's I-tunes was denied rights to music by the major labels even though full payment to all copyright owners was available. In 2002 Musicmaker went out of business though it represented a great opportunity to embrace the digital music world and provide a pathway to offset "free" music. It was not until 2004 before Apple and I-tunes entered the picture.

Although most consumers wanted to buy music by the song, the major music labels still offered only subscription models with copy protection through 2001. In 2002 BMG bought Napster and, with it, lawsuits from Universal, Song Informed and EMI for Copyright violations. Finally, after a massive global loss of sales as high as $15 Billion when comparing 2006 to 1996, along came Steve Jobs in 2004 with Apple I-tunes and "track" sales for 99 cents. Now people could pay once for possession of a song, along with limited burning to CD by encryption and they could play this song on the I-pod. I-tunes was fully embraced by the industry as a successful alternative to pirated downloads.

The I-pod unlocked digital music from the computer. The I-tunes I-pod solved the problem of digital music for the music labels and the consumers. Unlike Toyota, the music industry did not embrace changes as Toyota did with the Prius 16 years before. The recovery of massive sales volume losses despite newly developing digital revenues streams remain in question. Anticipating, adjusting and embracing the new are all key concepts as, for example, the mobile phone invades the music industry.

United States CD album sales declined by 5% in 2005, reaching 588 Million CD Units, while offset by 582 million digital track downloads (58 million album equivalent), virtually offsetting the CD sales decline.

Here are the industry players and their percentage of the market share in the USA at the end of 2006.

UMB-34.4%
Sony-BMG-28.1%
Warner Bros-16.9%
Independents-11.4%
EMI-Capitol-9.2%

As this chapter is being written, Warner Bros and EMI are contemplating a very necessary merger, driven by music industry decline. The following sales at retail revealed that online and non-traditional retailers grew while traditional independents and mass merchandisers lost volume, exemplified by bankruptcies at Tower Records and Musicland.

UMG's USA sales volume is estimated to be $2.2 billion at their buying level, thus indicating that USA records sales at wholesale would be about $6.5 billion, or about $9 billion dollars at retail. In 1996, this latter figure was $11 billion. Currently the USA music industry comprises about 1/3 of world volume suggesting a world retail volume between $30 and $33 billion as compared with $40 billion dollars in 1996.

From these figures one notes the music industry is expanding and contracting at the same time. Technology will continue to drive the contraction / expansion as music downloads, ring tones, podcasts and streams in new and varied forms via DVR's Cell Phones and Satellite, while Google, Apple and Microsoft fight for a worldwide 6 billion person market.

In the meantime, music industry labels must model themselves to function in the present and the future since revenue is 90% physical CD and 10% digital as this is being written. For example, during the 2nd week of February 2007, John Mellencamp's new CD release sold 157,000 physical copies in the first week of release. At present, neither the traditional CD nor the digital music world can be devalued, though the balance may certainly change.

As the industry moves to embrace the present and the future, a new and important position has evolved: the technology manager. This position will aggregate the many new revenue streams as well as introduce artists and artist promotions through the existing and proliferating appropriate websites. I believe this position will help diversify revenue, assist the labels' radio people to podcast and utilize HD and internet radio, and possibly become a vice-presidency position in the hierarchy of record labels.

The publishing world, having achieved a 9 cent per song mechanical license, is giving similar attention to peer to peer services, social networking sites, satellite radio and various other forms of downloading and streaming music, using litigation, bargaining and government regulation.

Artist performances and touring have been financially enhanced via simultaneous Multi-Theater Performances, reaching such massive audiences as to convince certain acts to perform "free" where attached to a major artist.

Will the year 2007 see digital sales outweigh physical sales as mobile music via the cell phone emerges? Music is rushing to embrace the digital world in all of its forms and hopefully, like Toyota, will *prevision* the windows of opportunity which bring new diversity to its revenues.

Historical Timeline of Recorded Music

1877   Thomas Edison invents sound recording using a recordable cylinder.

1878   Edison patents the phonograph.

1886   Alexander Graham Bell patents the gramophone.

1887   Emil Berliner patents 1st playback only gramophone (1st to use discs and a turntable).

1888   Bell's invention becomes the Columbia Phonograph Co.

1889   Leon Glass invents the coin-operated phonograph.

1906   Lee Deforest invents the vacuum tube, improving radio transmission and amplification of sound.

1913   *Billboard* magazine publishes a list of the most popular Vaudeville songs. It's the predecessor to their trademark charts.

1923   Bessie Smith records "Down Hearted Blues" which becomes an immediate success.

1933   Laurens Hammond introduces his Hammond Organ.

1936   Electric guitars debut.

1940   English Decca develops full frequency range recording.

1942   Bing Crosby releases the all-time top selling film song "White Christmas." RCA Victor creates the first "gold record."

1945   Fisher company markets the first component receivers.

1946   Peter Goldmark invents vinyl, a synthetic replacement for shellac, to make lighter, better sounding recordings for CBS.

1948   Columbia Records introduces the 33 1/3 LP record, increasing the 78-rpm record's 4 minutes per side to 25 minutes. Patty Page first overdubbed her own voice on "Confess"

Late 1940's   US companies begin to use magnetic tape in recording.

1949   45-rpm records are sold in the US. Original cast recording of "Oklahoma" becomes 1st LP to sell 1 million copies. Les Paul invents overdubbing.

1952   Gibson company's Les Paul electric guitar debuts.

1953   Columbia introduces the first portable record players.

1955   Ampex introduces a stereo reel-to-reel tape recorder for the home market.

1957	First stereo records introduced.
1958	*Billboard* debuts its Hot 100 chart.
1959	National Academy of Recording Arts and Sciences sponsors the first Grammy Award ceremony for recorded music. First transistor radios appear in the US.
1960	New technology allows precision editing in stereo recordings.
1967	Beatles release *Sgt. Pepper's Lonely Hearts Club Band*, 1st concept album. R. A. Moog brings the Moog Synthesizer to market
1975	Disco fad stimulates record sales.
1978	Sony introduces the Walkman.
1979	Sugar Hill Gang releases first rap song, "Rapper's Delight."
1981	MTV goes on the air with around the clock music videos. Walkman II, smaller and cheaper than the original Walkman, debuts
1982	First Compact Discs (CD's) go on sale
1985	Madonna launches her first road show, Michael Jackson releases *Thriller*, selling more than 25 million copies, becoming the biggest selling album in history, and dozens of top-name acts perform at Live Aid concerts in Philadelphia and London to benefit African famine victims.
1988	CD's outsell vinyl records for the first time.
1990	Sony launches DAT (Digital Audio Tape).
1991	Phillips produces first DCC (Digital Compact Cassette).
1992	CD's surpass cassettes as the preferred medium for recorded music. MP3 first appears. Sony debuts the Minidisc.
1995	Rock & Roll Hall Of Fame opens in Cleveland.
1998	Website MP3.com begins. First portable MP3 players are sold.
1999	Napster uses new technology for sharing music files. Universal and PolyGram merge to form Universal Music Group, controlling 25% of the worldwide music market. Woodstock '99 kicks off in Rome amidst complaints of the original concert's spirit being compromised and commercialized.
2000	Court decision declares Napster file sharing illegal.
2001	Introduction of the iPOD. Radio stations begin broadcasting on the web.
2002	Satellite radio introduced in automobiles.
2003	Apple launches iTunes.

<u>**Chapter 1**</u>

Overview of the Music Business

Irwin Steinberg

The discovery of commercially unique talent is the foundation upon which every music label is built. The music value chain, the opportunity to monetize the physical and digital content begins with the ability to identify such talent. The value of the record label is established in this choice and with the decision as to the people who make these choices. Just as James Liener, Billboard May 10, 2008, said "If you don't have great music (music with wide appeal), it doesn't matter how much marketing is involved."

Somewhere in 1969, in Holland, I heard and had in my hand a CD, an experience I had with other CEO's of Polygram Music Companies throughout the world. It was a Phillips invention, Polygram's parent company. We had opened Pandora's Box, a digital, easily duplicable master. We voted to wait and the CD was not unveiled until the mid 1980's during an industry recession. When the CD began replacing the LP, the music industry resisted for as long as it could. However superior sound and convenience forced the industry to accept the CD which, in the long run, cost the music industry millions because it could be copied.

The music industry, by not engaging the opportunities available to potential new revenue models, allowed the pirates and digital duplicators (i.e., Napster) to fill the void. Some argue, even at this writing, 40% of global music sales are pirated or person-to-person exchanged with no compensation to artist, songwriter, or label. Contrast this with Toyota, via the Prius, building an electric car in 1980. And Music Maker, a precursor to iTunes, founded and financed in 1996, could not license adequate music to proceed. iTunes and Toyota were visionaries. The music industry was not.

IFPI indicates that at the end of 2007 recorded music sales, at retail, worldwide, generated 31.8 billion dollars. This was down from 40 billion in the year 2000. Digital revenue, though growing through this period, could not and has not overcome the loss of and continuing decline of physical CD sales. Clearly we have an industry still in transition seeking new business solutions and new business models are in search of digital partners with whom to monetize music content to its fullest extent.

In addition, to expand revenues as sales revenue fall, music labels are expanding participation in image and brand rights associated with artists, including merchandising, sponsorships, touring, and artist management. This participation is illustrated by the new 360 degree artist contracts, providing income participation based upon the rationale that the music label gives ignition to all of these artist sources of revenue.

The four largest worldwide music labels at the end of 2008 based upon percentage of the global market were Universal (26%), Sony-BMG (21%), Warner Music (14%), and EMI (13%). The independent labels account for an astounding 26%, up from 2% in 1980 aided by easy availability to information via BDS (airplay) and Soundscan (retail sales, physical and digital). Also the major companies wished to partner with these less bureaucratic and more "street" oriented companies. The most successful indie labels at this time are TVT, Koch, Victory, Epitaph, and Roadrunner (in the process of being sold to Warner).

On the digital side, revenue is sought from different digital models, including digital downloads of single tracks and albums, online subscription services, interactive webcasting, video streaming and downloads, mobile music in the form of ringtones, ringback tones, and full track downloads. Content distribution agreements with mobile operators can be sought around the world with Vimpelcom (Russia), Docomo (Japan), Telefonca (Spain), Telenor (Scandinavia), and other such worldwide mobile operators as they develop.

Typically, in the USA, partnerships with such online and mobile operators must be carried out with iTunes, Microsoft, Napster, Rhapsody, Yahoo, YouTube, Lala, AT&T, Sprint, T-Mobile, Verizon, Orange, Vodaphone, KDDI, and worldwide social media communities with close to one billion visitors. And emerging are music enabled phones from Sony Ericsson, Nokia, and iPhone.

Digital service providers receive a master for sale in the digital format and thus monetize the music based upon agreements which establish wholesale prices, license fees, advances and/or equity arrangements, and/or participating in related advertising revenues.

It should be noted here that while most mobile revenue is still currently derived from ringtones, phones equipped with new capabilities can offer full track downloads, streaming audio, and video, further expanding the monetization process. Music products are sold in physical form to online physical retailers such as Amazon.com, Barnes & Noble.com, and BestBuy.com, plus terrestrial retailers such as Wal-Mart.

According to the RIAA (The Recording Industry Association of America), the USA grew at an annual compound growth rate of 7.6% from 1990 to 1999. Since that time annual dollar sales of the physical CD declined at an annual rate of 8%. If annual digital track sales are included, the 8% rate declines slightly to 7%, obviously not as yet able to stem the negative tide. As this is written, global sales are 77% physical and 23% digital. It is prognosticated that by 2012 sales will be 50% physical and 50% digital.

In 2008 market share by both physical and digital retailers and/or combinations of both were as follows:

Rank	Account	Share of USA (in percentage)
1	iTunes	17.83
2	Wal-Mart	15.14
3	Best Buy	13.14
4	Target	10.22
5	Alliance	9.72
6	Amazon	4.57
7	Borders	5.2
8	Transworld	3.2
9	Verizon	2.0
10	Handleman	1.39
11	Baker & Taylor	1.18
12	Super D	0.95
13	Sprint	0.93
14	Hastings	0.87
15	Virgin	0.86
16	Rhapsody	0.70
17	AT&T	0.66
18	Cosco	0.59
19	Napster	0.59
20	T-Mobile	0.58
21	L Music	0.58

iTunes is doing 70% of the USA digital market share.

According to IFPI in 2008, based upon worldwide recorded music sold, the following countries account for 75% of the market: United States, Japan, United Kingdom, Germany, and France. Currently, the U.S. does about 1/3 of the world market sales. In 1980, the U.S. was represented in 2/3 of the world's recorded music sales. The change reflects the more inclusionary global world.

This indicates the opportunity to synergize the earnings opportunity of an artist's contract by including world rights in such contracts. It provides the artist and the label with a revenue opportunity via licensing such music outside the U.S. Good examples of this are shown in ABBA licensed to a U.S. company from Sweden and Michael Jackson licensed by the U.S. contract to the rest of the world. Some music will cross cultures while others are indigenous to the country of origin.

About the artist contract, it is a music for hire agreement where the label pays for the cost of production and thus is the owner of the master. The collection of such masters is the value of the company. The recorded music is a copyright belonging to the label and remains so for 95 years beyond its first issuance. It is a copyright separate from the songs used in the recording and those songs must be separately registered. Artists are now seeking a 35 year life on the recorded master with the master then reverting to the artist. The details of the entire artist contract and the basis for its major concepts can be studied in Chapter 5 and there you will also learn of the major changes to the contract caused by the digital world. Of note, too, is the 360 degree aspect of the contract which provides for label participation from a revenue standpoint in areas such as touring, merchandising, and brand opportunities.

Artists out of contract such as AC/DC, the Eagles, Journey, and Radiohead have taken advantage of the digital opportunity by going directly to the public via the internet offering their music via websites turned social network. The advantage is in the unshared revenue, obtaining detailed information on the customer, selling advertising and merchandising, and control of the content. For example, when the physical CD is released, Wal-Mart is given an exclusive and for some well known groups, sales have reached as high as 850,000 units.

Also new to the music business is the technology manager, often an executive vice president whose role is to act on every known and potentially existent method for the maximum monetization of all that is digital, whether online or mobile, and influencing the use of the internet for exposure of the artist. Because of the low cost of storing music and making that music easily transferable in this digital world, music catalogs can be and are stored without deletion. So millions of tracks of music are available and thus we have the "Long Tail." That is, we can now appeal to broader, more segmented society with very broad and fragmented musical tastes. All the music ever recorded can now become available. Every label's past catalog, much of it deleted in the physical world, is now available for sale.

With tastes being so varied, the musical marketplace, radio, and touring companies can target small but specific demographics if they so choose. Radio's product is the audience and its demographics/psychographics which it attracts through its choice of music programmed. Radio attracts advertisers specific to the audience targeted. The touring companies not only attract the specific audience but also have their identity and email. Infinity and Clear Channel own radio stations which reach 70% of the listening audience. And those two companies own 135 of the arenas, 39 television stations, and carry out many projected concerts.

This brings us to the realization that the recorded music industry is an oligopoly in many ways:

1. Four major labels account for 74% of the global market.
2. Infinity and Clear Channels control 80% of radio's music audience as well as dominate arenas in the U.S.
3. 13 retail entities sell 80% of the CD's in the U.S.
4. iTunes controls 70% of digital sales.

Employees and students of the music business need to know how the oligopoly and those outside the oligopoly affect how the market is approached by an established artist as opposed to an artist newly introduced to the market.

In this chapter we have discussed revenue sources such as CD sales, online and mobile sources, and the 360 degree contract of "To and Fro" licensing involving markets outside the U.S. Another major revenue source is music publishing royalties. These royalties come from copyrighted musical compositions residing in company-owned publishing or inherent in the artist contract where the artist is also a songwriter. The music label as a copyright owner and/or administrator of copyrighted musical compositions is entitled to royalties for the exploitation of musical compositions which will generate revenue over long periods of time. Music publishers receive royalties pursuant to mechanical, public performance, and synchronization (see this book's chapter on music publishing). Four music publishers, collectively, account for 65% of the world market. They are: Universal (22%), EMI (20%), Warner (15%), and Sony/ATV (7%). Of Warner Music Groups $3.4 billion in total revenue, $620 million was from music publishing, a very important complement to any recorded music label.

Earlier in this chapter I referred to the choice of commercially unique music as crucial. A great background for this choice is the various exclusive charts in Billboard Magazine. This study of the charts, I believe, is not to duplicate existent success but rather to bring the unique music to those charts. The idea is to bring a new niche to those charts, a new sound, a uniquely identifiable sound.

In 1994, a guru by the name of Esther Dyson (says Paul Krugman of the New York Times) made a striking prediction: that the ease with which digital content can be copied and disseminated would eventually force business to sell the results of creative activity cheaply or even give it away. Whatever the product, software, news, books, music, movies, and the cost of creation would have to be recouped indirectly. Businesses would have to distribute intellectual property free in order to sell services and relationships. For example, music can be used as a vehicle to sell Coca Cola, or to experience a percentage of related advertising revenue.

In the case of record sales, an offset to free music may be in the economic model which converts airplay and YouTube into making money through publishing, touring, merchandising, and licensing. It took the music industry too long to recognize the digital damage.

Information wants to be free, but free will not support the cost of great and important newspapers like *The New York Times*, *The Philadelphia Inquirer*, and *The Washington Post*. Being tied to a percentage of web advertising will not provide enough money for any intellectual property to survive as free. Maybe we simply must institute a charge, per user, per intellectual category, at the ISP (Internet Service Provider) level.

Chapter 2

The Organization of a Record Company

Bill Stafford

Bill Stafford currently works with Missing Link Music, and enjoys participating in educational outreach programs in public schools. Prior to this he held the position of Vice President, Copyright, at SonyBMG in New York, overseeing the mechanical and synchronization licensing activities of Arista, RCA, Zomba, and other labels.

The successful operation of a record company depends upon the performance and interaction of its many divisions. In general, a record company acquires talent, manufactures recordings, and sells its products via traditional and electronic distribution networks. Marketing and promotional efforts are enacted to create awareness about an artist or upcoming release, and to stimulate sales through various channels.

Major record companies, like other major corporations, have multinational divisions which can be numerous and complex. A major record company's president is responsible to the board of directors for running the business and overseeing the direction of the corporation. The board members may consist of high-level executives from the record company's parent corporation, or shareholders who are not employed by the company but maintain a large financial interest in the corporation. Independent, or "indie" record companies operate on comparatively small budgets, are structured more basically, and tend to retain a musical focus or identity.

RECORD COMPANY STRUCTURE

The following core divisions exist and interact within most record companies to form the basis of their operation:

The A&R (Artist and Repertoire) Department seeks out talented artists by attending concerts, listening to demonstration recordings (demos), and following trends within the music industry. Once an A&R "scout" finds a desirable artist, an A&R manager or director must approve the signing of this artist to the label. The next important step is to convince the artist to sign a recording agreement. The hands-on creative positions within the A&R Department are often tied to the pressures of trying to sign the next "superstar" in the midst of the competition with other record companies vying for the same artist. In addition to full artist signings, today's recording technology and the proliferation of independent labels are leading to an increasing number of deals being structured for the distribution of existing recordings, purchases of existing master recordings, and even subsidiary relationships with the independent labels.

The Production Department ensures that recordings are manufactured, packaged and released according to schedule. The product manager is responsible for coordinating the delivery of packaging materials such as sleeves, labels and inserts with the actual CDs. Before the products are manufactured, product managers work with the A&R Department to ensure that the mastering and pressing of a recording is proceeding on time to achieve the scheduled release date. The distributors of a recording notify the Production Department regarding the number of products to assemble and ship. This communication allows Production to keep abreast of supply and demand, and maintain a product level without over or under stocking its inventory. The Production Department is also involved in coordinating the preparation of releases for digital distribution.

The Creative Services Department designs cover art for recordings, advertisements, and posters while working closely with the Production and Marketing Departments. Creative Services may also assist with the backdrops and graphics of video production, as well as the set design for certain tours. Projects with artwork involving 3-D, holograms, and other special effects are often contracted out to companies specializing in design. The Creative Services personnel often work in concert with technology managers to support the graphics, pictures, and artwork used on the company's website and for online digital music sales.

The Promotion Department sends recordings to radio stations and college campuses, and develops online promotional events such as contests in an effort to promote airplay and awareness of new releases. Recording artists, in conjunction with the Promotion Department, may embark on a "theme" promotion based on the most promising single from their new album. Short excerpts, or sometimes the entire single, may be offered for sale online at a discount price, or even for free as a download to stimulate a "buzz." The appropriate radio stations will be serviced with recordings, including singles containing numerous re-mixes, as well as merchandise relating to the artist's tour. Radio station ticket giveaways and other campaigns utilizing phones, e-mail, and text messaging may also be arranged by the Promotion Department. With the mainstream use of web-streamed radio simulcasts, stations that were once limited to a particular listening area are now heard around the world.

Each promotion department also has separate employees or hires independent promotion companies to help promote new video releases. Their main job is to get the label's videos played on MTV, VH1 and on all of the many independent programs that air videos on national, local, and cable TV and through authorized streaming sites through the internet. Another part of the job is to service the video displays at retail stores, which play promotional clips of new releases. Video monitors playing selections such as "Top 10 Videos" or "Video Picks of the Week" generate attention as well as help the sales of videos, CD's, and downloads.

Video pools are businesses which request videos from the promotion departments of record companies (usually without cost), which then re-record the various videos onto digitally looped reels and sell them to retail businesses for in-store play. These compilations are created by the video pools VJ's (video jockeys) and can be seen on monitors in many restaurants, clubs and retail stores such as Wal-Mart and Sears.

The Marketing Department advertises artists throughout the media, seeks ongoing publicity, and creates visibility at retail outlets. Working with the A&R Department and the artist's management, the Marketing Department also interfaces with technology managers to create and maintain blogs and other online "viral" marketing tools. Timing is important as the Marketing Department arranges events such as regional media coverage to coordinate with an artist's tour appearances in key cities around the country. In addition, in-store displays are arranged by the Marketing Department to influence impulse buyers and create awareness at select retail outlets.

The Sales Department works to get product into stores and to online retailers, and to maintain the supply necessary to satisfy the purchasing needs of the consumers. Some record companies combine Sales and Distribution into one department, so they can both coordinate with the Production Department to maintain an adequate supply of product as a marketing campaign is launched. Record orders taken from the large retailers are often scanned from the bar codes contained in an elaborately printed monthly release guide. This scanned information is loaded into the record company's sales database, triggering the shipments of product by the distributors to the retailers. In addition to commercial recordings, the Sales Department supplies retailers with promotional material such as stickers, T-shirts, posters, and free CD copies.

The Business Affairs Department negotiates artist agreements, tracks costs associated with an artist's recording fund, and licenses various types of repertoire usage. The divisions within business affairs include: A&R Administration, Copyright, Rights and Clearances, and Contract Administration. Many record companies combine their Business Affairs with their in-house legal personnel. In practice, litigation and major legal matters such as anti-trust or compliance with Federal investigations are almost always outsourced to law firms experienced with those matters. Most of the activity within the record company by business affairs and the legal department involve deals with artists, producers, publishers, joint venture partners, pressing plants, distributors, and internal matters such as building contracts, leases, service agreements, and employee agreement in conjunction with the Human Resources or Personnel Department. , The archiving of signed documents and the tracking of licenses and recording options, as well as the company's terms of use for online activities are also functions of the business affairs department.

The Finance Department processes all royalty payments and handles the company's income, expenses, and tax issues. The chief financial officer often meets with the company president regarding the impact certain financial decisions may have on the company. Executives within the finance department must approve large purchases such as catalog acquisitions and office equipment to insure that it fits within the annual budget created for each department. Another division of Finance, the Royalty Department, maintains a complex database capable of matching sales information with royalty rates, contractual information, and account histories for the mechanical and artist royalties paid out each quarter. The Royalty Department increasingly works with technology managers to accommodate the growing number of digital accounting transactions. Taxation, a sub-division of finance, works to help the company comply with the most recent tax rulings while taking advantage of as many corporate tax benefits as possible.

The International Department coordinates the releases of albums around the world in select territories. As far as marketing an international release, territories are identified with respect to their geography and cultural traits. The United States is considered a territory, as is Australia and New Zealand together (called Australasia). Once a release has been negotiated with a foreign licensee, the international department must arrange for the publicity and artist's tour dates to correspond with the album's release. The foreign licensee may ideally be a division of the record company, or it may be a non-affiliated manufacturer. Timing, boundaries regarding online sales, and the issues involved with marketing abroad make international exploitation a challenging procedure.

OTHER DEPARTMENTS IN A RECORD COMPANY

The departments detailed above are unique to the record industry and exist based on the dynamics by which recorded music is manufactured and sold. In addition to these departments are areas within all major record companies that are essential to the basic business functions of any large company in the United States. Among the administrative departments within a major record company that are not directly associated with the music industry are: Human Resources, which hires employees, implements policies and maintains personnel records; IST (Information System Technologies), which maintains computer networks and provides user support; Administrative Services, which moves office furniture and provides maintenance for equipment; and Corporate Communications, which works closely with the media and announces employee promotions and company-sponsored events.

As a whole, the music business and administrative departments within a record company interact to form a complex system geared to meet the demands of today's music marketplace. The advent of the digital encoding and distribution of music has created a need for many of the departments within a record company to work more closely, with technology being the core base. Many record companies have formed divisions called "Technology", "New Technology", or even "Global Digital Business" to accommodate the rapidly expanding digital music and video platforms. Employees including the technology managers, senior vice presidents, and presidents of these divisions have become key people, taking their places next to A&R, marketing, sales and the others in their importance to the industry.

Chapter 3

Record Company Profit and Loss

Irwin H. Steinberg

INTRODUCTION

This chapter examines the key elements which must be considered by any manager or manager aspirant in running a record company. In seeking advice from the chief financial officer (CFO) and/or the controller, the manager should be alert to key items in the profit and loss (P&L) statement which affect him or her, as well as to meet the demands of the investors.

This chapter refers to two charts which appear at the end of the chapter: the first, marked Chart 2, refers to the Mythical Records Incorporated pro forma profit and loss as expressed in thousands of dollars; the second, marked Chart 3, is a proposed break-even formula for determining the number of units needed to break even with a specific recording project, assuming one knows the recording cost.

BACKGROUND

In the 1980s, the Big 6 record companies had already established their distribution systems, primarily because they wanted to concentrate their marketing attention on their own products. What this P&L statement in part reveals is that in the process of going to company-owned distribution, the major labels discovered they had insufficient volume to justify carrying out their own distribution. This resulted in the acquisition of many smaller labels by each company to increase volume and support the enormous expense of maintaining the distribution systems which each label had set up.

In looking at the figures, note how the profitability of the Mythical Record Company of that date was primarily a function of its foreign income, which is marked as license income and as an additional function of the domestic license income, which is found on the fifth line of the pro forma profit/loss statement. Without these two areas of income, the Mythical Record Company would have experienced a loss, and this relates directly to the need at that time for the majors to expand their volume. In other words, once they had chosen to control their own distribution systems, each of the major companies had to increase its percentage of the marketplace by absorbing other companies in order to achieve profitability. Company owned distribution required a significant amount of additional volume in order to justify its existence.

COMPONENTS OF PROFIT AND LOSS

While referring to the Mythical Records P&L statement, there are certain key items which need the manager's attention, evaluation, and guidance, in the sense that the guidance will either flow from the manager, or in conjunction with discussions with the chief financial officer or controller. The items are:

1. recording costs
2. inventory
3. returns
4. royalty costs
5. international income
6. domestic income
7. operating overhead
8. net volume
9. profit, and opportunities for profit

Recording Costs

Recording costs are a result of all of the activities that surround the recording of music for the purpose of creating a single record, or a related album. This includes all of those costs incurred with the use of the recording studio, the musicians involved and all of the related matters which surround recording the album (see Chapter 5 on the artist contract for recording cost details). It should be understood at this point that recording costs are different from those which are referred to as music costs. Recording costs, generally speaking, are those costs that represent an advance against royalties due to the artist. At that point, since they are an advance against royalties and can be earned back through royalty payments, those costs represent an asset to the company. If the royalties to the artist exceed the recording costs, and are thus absorbed, then there is no music cost in that instance to the record company. However, as is more often the case, over an average year, a certain proportion of recording costs will not be absorbed through royalties, as there will be insufficient sales to permit such recoupment. Therefore, at some point the difference which results from the failure of the recording cost to be absorbed by the royalty cost will have to be written into the P&L statement.

The better the decision making of the A&R staff as to the artists and music chosen, the less likely there will be a disproportionate amount of music cost reflected in the profit and loss statement. Managers' effectiveness becomes important in the choice of the A&R staff who select the artists on the label's roster, as well as the choice of producers, and sometimes the songs as well. In addition, it is also a reflection of the way the manager or managers coordinate all of the functions of staff with relation to music, including radio, marketing, touring, etc., in order to maximize the potential of a specific single and/or related album. Looking at the P&L statement, we see that music costs based upon the definition just given, resulted in a cost of two million, nine hundred seventy thousand dollars or 2 to 3% of the net dollar volume. This would be an extraordinarily low cost. Typically, music costs in an effectively operated company will come to about 5% of net sales volume before foreign income and after domestic licensing income.

Inventory

Management would like to turn inventory over as frequently as possible during the year in relation to volume, and to experience as little obsolescence, that is, unsold inventory, as possible. One of the ways to accomplish this is not only to produce inventory related to past experience, but, when there is no past history, to try to meet the need of the marketplace without lowering sales. Inventory created in excess of demand becomes unsalable and must be carried as a cost rather than as an asset. Salable inventory remains an asset to the company.

Returns

Most record companies have a return policy that results in about 20% of its goods being returned when unsold at retail. Without the return policy there would be very little opportunity to take risks in the marketplace, especially with new artists. Record companies must give the marketplace a chance and have the product in the marketplace when the marketing and radio promotions are in effect. Returns are, therefore, inevitable. The manager must create an artist policy that minimizes the risks taken and prevents feeding goods into the marketplace in excess of need, which would create unnecessary returns and, eventually, a financial burden.

Royalty Costs

It's not well known to aspiring managers or to the public that royalty costs represent the largest single cost related to volume in any record company. The royalty costs that are paid to artists, to the publishers, and to the American Federation of Musicians, taken together with relation to the wholesale selling price, will average out somewhere around 30% of net dollar volume, a very major cost. This percentage can go as high as 50% in the case of an artist like Michael Jackson, who might receive 20 to 25% of retail selling price as his royalty rate. It is the author's opinion that this cost has a great deal to do with how artists are regarded at the outset, how they are rewarded as volume increases, and whether in some cases a manager is willing to pay a confiscatory royalty rate in order to hold an artist for image and/or marketing position purposes.

Royalty cost is a function of the negotiation of the contract, the attempt to create a realistic royalty rate in the present and in the future, so that it does not confiscate, or take all the possibility of profitability away, while also permitting a company to be attractive to new and growing artists.

Operating Overhead

The manager has the obligation to oversee the operating overhead of the company, which is reflected in its marketing organization, its administration departments, including finance, inventory control, etc., and in the kind of overhead incurred in the operation of the promotion department.

International Income

How does international income or international licensing occur? This income is the result of the relationship among the American company and companies outside the United States and/or Canada to which the American record company grants licenses. The label may license to independent record companies outside the United States or it may be licensing to companies within its own corporate structure that are a part of the world-wide operation typical of the Big Six companies. Nevertheless, in each of the instances described, music that is recorded in the United States and becomes attractive to countries outside the United States is licensable, and in the process of carrying out that license, there is an additional opportunity for profitability for the originating record company. Such a relationship could also occur as a result of an artist developed outside of the U.S. and licensed to an American record company, in which case the license fee is paid by the American record company to the foreign owner. In both situations there is an opportunity for income that must be recognized by the manager.

The manager has to be observant of the structure of his or her own company in order to assure that it has a person or a department functioning for the purpose of seeking to license music which it has created in its own company. This department should also be alert and sensitive to music being created outside the United States that is licensable in the United States. The opportunity for income is inherent in the licensing agreement, which generally calls for a percentage of the retail selling price to the licensing company, and which is generally shared on a 50/50 basis between the artist and the licensing record company. The licensee, the recipient of the license master, pays a percentage of the retail selling price in his or her country to the licensor or the originator of the music. When that money is received by the licensor it is shared between the artist and the record company and can be a substantial amount of income to the licensor, as well as creating royalty flow to the artist. This is also true for the licensee, despite paying what might be a substantial licensing fee, the licensee experiences a sale of an artist's music even though that artist is not a result of discovery within its own company. (For further detail on International Income, see Chapter 10)

Domestic Income

Another opportunity for bolstering the bottom line of a record company can occur with what is called domestic licensing income. Domestic licensing occurs between the record company and a record club, or an infomercial organization. The arrangement can also occur between a record company and a film organization which elects to license recorded music of the record company for use in a film. Again, the label should not only do the licensing but also have the kind of organizational set-up that can take advantage of these kinds of opportunities. (For further detail on domestic licensing, see Chapter 9)

Profit

A manager can organize to exercise control over profit and cost in two ways: first, conduct a break-even study related to each specific recording project, such as the one in Chart 3; and second, through the budget process. In this example, one half of the recording costs of the example project shown here will be recovered through royalty payments. We also learn from the example that the overall recording costs for this project are $100,000.

This selling price is reflected by the x in the break-even formula and in the example. The example also gives the percentages that manufacturing, royalties, distribution, selling, and administration add to this selling price. In this example, the company requires $356,000 to break even, working on the assumption that the selling price to the middleman is roughly $5.00, which was the selling price for a cassette at the time of this study. Under the cost structure, it requires about 70,000 cassette units to break even on a recording which involved $100,000 in recording costs and which effectively recovered half of the recording costs through the royalty rate expressed in the formula.

The second opportunity to affect the profitability of the record company occurs at the time when the budget is created. Major items for the manager to consider and to discuss with his staff in looking ahead at an existing operation would be to determine what kind of net volume can be expected by the company (the basis for this could be a study of the artist roster); looking at the artist roster in terms of which artists had made a contribution in past years or year; determining what the upcoming year's volume might be using past years as a yardstick; and estimating volume for artists not yet on the artist roster. The projected net volume would be the top line of the budget or the pro-forma profit and loss statement form. The bottom line would be the profit target. For example, if one were looking at a budgeted year to achieve $100 million in net volume and the pre-tax profit target is 12%, then the bottom line would read $12 million. The difference between net volume and the profit the company seeks is $88 million. Knowing the volume objective enables the company to then know what the manufacturing cost is going to be based upon experience with manufacturing policy and return policy as to how much merchandise must be manufactured in order to reach the $100 million in net volume. The company would also use its experience to determine what the music cost would be, knowing which artists were on the artist roster, what past recording costs have been, and what the recovery rate would be through royalties to come. Also, the average royalty would be entered into the budget projected as a percentage of volume. Inherent in the data in arriving at the $12 million bottom line, and as either an addition to the net volume or as an addition to the profit line, is domestic and international income (again, past years' experience would dictate the numbers).

Finally, the company would utilize its experience as to overhead; in this case overhead which is primarily administrative, to determine that cost. The label would then be left with an amount to be budgeted for marketing: marketing staff salaries, touring, radio promotion staff salaries, advertising and so forth. The final item thus would be a sort of bushel basket of costs which can be devoted to the purpose of supporting the artists in the marketplace. To give a further handle on this idea, assume this company had achieved its 100 million dollar objective and its profit margin of $12 million, which would leave $88 million to cover various costs typical of a record company's profit and loss statement. Assume for this exercise that of the $88 million, royalties (the established average royalty cost being 30% of selling price) account for $30 million, $20 million represents manufacturing costs, and $16 million represents the distribution system. Also assume that $10 million represents administrative overhead, for a total of $76 million. This leaves $12 million at the label's discretion to utilize in the marketing area, which includes touring, radio promotion, print advertising, and publicity.

In short, managers have two pre-planning instruments, the break-even point to make a determination about specific recording projects, and the annual budgeting tool.

CONCLUSION

By understanding the role of costs with relation to volume and the profit objective, the manager can play a very large role in the kinds of decision-making that control royalty costs, inventory costs, and other costs, and he or she can also play a major role in structuring the organization so that it can maximize areas of income such as international and domestic licensing income.

Chart 2
MYTHICAL RECORDS, INC.
PRO FORMA PROFIT AND LOSS (000s)

INCOME		
Gross sales	$ 133,000	
Returns @ 24.8%	(32,791)	
Effective cash discount	(1,887)	
Net music sales	98,322	
Domestic license income	3,000	
TOTAL INCOME:	101,322	
EXPENSES		
Cost of goods sold	$ 26,980	
Music costs	2,970	
Royalties (artists, pub.)	29,360	
Commercial/mgr. expense	25,910	
Gen. expenses (interest, etc.)	1,927	
Distribution	15,161	
TOTAL EXPENSE		102,308
SUB-TOTAL		(986)
ADJUSTMENTS		
License income received	$ 8,000	
Royalty expense (50%)	(4,000)	
TOTAL ADJUSTMENTS		4,000
PROFIT BEFORE TAXES		3,014

Chart 3
BREAK EVEN ANALYSIS

BREAK EVEN	MANUFACTURING	ROYALTIES	DISTR	SELL/ADM
X = 1/2 (Recording Cost)	+ .20 X	+ .30 X	+ .16 X	+ .20 X
EXAMPLE				
X = 1/2 ($100,000)	+ .20 X	+ .30 X	+ .16 X	+ .20 X
.14 X = $50,000				
X = $356,000				
X = 70,000 units				

NOTE: An important investment factor: usually money spent on a somewhat successful new rock, urban, or country act will translate into a higher sales base from which to begin the next album. In the case of a CHR (Contemporary Hits Radio) act, the large cost of breaking a hit single must be repeated three to four times before a self-sustaining name for the act is created. Over time, the pop act may cost more to establish and will disappear more quickly from the scene.

As this edition goes to press, Apple Corporation, through its I-Tunes subsidiary, sells music online for $ .99 per song. This technology provides for a legal way for consumers to download music, and also a new equation for labels, artists, and others to receive income for their music. The way this $ .99 pie will be divided is:

Label	47
Artist	7
Producer	3
Publisher	8
Service Provider	17
Bandwidth Cost	12
Credit Card Fees	5

Legally downloaded music provides a budget line to the record company's budget and, depending on consumer's adoption of downloading as a system of delivering music into the home, may significantly affect the company's profitability.

Chart 4
10K Report of 2008

RESULTS OF OPERATIONS

Fiscal Year Ended September 30, 2008 Compared with Fiscal Year Ended September 30, 2007 and Fiscal Year Ended September 30, 2007 Compared with Fiscal Year Ended September 30, 2006

Consolidated Historical Results

Revenues

Our revenues were composed of the following amounts (in millions):

	For the Fiscal Years Ended September 30,			2008 vs 2007		2007 vs 2006	
	2008	2007	2006	$ Change	% Change	$ Change	% Change
Revenue by Type							
Physical sales	$2,040	$2,157	$2,484	$(117)	-5%	$(327)	-13%
Digital	599	434	335	165	38%	99	30%
Licensing	256	244	186	12	5%	58	31%
Total Recorded Music	**2,895**	**2,835**	**3,005**	**60**	**2%**	**(170)**	**-6%**
Mechanical	225	228	225	(3)	-1%	3	1%
Performance	243	213	191	30	14%	22	12%
Synchronization	99	91	83	8	9%	8	10%
Digital	40	27	20	13	48%	7	35%
Other	16	11	19	5	45%	(8)	-42%
Total Music Publishing	**623**	**570**	**538**	**53**	**9%**	**32**	**6%**
Intersegment elimination	(27)	(22)	(27)	(5)	-23%	5	19%
Total Revenue	**$3,491**	**$3,383**	**$3,516**	**$ 108**	**3%**	**$(133)**	**-4%**
Revenue by Geographical Location							
U.S. Recorded Music	$1,380	$1,459	$1,483	$ (79)	-5%	$ (24)	-2%
U.S. Publishing	225	212	220	13	6%	(8)	-4%
Total U.S.	**1,605**	**1,671**	**1,703**	**(66)**	**-4%**	**(32)**	**-2%**
International Recorded Music	1,515	1,376	1,522	139	10%	(146)	-10%
International Publishing	398	358	318	40	11%	40	13%
Total International	**1,913**	**1,734**	**1,840**	**179**	**10%**	**(106)**	**-6%**
Intersegment eliminations	(27)	(22)	(27)	(5)	-23%	5	19%
Total Revenue	**$3,491**	**$3,383**	**$3,516**	**$ 108**	**3%**	**$(133)**	**-4%**

50

Note the importance of revenue outside the U.S. through related companies (50) throughout the world. Note also the contribution of licensing and publishing further emphasizing the search for the organization for such income needed to offset other areas of decline. All of the foregoing is noted in Chapter One. These areas of income allowed the company to break even in 2008.

The Music Business in Action:
Value of Music Eroded
Effect of Higher Digital Rates

In 2003, Pennsylvania State University became the first institution of higher education to provide students with low cost access to music via low price music subscriptions and downloads. Eighty campuses have followed. Labels and publishers have endorsed this, succumbing to large negotiated advances. The students pay discounted fees for downloads and tethering. 20,000 students at Penn State signed up. Duke University offers each student a 20GB Apple computer iPod upon entering the University. Cornell University's 13,000 students accessed 10,000,000 songs in a year. Some industry observers argue that this arrangement erodes music's value and jeopardizes the industry's revenue stream. For example, the average music retailer in a college market loses about 40% of its store's business. What will be the impact on the retail music business?

Looking back at this chapter, observe how the online subscription fee is shared by the label, songwriter, and provider. The provider's margin is insignificant, leading one to believe that the high concept of online music providers is to sell hardware and/or to attract advertising revenues. Causing an interruptus for the online providers is a mechanical rights owner's drive to seek substantially higher royalty rates for music used in all subscriptions services and the triggering of new rates for all demand streams, casting and tethered and untethered downloads.

Look for higher online subscription fees as these new rates devour subscription profit margins. The recently proposed increases fees have been met with protests by online radio stations, fearing that the substantial increases for use of copyrighted music will put them out of business. As we go to press, the issue is anything but settled. Look forward to much more wrangling and political wheeling and dealing in the near future.

The Music Business in Action 2:
McCartney and Starbucks

In this day of multinational corporations owning everything there is to own, the possibility exists that one day Rolls Royce might own the Rolling Stones' contract. That may seem an exaggeration to you. BUT, now in fact, here comes Paul McCartney, former Beatle, in a contract with Starbucks, having left EMI group's Capitol Records. McCartney becomes the first artist to sign with Hear Music, a label created by Starbucks. In this arrangement, McCartney will retain ownership of the resultant master recordings. Recently, Wal-Mart made a similar arrangement with Garth Brooks and The Eagles, and Target with Kenny Loggins. The non-traditional approach is gaining momentum.

 The recording industry continues to suffer revenue losses, exacerbated by their high promotion costs. Here are five business approaches which might be chosen by labels to offset this downward spiral:

The first speculated approach was to tie-in to the corporate word and their major agencies with regards to promotions that seek to sell brand named products propelled by certain artist's CD's and downloads.

The marketers, working with current releases, benefit from the star power of stars such as Gwen Stefani, The Black Eyed Peas, or Michael Buble. In turn the record labels benefit from the multi-million dollar budgets supporting the artist – brand name campaign.

Such a campaign involving a digital camera was carried out with Stefani, Interscope, and Hewlett Packard.

Buble and Starbucks, over Frappaccino coffee are in a similar venture.

And Black Eyed Peas and again Interscope are another such team as it involves American Eagle Outfitters.

All of the foregoing causes the age old argument about selling out to Madison Avenue to recede in view of present day cost reduction needs and the positive results of the foregoing promotions.

Given this search when will Rolls Royce sign such a contract with the Rolling Stones?

Chapter 4

Defining Talent

Irwin H. Steinberg and Jennifer Fischer

Many will argue that any attempt to define musical talent is self-defeating. Talent is a concept given to many interpretations and philosophies, and a discussion of talent on purely artistic terms could last for centuries. For the purposes of this chapter, it is important to determine the components of talent and their relevance to commercial success within the popular music market.

The relationship between technical talent and commercial talent is a shaky one. Technically speaking, an artist could be a master at his or her craft, yet may lack the special qualities that constitute commercial viability. Jules Shear writes hit songs, yet he hasn't achieved popular success as a solo artist. Conversely, from a purely technical standpoint, the band R.E.M., as musicians, are self-taught hacks. Bob Dylan's singing voice is pathetic if one is discussing virtuosity. These factors alone are all meaningless, because these artists have a chemistry combining artistic charisma with the fundamental components of technical talent.

Of all the concepts covered in this book, the most elusive is how a record company defines and selects talent. Frequently, record company people will say their decisions are based on instinct—that they can see a band perform and tell on the spot whether that band has what it takes to be successful. Traditionally, A&R people say that they have "ears"—that they can listen to a song once and discern whether it will be a hit. Others say they watch what others do and copy what is successful. However successful A&R people describe it, science or art, their magic can be examined in the context of a series of key factors that enter into a record company's evaluation of commercial viability.

COMMERCIALLY UNIQUE

Foremost among the components of success is commercial uniqueness: the group or individual must have a sound that doesn't already exist on the air. The artist, the artistic concept, the songwriting, the arrangements, and the musicianship must be special, particularly identifiable. The artist must be able to find a special niche rather than follow a trend or simply duplicate what already exists. In a business where copycatting is rampant, the importance of this aspect may be hard to believe. But virtually everyone in the business is looking for the next trend, or at least a new sound within an existing trend. Commercial uniqueness is the single most vital component of a group's success in the record business. Will the act draw a large enough record-buying audience to justify the label's investment of its funds? At an independent label, the investment and the return needed are much less than at the major labels. But unique and commercial are not contradictions; A&R people look for more of a balancing act. An artist who is going to make it big must have successful precursors, but must also be special enough to attract listeners. If an artist is commercially unique, a record company will then go on to evaluate other components. If the artist is not commercially unique, the remaining components are not even considered.

PERSONA

How well does the act perform on stage? How does the act dress? Is their movement on stage effective? What is their live show like? These are the questions an A&R executive asks to determine whether the artist has the requisite persona to capture the more visceral emotions of the music consumer. Musical eras have defined categories of persona: disco required a "glam" persona, new wave required a counter-cultural, almost nerdish persona, and alternative rock requires a "we don't care about persona" persona. Whatever it is, however, an artist must have it.

SONGWRITING

Is the artist or group self-sufficient as songwriters? Publishers no longer bring songs to artists, and most of the successful groups now write and perform their own original material. However, country artists are often performers of other people's music. This pressure to write is being felt by the newer country artists who are beginning to venture into that arena. Many people also believe that artists who write their own music have a greater emotional relationship with that music, and, because of this relationship, can perform it with more meaning than any other performer can. This point may be debatable, but most currently successful groups are writers as well as performers, so compositional skills must rank high on the list of components for success. Furthermore, the lyrics and the music must support the "commercially unique" concept.

MOTIVATION

The artist or group must have an overwhelming desire to be successful performing artists not only for the present but also for the reasonably distant future. The group should have long-range as well as short-range goals in addition to a commitment to stay together and to work hard to build on their natural talent.

STABILITY

It is no longer acceptable for an artist to have a lifestyle that is likely to self-destruct. If the act is a group, there must be a cohesiveness that assures continuity. Record companies are in business for the long haul. If a company invests its resources in an act, it wants to be able to reap the benefits of that investment over a long period of time. If there are obvious signs of trouble within the group, such as constant disagreement among the members, lack of commitment to the group's longevity or heavy drug use, the company may not want to invest in the act.

GROWTH/CHANGE

This is difficult to evaluate on a first hearing. If the group is going to be in business for a long time, they must have enough musical intelligence to grow, change, and evolve so that they have the potential for a long-term career. The second album should not sound exactly like the first. Strong songwriting talent, mentioned previously, may be one gauge of the ability of the artist to grow and develop.

MANAGEMENT

Does it exist? Will the management team give the artist good guidance, financial support, skilled booking and negotiating skills? Most record companies won't even consider an act unless it has a manager. The manager, not the artists themselves, is the main contact with the record company, the publisher, MTV, agents, and promoters. Therefore, the manager must be someone with whom the record company feels comfortable working.

MUSICIANSHIP

The perceptions of the importance of musical virtuosity, or even simple musical ability, vary with the audience. It may be a lay person's view that technical musical ability is extremely, or even primarily, important. But the industry views musical talent with varying degrees of significance. Certainly in the jazz arena, technical virtuosity is usually all-important. In the country arena, the artist's vocal talents are extremely important. But in rock the significance of musicianship varies. Recent trends have even appeared to discourage any sort of musical virtuosity.

Generally, in the rock arena, musical virtuosity is just one of many factors that a record executive will consider in making a decision to sign. The current view among many aspiring recording artists is that talent "won't get you anywhere." But without it, the road is certainly more difficult.

CONCEPTS INTO PRACTICE: TRUE STORIES

With these concepts in mind, consider some of today's artists. How might their success (or lack of it) be defined by the components of success as described above? Think of the difference between artistic talent and commercial talent. Are there differences? Do the two co-exist or are they mutually exclusive? Take a marketing perspective (it isn't called the music business for nothing) and shape your own ideas of the most important elements of talent. At the same time, try to pin down the common components that the real movers and shakers in the record business are considering.

Metallica

Heavy metal gods to millions of kids, Metallica's fans are mostly male, mostly white, and mostly between the all-important record-buying ages of 12 to 19. Commercially the most successful at their craft, Elektra artists Metallica have sold millions of records with virtually no radio exposure. Rap and hip-hop artists proved that work on the street is just as powerful a promotional tool as radio. Metallica manages to combine technical prowess (their lead guitarist is considered a wizard by many) with sheer power and lasting visual impact. In 1991, Metallica's album Metallica hit the charts at #1 at entry (Billboard 8/31/91). Interestingly, just a short time later, Garth Brooks was #1 on the charts. Certainly Metallica has exhibited strong persona, songwriting, motivation, stability, management and musicianship. Are they commercially unique? They have proven unique enough to sell millions of records.

Wilco

Wilco is a Chicago-based band that is most often associated with indie rock despite their long term career with major record labels. A two-time Grammy winning group, Wilco has gone through many transformations and has managed to stay relevant with true musical talent, song-writing skills, and dedicated fans. Since their inception in 1994, the lead singer/guitarist Jeff Tweedy and the bassist, John Stirrat, are the two remaining original members, while their manager, Tony Margherita has been with them all along as well. Their seventh album is highly anticipated and scheduled for release in June of 2009, as their previous album released in 2007, *Sky Blue Sky*, has been their most commercially popular to date. To promote *Sky Blue Sky*, Wilco offered several songs as free downloads as well as licensed several songs to a Volkswagon campaign. This move was highly criticized by fans that viewed Wilco as "their" band and called the move "selling out". Regardless, the move made Wilco a commercial success and a household name. No longer just a critically acclaimed group, Wilco is a great example of traditional talent, strong management, and long-term motivation.

Lil Wayne

Rap and Hip-Hop artist, Lil Wayne hails from New Orleans. The twenty-six year old has earned Gold, Platinum and two Multi-Platinum awards in his thirteen-year career. Signed to Cash Money Records (Universal) in his pre-teen years, Lil Wayne has enjoyed great commercial success through a combination of natural songwriting ability and an entrepreneurial mindset: he founded Young Money Entertainment, and served as president of Cash Money Records. He has very much put Hip Hop on a mainstream level by maintaining a balance between hardcore New Orleans rap and modern, popular music. Lil Wayne has a certain commercial uniqueness that stems from his intelligent and observant yet edgy lyrics, and contrasting melodic auto-tuned vocals. 2009 sees Lil Wayne's fans awaiting the release of "Rebirth", his attempt to break into the rock scene. It remains to be seen if this change in genre will be as popular as his previous work, but the first single, "Prom Queen" has had notable success in the Billboard charts.

Mariah Carey

She's young with fashion-model looks, confidence, and enough vocal chops to go with her physical appeal. Mariah Carey was signed by Tommy Mottola, CBS Records chief, after hearing some demos she made in 1988 while earning a part-time wage as a background session singer. Her self-titled debut album landed in the top ten on Billboard's Pop Album chart. Her first single, "Vision of Love," was #1 at both Pop and Black radio. Her launch at CBS was supported by extensive trade advertising, TV appearances (the Arsenio Hall Show) and other media advertising. Mariah Carey provided an opportunity for Donnie Lenner, president of Columbia Records, to try to duplicate or surpass the success he enjoyed in promoting Whitney Houston at Arista. Often compared to Houston, Mariah Carey has received critical acclaim for her technical proficiency, wide vocal range and blues inflections. In September, 1993, Mariah Carey was part of a trio of "adult" acts in positions one, two and three on the charts; Garth Brooks and Billy Joel were in the other two positions. After a brief hiatus, Mariah returned to the pop chart in 2005 and has remained there since. To date, she is ranked second as the artist with the most #1 singles, only behind the Beatles. Her 2008 hit, "Touch My Body" pushed her past Elvis to second place.

Bonnie Raitt

After twenty years of making great music, Bonnie Raitt has finally made it commercially. Hers is an obvious example of pure artistic talent that, until recently, never realized commercial success. She has always enjoyed the respect of her peers and has defined a style of music that many have co-opted. Her 1989 release, Nick of Time, brought her four Grammies and allowed her next release Luck of the Draw, to hit the tracks running. The album made it to #2. Nick of Time was in the Top 100 for more than 118 weeks! Bonnie Raitt's belated success is certainly not due to a change in musical style; if anything her roots and her style have become even more highly defined. In fact, her one attempt at pure commercial appeal, The Glow, failed miserably (more miserably than her previous albums, that is).

Radiohead

Radiohead is an English alternative rock band from Abingdon, Oxfordshire. They released their first single, "Creep," in 1992. While initially the song was unsuccessful, it became a worldwide hit several months after the release of their debut album, *Pablo* Honey in 1993. Fans and critics alike had a positive response to Thom Yorke's falsetto voice and Radiohead's all-around distinct sound. However it was with Radiohead's third album, *OK Computer* in 1997 that the band rose to international fame. Featuring an expansive sound and themes of modern alienation, *OK Computer* has often been acclaimed as a landmark record of the 1990s. *Kid A* and *Amnesiac* were released in 2000 and 2001 respectively, and marked an evolution in Radiohead's musical style. *Hail to the Thief,* released in 2003, was the band's final album for their major record label, EMI. On October 1, 2007, the band announced that they had finished their seventh album, *In Rainbows*, and that it would be "out" in a matter of ten days. Giving fans the option to pay whatever they'd like for the album as a zip file of MP3s, Radiohead also devised a pre-order system for the physical version of the album -- a "discbox" containing a double-vinyl version, a CD copy with an enhanced six-track bonus disc, a lyric book, and photos -- which they planned on shipping by early December. This was done without the involvement of a record label.

Amy Winehouse

The UK's modern answer to Courtney Love, Amy Winehouse, signed to Island Records (Universal), is a singer-songwriter known for her impressive voice and her turbulent personal life. She holds the record for the most Grammy wins for a British female artist, winning 5 Grammys in one night for her album "Back in Black" and song "Rehab". Her predominant jazz influence and 60s soul sound is a large part of her success, and in combining so many musical styles with a diva versus rock star attitude has very much made Amy Winehouse the ultimate female artist of the 21st Century. People copy her style, buy her music, and love to hate her. Winehouse's long history of drug and alcohol abuse alongside several related health problems has resulted in extensive media coverage, almost transforming her from a pop star to a reality media star. Her distinctive sound and seductive image has helped her transition from British stardom to US Billboard success.

Taylor Swift

Taylor Swift is an all-American girl with an exceptional talent for singing and songwriting. Her first single was released in 2006 when she was only 16 and started her journey as one of country music's youngest and brightest stars. Although she is new to the industry, she has managed to make her mark, winning many awards and even be successful on pop charts. Her album *Fearless* was released in late 2008 and debuted at #1 on the Billboard 200 Album Chart. This was the largest opening for any female of any genre of that year. The first single, "Love Story," was popular on both the pop and country charts, a hard feat to accomplish.

Madonna

Either you love her or you hate her, but in a discussion of talent, whatever that may be, her success must be noted and considered, which is probably all she ever wanted. The Economist (July, 1991) said she had labored relentlessly to make herself into an icon, striving to become a celebrity in the ranks of Elvis, James Dean and Marilyn Monroe. As the magazine suggests, "Her fans don't mind if she pushes their buttons." The writers also suggest that pop culture's real appeal is, in fact, "[This] joy of surrender, the guilty pleasure of being willfully taken in." (Economist, July, 1991) Although Madonna's talent as a musician and dancer is questionable, she has been given her own entertainment conglomerate, compliments of Time Warner, and an inside source reports her annual income at well above eight digits. Madonna is a real study in what is talent, and what is commercially unique. She clearly has it all. She is a case study on the importance of each factor discussed at the beginning of this chapter.

Elvis Presley

Elvis Presley hit conservative 1950's America like a freight train: a fresh new sound, great looks, a great voice, and boundless sexual charisma. And this dream combination was not the extent of Presley's massive appeal. To a post-war generation of youth trying to find their way in a new era, Presley pointed to a new direction. He was one of them, traditional yet irreverent, wanting something bigger and better and willing to live out his fantasies without compromise. Presley's sound was so unique at the time (combining "black" gospel, blues, and rhythm and blues with "white" bluegrass and country and western) that it created an entirely new genre: rock 'n' roll. While swiveling hips, pulsing rhythm and sexual innuendo were nothing new to black audiences, they came as a shock to white middle-class America. After all, Presley was only shown from the waist up in one of his first prime-time television appearances. His cool charisma and manner of dress excited females and made males want to emulate him. While not a songwriter, Elvis had strong talent as a singer. He was able to cover styles from blues to country and western to gospel.

The Beatles

The Beatles, passed on by several major labels, became one of the biggest acts in history. The group's appeal was multi-fold: superb songwriting and strong musical talent, an exciting stage presence honed by long and arduous gigs in Liverpool and Hamburg, and a unique look and photogenic image. Later, innovation and experimentation with the aid of a strong producer, George Martin, carried the band and popular music into previously unexplored territory. Strong management helped the group garner recording deals on both sides of the Atlantic, key television appearances, and product marketing. The group began to unravel after manager Brian Epstein's death in 1967. Sometimes overlooked was the band's tremendous work ethic. During the years 1964-66, the Beatles produced nine albums of new material and two movies while touring constantly. From 1967 to 1969, while no longer performing publicly, the group released six more albums of new, increasingly complex material while shooting two more movies. In addition, during this time the individual members were involved in solo projects.

The Seattle Sound

As recently as a few years ago, to a student of rock music Seattle was just a city in the Pacific Northwest. Within those few years, Seattle became the birthplace and childhood home of the alternative music movement, which has changed the entire direction of rock. This music has evolved quickly from its infancy as grungy, talentless and spoiled-brattish in its approach to a musical direction that is more sophisticated, a bit more joyful, more melodic and certainly more talented. The sound began as pure and simple grunge, the stuff college radio stations had been playing on the sly for several years prior. Why the sudden interest? Beginning in 1991, college radio began to be regarded as an important step in breaking new bands. This increase in importance, some have said, was a direct response to the continued conservative programming of many commercial stations, particularly those stations that describe their format as AOR (album oriented rock). Most commercial radio programmers countered that they were just spotlighting the music that appeals to their listeners, and that most new or alternative/college radio-oriented artists were too challenging and did not mix well with the safer material. Thus it seems that programmers were indirectly saying that their listeners had a different perception of talent. College radio, however, has now gained the respect of labels and artists. This evolution provided the fertile soil for the movement of a trend from the limited listenership of college radio stations to the playlists of the big commercial stations.

Beethoven

The 10th edition of Scholes's The Oxford Companion to Music marvelously and cogently describes Beethoven's uniqueness:

> More than any other composer he deserves to be called the Shakespeare of music, for he reaches to the heights and plumbs the depths of the human spirit as no other composer has done, and it was his own ambition to be called 'Tone Poet.' In him were combined, in a measure that remains (and may forever remain) unique, the power to feel both passionately and tenderly and the mastery of musical resources necessary to express his feelings in the (1) command of pregnant melodic phraseology and of varied, original, and sometimes daring harmonic idiom, with (2) sense of the innate principles of form as went far beyond a mere successful adherence to the conventions of balance and variety of material and key, and (3) ability to imagine his melodies and harmonies in gabs of glowing instrumental colour, whether this be drawn from the more restricted prismatic scale of the pianoforte or string quartet or from the wider ranging one of the full orchestra.
>
> His work may, on one side of it, be regarded as the continuation of that of Haydn and Mozart and, on another, as the inspiration of that of Wagner. Such a placing in succession of four great names does not, however, hint at degrees of perfection, but only at that process of development from simplicity to complexity which, in harmony, form, and instrumental treatment, went on consistently from about the middle of the eighteenth century to near the end of the nineteenth—and for that matter is in certain ways still in progress.

Looked at in this manner, and with an eye to the type of feeling he expressed, Beethoven may be considered the last of the classical and first of the modern composers, or the last of the classical and the first of the romantic composers.

THE "DISCOVERY" MYTH

The common romantic notion of the A&R "find" or "discovery" involves a label scout who stumbles onto a unique and important artist playing in a small club in an out-of-the-way market. Bruce Springsteen was a classic rock and roll "discovery," which fueled his appeal. Springsteen had a bar band in New Jersey, unknown outside of his neighborhood until John Hammond and CBS got the wheels turning. This situation, however, does not present itself often. Most signings today hinge on whether an artist has proven performance behind him or her including strong independent record sales, European market performance, familiar image or press attention, in conjunction with the other factors described above.

The U.S. market may never have heard of the Sugarcubes, a band from Iceland. However, this was a band that was huge in their native country (as huge as a band could be in Iceland) and sold many records in Europe prior to their domestic deal. In the U.S., such regional success now grabs the attention of labels. Edie Brickell and the New Bohemians were a strong draw in south Texas clubs before being signed to a label deal. Soul II Soul's introduction to the U.S. market was based on incredible response in the U.K. It is obvious that more than just so-called raw talent influences the decisions of record labels.

MARKET REALITIES: SUCCESS AFTER SIGNING

Obviously, there are other qualities of talent which transcend strict technical accomplishment. The mechanics of marketing a record or artist must be in full gear in order for the public to get its chance at making the final judgment. A great record by a talented artist does not automatically and effortlessly rise to the top like cream. The key to a record's success, regardless of talent, is hard work by both the record company and band alike. A promising signing by a label can be buried by a promotion staff that's not fully behind the release. An artist unwilling to participate in interviews, store appearances, and other legwork may seriously hinder the progress of his or her record, in spite of talent or lack of it.

Radio stations and MTV only have so many programming hours per day. There is no way that the mainstream media can support all music that's considered to be important. In answer to this limitation, some labels have developed alternative marketing departments to exploit avenues other than the mainstream media, such as college radio fanzines, smaller markets, etc. A problem arises when these departments are strapped with limited budgets and hindered by lack of support from other promotion departments. The problem is exacerbated further by restrictive formats like classic rock and satellite-delivered programming.

AGENTS, MANAGERS AND LAWYERS

Agents, managers, and lawyers play an important role in the shaping of talent. Often a manager or lawyer representing an artist of questionable prospects can successfully negotiate a deal with a label on speculation that, with the right support, the artist will gel. The remainder bins at record stores are replete with releases by unknown artists, likely signed through the influence of a well-connected lawyer or manager. For example, did you ever come across a record by Broken Homes on MCA? Little America or Tommy Keene on Geffen?

The following example illustrates a case in which the mechanics of marketing and business broke down and led to the aborted career of an otherwise promising artist:
Dwight Twilley had a hit record in the early 1970s with "I'm On Fire." It reached #16 on Billboard's Hot 100. Twilley's career was soon destroyed by a bizarre series of unfortunate circumstances. Twilley had moved his band from Tulsa, Oklahoma, to Los Angeles to pursue a record company contract. The band signed with Leon Russell's Shelter Records and the "I'm on Fire" single was released. Shelter folded but was incorporated into Shelter/ABC just before the album Sincerely, which contained the "Fire" single, was released. The album didn't do as well as the single, due to delays between single and album release. Shelter struck a deal with Arista, who released Twilley's second and third albums.

Unbelievably, Shelter forgot to pick up the option on Twilley when his contract expired. This left the artist in a state of limbo regarding his relationship with Arista. To avoid legal problems, Arista's president, Clive Davis, put Twilley on indefinite hold until they figured out what to do. Meanwhile, EMI approached Arista and made a successful offer for Twilley's contract and his next two albums. Personnel changes at EMI upset Twilley and he was later released from his contract. Twilley then met Joe Isgro of Private Eye Records (Isgro later went on to play a major role in the indie-payola scandal). Private Eye obtained a distribution deal with CBS for Twilley's new album, but CBS killed the record after the scandal broke. Twilley was eventually released from his CBS contract.

Because Twilley had no representation when he signed his first contract with Shelter, he received no royalties from "I'm on Fire" or 98 other songs that Shelter owns. At last sighting, Twilley was playing at a local club, backed up by a heavy metal band, for an audience of about 40 people.

CONCLUSION

In this business, there are few absolutes. The subjective analysis of talent means little if all the goods don't coalesce into a decent song. The points discussed here are not absolute. Ultimately, music strikes an emotional response, and how can that be measured with any degree of certainty? Looking at talent from a commercial perspective, one has to take into account tested parameters of taste as well as gut reaction. If commerce in general were a supermarket, the music business would be the cereal aisle. How is a particular box going to stand out? Certainly, it has to be different, but it also should strike a satisfying chord of familiarity. If talent is attempting to reach the mass public, which qualities will appeal to the greatest number of people? On the other hand, which qualities will further the art form instead of relying on tired clichés and overwrought styles?

Think of these things as you watch the next video or see the cover of *Rolling Stone* (one without a movie star on it). Ask yourself how four longhaired guys from Tucson can compete with a number one record by a former Lakers cheerleader. The answer may be obvious to some and not so obvious to others. Surprises do happen in the record industry, and it's the qualities that prompt these surprise performances that need to be examined.

The Billboard charts of May 11, 2009 shows such artists as Taylor Swift, Kings of Leon, Rascal Flatts, The Black Eyed Peas, Lady GaGa, and Bob Dylan among the top ten sellers in the U.S. The principles discussed in this chapter apply to these artists as well as to those mentioned in the text.

It makes sense, at the end of this chapter, for everyone to try his or her hand at being an A&R scout. Consider the groups in the preceding paragraph. Every one of them is currently extremely popular, but do they measure up on our list of criteria for defining talent? A good first step is to choose one or two of the groups or individuals and go through each of the criteria to see how they rate. Here is a start:

Kings of Leon

1. Commercially unique:
2. Persona:
3. Songwriting:
4. Motivation:
5. Stability:
6. Growth/Change:
7. Management:
8. Musicianship:

Rascal Flatts

1. Commercially unique:
2. Persona:
3. Songwriting:
4. Motivation:
5. Stability:
6. Growth/Change:
7. Management:
8. Musicianship:

Using these same criteria, evaluate the following performers:
    Rick Ross
    Depeche Mode
    Lady GaGa
    T.I.
    Nickelback
    Keith Urban
    Beyonce'
    Jars of Clay
    Bon Jovi
    Britney Spears

A good next step might be to compare the chosen groups' music to other established groups or individuals performing the same type of music. If the example is a solo country artist, compare him or her to top country performers. The top performers in any category have very good reasons why they have risen to the top. How does a superstar country performer like Garth Brooks score on the chart?

Kenny Chesney

1. Commercially unique:
2. Persona:
3. Songwriting:
4. Motivation:
5. Stability:
6. Growth/Change:
7. Management:
8. Musicianship:

A good next step would be to compare these performers with some of the real veteran performers. If we stay with the male country vocalist example, Johnny Cash would be an excellent case or, going back a little further, Merle Travis.

Johnny Cash and/or Merle Travis

1. Commercially unique:
2. Persona:
3. Songwriting:
4. Motivation:
5. Stability:
6. Growth/Change:
7. Management:
8. Musicianship:

This is just a rough outline of what should be a new way of looking at music, performers, and what to look out for as music business professionals. Do not limit your thinking to these few examples. Ask yourself how a contemporary girl group, the Spice Girls, for example, would compare to successful groups of the past, like the Shirelles or the Crystals or the Supremes.

Pussycat Dolls

1. Commercially unique:
2. Persona:
3. Songwriting:
4. Motivation:
5. Stability:
6. Growth/Change:
7. Management:
8. Musicianship:

Supremes

1. Commercially unique:
2. Persona:
3. Songwriting:
4. Motivation:

5. Stability:
6. Growth/Change:
7. Management:
8. Musicianship:

Though the times and music are different, the same qualities that made groups and individuals successful in the past, all the way back to Beethoven, are the same qualities that are making them successful now, and will continue to do so in the future.

Speaking of Beethoven, these criteria work equally well for classical musicians. There may be a stronger emphasis on musicianship in classical music, but a pianist can win the Van Cliburn or Tchaikovsky competition and not have a major career. Musicianship alone will not make a successful soloist; the other qualities must be there as well. What makes Murray Peraiha one of the most highly respected of all pianists performing today? What about the legendary pianists of the past, Horowitz, Rubenstein, and Serkin? What made them great, and what do young classical musicians need to do in order not to imitate them, but to establish their own personalities in the concert scene?

The music managers and A&R people understand this, and develop and nurture talent that they find. The next top performer may be just around the corner; these are the tools by which we can recognize talent.

The Music Business in Action:
Music Intelligence

Computer programmers working in a new field called "music intelligence" are developing software capable of predicting which songs will become hits. Capitol Records, Universal Music, and Sony are using this software and finding it surprisingly accurate.

The software uses a process called "special deconvolution" to isolate and analyze such things as sonic brilliance, octave, cadence, frequency range, fullness of sound, chord progression, pitch, and timbre, all of which define any selection of music. The music intelligence developers argue that it does not matter that music, so analyzed, comes from different eras. They argue that the underlying parameters encompass successful music in any genre in any time.

In addition to record labels, radio programmers are using this technology. This technology is called "music science" by the company Platinum Blue, "Hit Song Science" by Orixa of Madrid and includes a company called Polyphonic HMI.

Bulls-eye predictions were made with music intelligence software for *Candy Shop* by 50 Cent, *Be the Girl* by Aslyn, *Unwritten* by Bedingfield, and *She Says* by Howie Day.

Why have we not heard more about this? Probably no one wants others to know that a "box" is making their decisions, but if "music intelligence" is the way that the hits of the future are going to be made, then all of the parameters discussed in defining may take a back seat to the "ears" of the computer.

THE RECORDING ARTIST'S WORLD

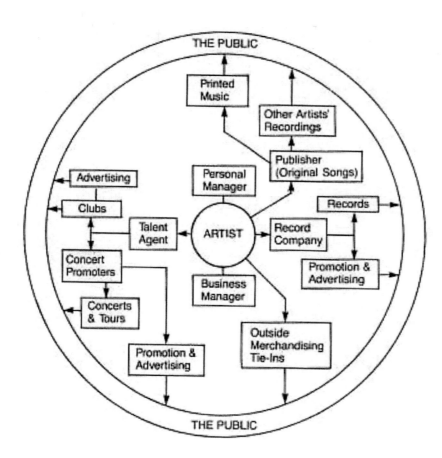

Reproduced with permission of Schirmer Books, an imprint of Simon & Schuster Macmillan, from *Inside the Music Business* by Michael Fink. Copyright ©1989 by Schirmer Books.

Chapter 5

The Artist Recording Contract

Irwin H. Steinberg

Note: Chapter Five deals with artist contract matters in general and with a contract written in the mid 1980's. This is done to give historical perspective and understanding regarding how technological advances have changed artist contracts over time. It then moves to Chapter 5A, current day digital rights issues in the contract of today. It then moves to Ch. 5B where provisions of a current day contract inclusive of the digital world are explained in detail.

INTRODUCTION

It is hard for anyone who hasn't gone through the experience to imagine the euphoria a band feels when it receives the news that a major record company wants to sign the band to a contract. Years of toil, sweat, playing for little or nothing, has finally paid off. Someone has finally noticed what the band members have known all along; this is a special group, whose music deserves to be heard by a large public.

This euphoria soon turns to anger and confusion when the mail brings a contract that, the members feel, can't be figured out by any lawyer since Clarence Darrow, and maybe not him either. Should they sign a contract they don't understand? They are sure they are being cheated, but don't understand how. To not sign the contract, however, may mean passing up the chance of a lifetime. Many bands, regretfully, sign first and regret later. Others have the wisdom to hire a good lawyer to protect their interests, or have a manager present to help with the negotiations.

This chapter provides an analysis of a typical record company contract and explains why each clause is included. It is not a substitute for a good lawyer, but it is designed to give the reader some insight as to the legal relationship a record company is to have with the artist.

This contract was written at the introduction of the CD, which makes the related part of the contract interesting in itself. But it is also the precursor of the contract approach for online sales. Further, this contract was chosen for its complexity and for its obvious call for balanced and fair negotiation.

THE CONTRACT: BACKGROUND

In this chapter, we will be referring to a recording contract which is an actual contract written in the late 1980's for an artist of major significance. We have chosen this contract because of some interesting innovations and adaptations in respect to typically controversial areas of a recording agreement. Thus think CD where you see LP and think singles where you see EP and when you see 45, think online (see end of chapter 3).

Before referring to the details of the typical recording agreement, consider who negotiates such an agreement. On behalf of the artist, any one of the following could be present, or any combination thereof: the artist, the artist's manager, or the artist's attorney. On behalf of the record company, the business affairs head, a corporate legal officer who is a senior vice-president, the president of the company, and possibly the A&R (Artist and Repertoire) director who has selected the artist could be present. Very rarely will the A&R director be there for negotiation on his own; either the president or the business affairs chief will be present or both might be present.

Should the artist be at the negotiation? This author contends that it is not a good idea because negotiations can be confrontational, and thus not a good way to initiate a relationship between the artist and the record company management.

WHAT THE PARTIES SEEK

The recording contract should never be seen as a document that cannot be altered. Rather, the contract is a starting point for negotiation. The object of the contract is to provide a landscape for negotiation, resulting in a document that makes both parties happy. So the question is, what will satisfy each side?

In a recording contract, the artist seeks:

1. exposure, an opportunity for income.
2. freedom of expression.
3. a stable financial and management atmosphere in which to work.
4. guidance from the record company and a generally collegial atmosphere.
5. future rewards should he demonstrate longevity.

The record company seeks:

1. unique commercial music from the artist.
2. an opportunity for profit, which is reflected in the construction of the agreement allowing the music to be recorded and sold at a reasonable cost.
3. the opportunity to extend the contract should the initial exposure be successful.
4. communication with the artist and with his/her management.
5. opportunity to be involved in artistic decisions.

Power

Power becomes a factor in negotiation and a question when discussing the artist's contract. Obviously, when the artist is established he/she might have equity from a power standpoint in dealing with a record company regarding royalty rates, exposure in terms of radio or video play, general merchandising, and the kind of exposure in foreign markets. An artist without power, such as a new artist, can't push past reasonable economics of the contract since the risk is, at the outset, solely in the hands of the record company. The company might contribute an advance, it will pay for the recording costs, and it will pay for the initial exposure. The advance to the artist could be as much as $500,000. That $500,000, constructed as recoupable from royalties, may or may not be recovered by the record company and if not results in a cost in a record company's financial statement, as opposed to an asset. The artist with power can negotiate most of the elements of the contract to receive a higher royalty rate and to establish higher supporting costs and guarantees of that kind of support. On the other hand, the new artist might have to accept a relatively low royalty rate and also stand certain costs against the royalty rate, which might include the use of independent radio, video, and of course, recording costs in general.

However, there are ways of mitigating a new artist's lack of power. In the sample contract, note that it includes an escalating royalty rate based upon the achievement of different sales volume levels. This is one of the ways of mitigating a lack of power. That is, one might start with limited requests as to royalty rate and support costs, but when successful those rates and costs would be altered accordingly.

It must be recognized by all the participants in the agreement that the bulk of the volume done in the industry and perhaps 90% of the volume done worldwide is done by members of the record industry oligopoly (the four companies who comprise the oligopoly being SONY/BMG, EMI/Capitol, Universal, and WEA). These companies are publicly held, and with public ownership come responsibility for the bottom line and for producing not only dividends but evidence of a growing income per share. What does this mean to the people who negotiate on both sides? It means that the objectives of both the artists and those representing the record company have to be such that they permit a cost structure that provides an opportunity for profit. In the case of the Michael Jackson-SONY contract at a 25% royalty rate (25% of retail), for example, the structure might translate into as much as 50% of the selling price of the record company to the middleman (the retailer or the level of distribution which precedes the retailer). There are, therefore, limiting factors on both parties which must be realistically viewed. Overall, with the royalties that must be paid by a record company to the American Federation of Musicians, and for royalty payment to the artist, and the publisher's royalty, the average for most record companies is somewhere in the area of 30% of the record company's wholesale selling price.

THE CONTRACT: IMPORTANT CLAUSES

Referring to the artist contract appended to this chapter, paragraph 1(d) and paragraph 1(e) are written so as to encompass any and all technology which is used now or in the future to transport recorded music. Paragraph 2(g) calls for a minimum amount of playing time, to assure that there is sufficient music recorded and scheduled for the particular album to justify calling it an album and to justify the selling price attached to an album.

Paragraphs 1(k)(i) and 1(k)(ii) have to do with the basis for calculating the royalty. The retail selling price is described as the price at which the record is sold in the United States, and also defines retail selling price outside of the United States to provide a basis for calculating the royalty. For example, if the royalty rate is 10% and the retail selling price is $15.98, after certain deductions from the $15.98 (described later in the contract), the royalty rate is applied to the retail selling price and the artist is paid on that basis. On the other hand, paragraph 1(k)(ii) notes that should the company choose a wholesale basis, it would recalculate royalty rates using a wholesale price, which would leave the artist with a royalty no less than the rate calculated based upon the retail selling price.

Paragraph 1(l) covers recording costs and not only defines the recording costs but indicates that the costs will be deemed an advance recoupable from the royalties which might accrue based upon the sales which occur under the agreement. In other words, these advances must be recovered through royalty payments before any payment is made to the artist. What this paragraph indicates is that the artist is an employee of the record company and that the recording agreement is a kind of joint venture between the employee (in this case, the artist) and the record company. Should the advance not be recovered, then such advances become a cost of the record company and are in no way the responsibility of the artist to repay. Hence, the engagement of a record company with any artist is a risky venture in that if the record doesn't sell, the record company is stuck with the loss.

Paragraph 1(o) covers territory, and in this contract that means the entire world. This provision is for the benefit of both the artist and the record company, since there is always the possibility that the music produced could reach many cultures throughout the world. For example, certain Michael Jackson albums have sold as many as 25 million copies in the United States and 25 million copies outside the U.S. Most record companies, particularly major record companies, have offices throughout the world and are fully prepared to release recordings in many of those places. The contract, though signed in the United States, extends beyond the borders of the United States. Some artists sell more records overseas than in the U.S, so it is important to negotiate for the release of recordings in foreign countries if the artist has a potential market there.

Paragraph 1(q) refers to merchandising rights, and these rights are clearly defined in the paragraph. This agreement makes it clear that the revenue which flows from these merchandising rights will be split 50/50 between the artist and the record company. Most artists will negotiate this right, or ask for a right of first refusal rather than granting this stipulation outright.

Paragraph 1(r) gives the definition of a budget record. In this contract, records which are subject to being recategorized to reflect reduced demand experience a different royalty rate because of the reduced selling price. Paragraph 1(s) refers to and defines the word "advance," previously described as recording costs, a cash advance, or both, and this paragraph confirms that these advances are recoupable against the artist's royalties. In the case of this contract, however, cross-collateralization is prevented. The record company is barred from defining the mechanical royalties as part of that advance so that any songwriting done by the writer or the writer's publishing company must be paid despite the fact that the advance may not be recouped through royalties. In some contracts, the record company provides for cross-collateralization in order to reduce its risk. An example of cross-collateralization would be if an album fails to break even in a multi album deal, the royalties from subsequent albums would be used to offset the losses from the first album. Artists generally restrict cross-collateralization to protect their mechanical royalties from being used as a recoupment vehicle for the label. However, in over-budget situations and for tour support, an artist might ask for an advance against mechanicals.

Paragraph 2(a) provides for four separate options. The company will desire longevity of the contract should the artist be successful and the options referred to in this paragraph are held by the record company so that it can extend the agreement under clearly defined conditions. Each option is attended by an album and thereby rewards the record company and the artist should the initial year prove to be a success. Note in this paragraph the use of the word "exclusively." Obviously, without an exclusive arrangement with the artist, the contract loses a great deal of its value because of the possibility that other renditions by this artist will compete against the use of resources for this artist by the record company. Surprisingly, many naive artists feel that this exclusivity is unjustified. The leaving member clause discussed later in this chapter also deals with this issue.

Paragraph 2(b) indicates that the contract shall not exceed seven years and provides for the delivery of a specific number of LP's should the options be exercised, and also provides for the length of time given to make such delivery.

Paragraph 3(a) clearly expresses the fact that this agreement is exclusive as long as the contract is under term between the artist and the record company.
Paragraphs 3(c), 3(d), 3(e), and 3(f) refer specifically to the delivery of the second, third, and fourth albums, and also indicate that should the company fail to exercise its option, then the term of the agreement automatically expires at that point.

Paragraphs 3(h) and 3(i) have to do with the artist's performance, specifying that the recordings done by the performer shall be reasonably consistent in concept and style and similar to the songs previously recorded. This stipulation protects the record company by preventing the artist from simply creating an inconsistent and inconsequential album purposely to bring the contract to a close. The two paragraphs also indicate that what is delivered to the record company in the form of music shall be technically satisfactory for manufacture. For example, if the decibel level is so high that it distorts the music, the recording might not be considered technically satisfactory, and so re-record provisions are made in one of these two paragraphs.

It is important to understand that the value of any record company is in the form of the master recordings it owns, and the contracts which it holds. That's why contracts written between the artist and record company require the artist's exclusivity, and except for extremely rare instances, the masters when delivered to the record company are solely the property of the record company. Without these masters, record companies have far less value. Beginning with paragraph 4(b), in extending this idea of catalog value, note that the artist cannot under the agreement written here re-record any song done under the term of this agreement for five years, subject to the date at which the composition was recorded under this agreement. This provision protects the value of the catalog, and this contract indicates that, should the artist violate this stipulation, no royalties have to be paid to the artist on albums made under this agreement. This clause also covers uses in other media. In more recent agreements, record companies also seek revenue generated from motion picture soundtracks and other media through such a provision.

Paragraph 5 clearly describes the fact that all recordings, including both audio and audio-visual recordings delivered to the company, and any derivatives manufactured therefrom shall be the exclusive property of the record company. Again, the value of the company resides in its owning these recordings, and that's why this paragraph exists as written. This agreement states that ownership extends to the conversion of a recording to any or all forms of embodiment, that is any and all forms of transmission of the music under contract, whether it is by CD or any method in the future as yet unknown.

The subparagraphs under paragraph 5 should be read for the provisions that have to do with the company's right to couple other artists with the artist whose agreement is under consideration. The agreement also states other rights of the record company, to lend or lease the existent masters, whether to a "budget line" which it owns or to a record club or to a foreign organization. Also, these paragraphs deal with the right to broadcast or to carry out certain deletions or editing as might be done in altering a particular composition for dance clubs, the right to engage in the synchronization of the music with film, the right to use the artist's photo, name, and general biography, and the right to convey the rights to this master by license or assignment. Without paragraph 5(i), a record company could not sell itself as a company to another entity. The items discussed here, such as coupling, leasing masters, etc., are all negotiated issues, and require the artist's consent before entering into an agreement with another company.

Paragraph 6(a)(i) indicates that the company will pay for promotional videos. However, one-half of the costs of those videos will be chargeable against and recoupable from royalties. This stipulation can vary in contracts from 100% chargeable to not chargeable at all.

Paragraph 7 refers to the escalated royalty rate. Earlier in this chapter it was noted that it is possible to mitigate a lack of power by providing an escalating royalty rate based on volume levels achieved. Section 7 of the contract describes how the royalty rate changes at different sales volume levels. In paragraph 7(a)(i), based on the late 1980s when the manufacturing cost of CD's was high, it was recommended in this contract that the royalty be paid at the same level as a conventional vinyl disk. For some reason, the negotiators did not provide an addendum or alternative to this concept by suggesting that as the manufacturing cost came down, the artist would be paid on the full retail selling price of the CD as it grew in both the percentage of volume for the record company, and in terms that as the quantity got larger, the cost would come down.

Paragraph 7e deals with altering the royalty rate accompanying the licensing of the artist's masters to a record club.

Throughout this contract, for artists signed in the United States, the royalty rate is usually 10% to 20%. For all other uses of the music, such as licensing which occurs with foreign organizations, premium sales, synchronization with film, and record club royalty, such revenues are shared equally between the record company and the artist. There are various portions of this contract which stress this idea.

Paragraph 7g indicates the deductions for packaging or containers which are made from the retail selling price before calculating the royalty. The argument made by the record company is that it is paying its royalties based on the music and not on the packaging of that music. Therefore, those percentages as expressed in this paragraph indicate the kind of deduction made from the retail selling price for the container before the royalty calculation is made.

A very important and controversial paragraph, paragraph 7(l) indicates the conditions under which no royalties will be paid for certain kinds of record transactions. For example, records that are returned under the return privilege exercised between the record companies and their retailers will not be subject to the royalty calculation. Nor will records which are given away to radio stations, TV stations, publishers for publicity, or to dealers or consumers for various merchandising campaigns. But even more interesting is the provision that should the record company sell the album for less than a certain price because the records are no longer salable in the conventional marketplace at the conventional price, and so are considered deletes or cutouts, no royalty shall be paid. One might argue the equity of this provision, but without it, record companies would probably be less willing to take chances when going into the marketplace, especially for a new artist. Thus, if this paragraph did not exist, it might very well be that the coordination between radio play and MTV might not happen. The record company's position is that if the label takes the risk of placing the artist's records in the marketplace, and the consumer does not buy those albums, the label does not recover the cost of manufacture of the record and the container, and so no royalty is paid. The author believes there is equity in this argument. Without it, exposure would probably be very poorly coordinated.

Special sales plans referred to in paragraph 7(l)(i) also refer to the reduction of royalty rates should special sales plans take place. Later in the agreement limits are placed on this provision, as the record company can not create sales plans that extend beyond a certain percentage of the overall sale, and thus the artist is protected. On the other hand, the special sales plan might convince the dealer to give the artist special exposure when ordinarily it would not occur. This limit is expressed in paragraph 7(i)(iii).

Paragraph 7(v) refers to the sharing of public performance fees, should they be paid to the record company. Public performance fees are the result of payments made from specific artist songs played and broadcast over the air. At present, this fee is not being paid in the U.S to either the artist or the record companies. It is only being paid to the songwriter or the songwriter's publisher. Outside the U.S., there is a performance fee paid as the result of broadcast to both the artist and the record company, and what this paragraph indicates is that such fees, when paid, wherever they are paid, shall be shared equally between the record company and the artist.

Paragraph 8(c) has to do with the artist's right to audit, and sets forth specific provisions for this. According to this agreement, the audit must be conducted by a Certified Public Accountant and must be done within a certain period of time. If there is an error in the company's records, there are certain penalties to be paid as well as additional royalties which may have been overlooked. This is a very important paragraph, as it contains provisions under which the audit can be carried out.

Paragraph 9(a) states that in the case of this artist, the advance paid by the record company includes not only the cash advance but the recording money, placing this money in the hands of the artist to carry out the completion of the album. All of the money which is defined as recording costs in this contract come under the supervision of the artist but must be met within the payments of the 1st, 2nd, 3rd, 4th and 5th albums if they occur, based on the amounts advanced. Subsequent paragraphs note that these are non-returnable advances and are recoupable from royalties.

In paragraph 9(c), should the record company hire independent promotion people, that is, people not on the staff of the record company, to assist in the radio promotion of any of this artist's recordings, one half of such costs would be chargeable against the artist royalties. Very often, although not included in this contract, recording agreements include a provision that this stipulation must have the artist's approval before being carried out.

Beginning with paragraph 10(c)(i) are several paragraphs that have to do with controlled compositions. Controlled compositions are songs which are written by members of the recording group or a specific artist referred to in the agreement who have written the songs utilized in the album. In this case, the record company argues that the company should be co-owners of such songs, since it is the company which brings the compositions to radio, resulting in performance fees paid to the writers only, an area of revenue for the artist in which the record company does not share. In the case of this artist, the agreement reached was that the record company only pays 75% of the statutory royalty rate per composition. At the time this chapter is written, the statutory rate paid to a composer is 6.95 cents per five minutes of music. Under this agreement, multiply 9.1 cents by 75% to reduce the cost to the record company in the manner described previously. Some argue the equity of this provision of the agreement, but the argument stands that the record company carries out the promotion of the compositions which results in revenues not only from performance fees but also contributes to the publishing revenue for the writers and/or owners of the compositions.

Paragraph 12 has to do with the artist warranting that there are no restrictions of any kind that would prevent the artist from entering into this agreement. This provision is standard, and is for the protection of both the record company and the artist.

It was previously indicated that part of the income for both the record company and the artist derives from representing the licensing of the masters produced under this agreement to companies outside the U.S Such licensing results in the payment of royalties from the licensee to the record company or licenser as the result of the sales which occur. This paragraph is well-negotiated by the artist's representative, because 10 or 12 countries outside the U.S. may account for 70-80% of the income that comes from foreign sources. The artist argues that should the record company be unable to achieve a licensing agreement in the named countries, then the right to license reverts to the artist. However, should this provision be carried out by the artist there is still a small amount of income that will flow to the record company even though the artist carries out the licensing. The licensing rights, under the conditions of this paragraph, could revert to the artist under the terms of the contract should the company not achieve a licensing agreement in the named territories.

Finally, beginning with paragraph 20(b), the agreement states that the record company has the right to replace any leaving member of the group at its discretion and choice, and that it also has the right to hold the leaving member to a contract. An artist leaving the group is thus subject to a fully expressed and agreed-upon contract, should the record company choose to sign him. Signing the leaving artist is at the record company's option, and in addition, the record company is a full participant in choosing the replacement for the leaving member.

CONCLUSION

In summary, the attached contract includes the following particularly important points:
- the contract is exclusive.
- the recording costs advance and the cash advance are recoupable out of royalties, and royalties do not flow to the artist until this recoupment is fulfilled. In this particular contract, there is a unique effect caused by escalating the royalties on a volume basis.
- the standard deductions constitute reductions of the royalty base price prior to calculating the royalty to the artist.
- the royalty flow of money is shared between the artist and the record company when it involves a license to a foreign organization, to a record club, premium service, or film company.
- this contract attempts to recognize a technological change in altering the royalty rate for the CD. Consider how such a provision might be applied in the future.
- the contract is constructed for one year, but options can be carried out by the record company to extend the term of the agreement.
- the masters when completed by the artist are the property of the record company and give recognition of the fact that such property is where the record company's value resides. If record companies had not held the masters as their property they could not be experiencing the gains which have occurred with the new technology as represented by the CD, for example.
- a recording agreement is an employment contract. The artist retains no interest in the physical tapes or masters or the copyright in the sound recording.
- the right to audit clauses and the default clauses are both important to the construction of the agreement.
- the leaving member clauses are very important for the protection of the investment in the group by the record company.

Note: As this book goes to press, the issue of electronic transference of digital music by one-off encryption and direct downloading to a CD-Recordable (CD-R) is rapidly evolving, and is likely to affect future artist contracts. For further discussion of these technologies, see Chapter 16.

SAMPLE RECORDING CONTRACT

Date: _____

When signed by you and _____ a division of
_____ the following shall constitute an agreement
between you and _____

1. (a)   "Master", "Master Recording": Any recording of sound, whether or not coupled with visual image, by any method and on any substance or material, whether now or hereafter known, intended for reproduction in the form of Phonograph Records, or otherwise. An "Original" Master or "Original" Recording shall mean Recording which first fixes sounds in a medium sufficiently permanent or stable to permit it to be perceived, reproduced or otherwise communicated for a period of more than transitory duration, or, in the case of recordings which are made by process of mixing and fixing together independently fixed sounds, the recording which first fixes any mix of such sounds. "Copy" or "Duplicate" Masters are recordings derived from any Original Master without change other than is inherently introduced by the technical limitations of the re-recording process.

(b)   "Side": A recording of sufficient playing time to constitute one (1) side of a 7-inch, 45 rpm disk Phonograph Record but not less than two and one-half (2-1/2) minutes of continuous sounds, embodying performances of Artist.

(c)   "Matrix", "Derivative": Any device, now or hereafter used, directly or indirectly, in the manufacture of Phonograph Records or Audio-Visual Devices and which are derived from a Master Recording, inclusive of Copy Masters but not limited thereto.

(d)   "Records", "Recordings", "Phonograph Records": Any device on or by which sound may be recorded, reproductions of recordings, now or hereafter known, manufactured or distributed primarily for home and/or jukebox use and/or on or in means of transportation.

(e)   "Audio-Visual Devices": All forms of reproductions of Audio-Visual Recordings, now or hereafter known, manufactured or distributed primarily for home and/or jukebox use and/or on or in means of transportation. Audio-Visual Recordings means every form of recording containing masters recorded hereunder embodying performances of Artist wherein are fixed visual images whether of Artist or otherwise together with sound.

(f)   Purposely deleted

(g)   "LP": A 12 inch, 33-1/3 rpm double-sided long-play phonograph Record or the equivalent thereof embodying thereon the equivalent of not fewer than eight (8) Sides and not more than ten (10) Sides, and having not less than thirty-five (35) minutes playing time.

(h)   "Album": One or more 12 inch, 33-1/3 rpm Records, or the equivalent thereof, sold in a single package.

(i)   Purposely deleted.

(j)   "Long Play Single": A 12 inch, 33-1/3 rpm or 45 rpm double-sided long-play Phonograph Record embodying thereon not more than three (3) Sides.

(k)(i)   "Retail List Price": With respect to Records sold in the United States, company suggested Retail List Price in the United States, and, with respect to records sold outside the United States, Company's or its licensee's suggested retail price in the country of manufacture or sale, as Company is paid or credited, or, in the absence in a particular country of such suggested Retail List Price, the actual retail price as may be established by Company or its licensee(s) in conformity with the general practice of the Record industry in such country, provided that in such event Company shall be entitled to utilize the corresponding retail price adopted by the local mechanical copyright collection agency for the collection of mechanical copyright royalties without adjustment for packaging deductions. For purpose of royalty calculation, the Retail List Price shall be subject to the adjustments set forth in paragraph 7 hereof.

(ii) Company may at some time change the fee method by which it computes royalties from retail basis to some other basis, such as, without limitation, a wholesale basis. If Company changes the method to a new basis (the "New Basis") the New Basis will replace the current references to the Retail List Price and the royalty rates shall be adjusted to the appropriate royalty which would be applied to the New Basis so that upon the first change to the new basis the dollars-and-cents royalty amounts payable with respect to the top-line product being sold by Company would be the same as that which was payable at the instant prior to such change of methods of royalty computation. (By way of example, a New Basis, which would only be half the prior retail basis, would require an adjustment by doubling the royalty rate.) Once the New Basis and adjusted royalty are established, computations thereafter will proceed without further reference to the prior retail basis. It is specifically understood that in establishing the New Basis and computing the adjusted royalty, if there are other adjustments made by Company that would other wise make the New Basis more favorable (a particular example of which might be the distribution of smaller quantities of free goods than theretofore distributed) then the benefits of such other adjustments will be taken into consideration in adjusting the royalty rate.

(l)   "Recording Costs": All costs including pre- and post-production costs incurred for and with respect to the production of the Sides. Recording Costs include without limitation, union scale, the costs of all instruments, musicians, vocalists, conductors, arrangers, or orchestrators, copyists, etc., payments to a trustee or fund based on wages to the extent required by an agreement between Company and any labor organization or trustee, all individual producer's fees, all studio costs, tape, editing, mixing, mastering to tape, engineering, travel, per diems, production fees, rehearsal halls, cost of non-studio facilities and equipment, transportation of instrument and other costs and expenses incurred in producing the Sides hereunder, from time to time, and which are customarily recognized as Recording Costs in the Phonograph Record industry.

(m)   "Composition": A musical composition or medley consisting of words and/or music, or any dramatic performance, reading, monologue, dialogue and other performances in a unit of literary, dramatic or musical material, whether in the form of instrumental and/or vocal music, prose or otherwise, irrespective of length.

(n)   "Records Sold For Distribution In The United States": Records sold by PolyGram Records, or any independent distributors with whom Company may now or hereafter enter into arrangements or agreements for distribution to retail trade, which shall exclude, club and other mail order sales, "key outlet marketing" sales and Budget and Mid-Price sales.

(o)   "Territory": The world.

(p)   "Artist": The individual or individuals referred to as performing for the purpose of making Recordings pursuant to this agreement.

(q)   "Merchandising Rights": All rights with respect to printed material, endorsements and merchandising or commercial tie-ups in connection with the exploitation of physical property, including without limitation, toys, novelties, articles of apparel and juvenile and other publications (e.g., coloring books, paper cut-outs, activity books, etc.), for the purpose of paragraph 1(a) and limited solely thereto.

(r)   "Budget Records": Albums sold in a particular country of the Territory at a suggested Retail List Price which is seventy five (75%) percent or less of Company's suggested Retail List Price in such country of the Territory for top "pop" single LP Albums. A promotional Record released under Company's top "pop" label if otherwise it fulfills the criteria for Budget Record set forth above shall be subject to the provisions of this agreement related to Budget Records except that any release restrictions pertaining thereto shall not apply to such promotional Records.

(s)   "Advance": The word advance means a non-returnable prepayment of royalties. Company may recoup advances from royalties to be paid to or on behalf of you or Artist pursuant to this agreement only. Company will not recoup advances from mechanical royalties to be paid to or on behalf of you or the Artist or to your or the Artist's designated agent or collection agency concerned.

2. (a)   Company hereby engages you to furnish the services of Artist to perform for the recording of Phonograph Records, and you hereby accept such engagement, and agree to cause such services to be rendered exclusively to Company for the recording of one (1) LP ("Minimum Recording Obligation in the

Initial Period") in accordance herewith. You hereby grant to Company four (4) separate and consecutive option(s), the first of which shall be for sufficient additional Sides to constitute one (1) LP(s), the second and third of which shall be for sufficient Sides to constitute one (1) LP(s) each, and the fourth which shall be for sufficient Sides to constitute one (1) LP(S) ("Minimum Recording Obligation in each Option Period"). Each of such options shall be exercised, if at all, in accordance with the provisions of paragraph 3 below. The Minimum Recording Obligation in the Initial Period and the Minimum Recording Obligation in each Option Period shall hereinafter be referred to as the "Minimum Recording Obligation" for the applicable period of the Term. Company's execution hereof and Company's exercise of any of its options to extend the Term shall be deemed Company's request that Artist record the Minimum Recording Obligation for the applicable period of the Term.

(b)   The Term of this agreement shall be the period commencing on the date hereof and ending nine (9) months after delivery to Company of fully mixed and edited master tapes containing Sides constituting the last Recording to be recorded in accordance herewith but in no event shall the term exceed seven (7) years. The "initial Period" is the period of the Term commencing on execution hereof and ending upon exercise of the first option or upon expiration of the Term, whichever shall occur earlier. An "Option Period" is the Period of the Term commencing on exercise of an option for Sides constituting one or more LPs and expiring upon exercise of the next subsequent option, or upon expiration of the Term, whichever shall occur earlier.

3. (a)   During the Term, Artist shall perform for the purpose of recording phonograph Records exclusively for Company, and Company shall have the exclusive right for purposes as provided in this agreement to all record performances of Artist made throughout the Term.

(b)   Company's execution hereof shall be deemed its request that artist record Sides to constitute the first LP so that such Sides are delivered to Company within ninety (90) days following the date hereafter.

(c)(i) Not later than nine (9) months nor earlier than seven (7) months after delivery to Company of the Sides constituting the first LP referred to in paragraph 2 (a) above, Company shall, at its option, have the right to give you written notice of its request that Artist record sufficient additional Sides to constitute one LP (the "second LP") so that such Sides are delivered to Company within ninety (90) days of such request, and Artist shall record such Sides if so requested. If Company fails to exercise its right as set forth in this paragraph, the Term of this Agreement shall automatically expire.

(d)   Not later than nine (9) months after delivery to Company of the Sides comprising the second LP, Company shall, at its option, have the right to give you written notice of its request that Artist record Sides to constitute a third LP so that such Sides are delivered to Company within ninety (90) days of such request, and Artist shall record such Sides if so requested. If Company fails to exercise its right as set forth in this paragraph, the Term of this Agreement shall automatically expire.

(e)   Not later than nine (9) months after delivery to Company of the Sides comprising the third LP, Company shall, at its option, have the right to give you written notice of its request that Artist record Sides to constitute a fourth LP so that such Sides are delivered to Company within ninety (90) days of such request, and Artist shall record such Sides if so requested. If Company fails to exercise its right as set forth in this paragraph, the Term of this Agreement shall automatically expire.

(f)   Not later than nine (9) months after delivery to Company of the Sides comprising the fourth LP, Company shall, at its option, have the right to give you written notice of its request that Artist record Sides to constitute a fifth LP so that such Sides are delivered to Company within ninety (90) days of such request, and Artist shall record such Sides if so requested. If Company fails to exercise its right as set forth in this paragraph, the Term of this Agreement shall automatically expire.

(g)   Without limitation of any other rights and remedies of Company, if Artist fails to record and fails to deliver the Sides in accordance with this paragraph, then Company's obligations pursuant hereto shall be deemed automatically suspended for a number of days equal to that number of days that elapse between the last date on which the Sides are to be delivered and the date on which the Sides are actually delivered, and the then current period of the Term, the dates on which Company may exercise its options to extend the Term, the dates of commencement of subsequent periods of the Term, and the Term shall be expressed or implied herein, however, if any such suspension exceeds one hundred twenty (120) days, Company shall, in addition to its other rights and remedies, have the right to terminate this agreement by written notice to you at any time after said one hundred twenty (120) day period, and upon such termination Company shall have no further obligation to you hereunder, except the obligation to pay royalties, if earned.

(h)   Artist's performances hereunder shall be reasonably consistent in concept and style and Sides recorded hereunder will in general artistic concept and style be similar to the Sides previously recorded hereunder. The foregoing shall not restrict Artist from adjusting such artistic concept and style to reflect then current trends in rock music. If Artist desires to perform in any new concept or style, Company's prior written consent shall be required. You further agree that neither "live" performances nor multiple LP albums shall be recorded and accepted as a part of the Minimum Recording Obligation without Company's and your prior written consent, and Company agrees that it shall not require Artist to record any multiple LP Album hereunder. Without limitation to the generality of the foregoing, any multiple LP Album recorded hereunder shall be deemed a single LP for the purposes of fulfillment of the Minimum Recording Obligation and of payment unless Company explicitly in writing by an authorized officer agrees otherwise. In the event Company agrees to allow Artist to record a live LP, said LP shall be credited toward Artist's recording obligation hereunder and any advance which may be applicable as a result of such recording obligation shall apply to the live LP.

(i)   The Compositions to be recorded shall be selected by reasonable mutual agreement between Artist and Company. Each Master Recording shall be approved by Company as technically satisfactory for the Manufacture and sale of Phonograph Records. Upon Company's request and expense, Artist shall re-record any composition until a technically satisfactory Master Recording shall have been obtained. Should artist fail to appear at any recording session scheduled by Company during any period of the Term, of which Artist has been given reasonable written notice, due to a willful breach by Artist of this agreement, the minimum Recording Obligation for such period of the Term may, at Company's option, be reduced by the number of Sides which were scheduled to have been recorded at such session, and Company shall have the right to charge any of its out-of-pocket expenses in respect of such session against your royalties if and when earned.

(j)   For the purposes of paragraph 3 and 4 hereof the date of delivery of Sides to be delivered hereunder shall be that date which Company, by written notice to you informs you to be such delivery date provided that:

(i)   You shall have the right to object to such date by written notice to Company given within ten (10) days after receipt of the notice from Company as aforesaid. If you do so object, you and Company shall mutually and in good faith agree on the date to be deemed the delivery date, which shall be the earliest date to which Artist has so completely performed the producers set forth in paragraph 3 (j) (iv) with respect to such LP. If you do not respond to Company within the aforesaid ten (10) day period in which you may object, or do not otherwise object to the date given by Company as the date which Company deems to be the date of delivery, then the date given by Company shall be deemed to be the delivery date of the album in question.

(ii)   If Company does not send the notice referred to above to you on or before the date thirty (30) days following initial release of any LP hereunder, then you shall, not later than forty-five (45) days following such initial release, inform Company, by written notice of the date which you deem to be the delivery date of such LP. In such event Company shall have the right to object to such date by written notice to you as aforesaid. If Company does so object, you and Company shall mutually and in good faith agree on the date to be deemed the delivery date, which shall be the earliest date on which you have completely performed the procedures set forth in paragraph 3 (j) (iv) with respect to such LP. If Company does not respond to you within the aforesaid ten (10) day period in which it may object, or does not otherwise object to the date given by you as the date which you deemed to be the delivery date of the LP in question.

(iii)   If neither Company nor you give notice of the delivery date of any LP recorded hereunder to the other party as provided above, then the delivery date of such LP shall (subject to paragraph (v) below) be deemed to be thirty (30) days prior to the date of initial release of the LP in question.

(iv)   "Delivery" for the purpose of this agreement shall mean delivery to Company of fully mixed and edited master tapes for the applicable Single or LP and approval by Company of such master tapes and reference disk as technically satisfactory for the manufacture and sale of Phonograph Records.

(v) "initial commercial release" or "initial release" for the purposes of this agreement shall mean the first date on which finished commercial product is available to Company's distributors (including without limitation PolyGram's wholesale customers in the United States), as set forth on Company's regular release schedule for the applicable month.

4. (a) You agree not to license or consent to the use of Artist's name, likeness, voice, biographical material or other identification (hereinafter called "Artist's Identification") for or in connection with the recording or exploitation by anyone other than Company of Phonograph Records or Audio-Visual Recordings derived from Recordings made during the Term.

(b) You further agree that Artist will neither perform nor license nor consent to, nor permit the use by any one or more third parties of Artist's Identification for or in connection with the recording or exploitation of any Phonograph Record (including, without limitation, any Audio-Visual Device) embodying any composition recorded by Artist under this agreement prior to the date five (5) years subsequent to the date such Composition is recorded hereunder, or the date three (3) years subsequent to the expiration or other termination of the Term of this agreement, whichever is later. Should Artist so perform or should a licensed or consented or permitted use of Artist's Identification by any one or more third parties occur in connection with any such Composition during the period referred to above, then Company shall have the right, at its election and without limitation of its other rights and remedies, to terminate this agreement and Company shall have no further obligation to pay royalties to you which otherwise would accrue to you hereunder on Records which contain Artist's performance of such Composition. Nothing herein contained shall prevent the Artist from rendering its services as a performer for the purposes of so called free, pay and cable television, (including without limitation HBO, Showtime, or any future media analogous thereto of any length), radio broadcast, live performance, or motion pictures, if any member of Artist participated as an actor and that the product of such services and any recording thereof is not reproduced on the records or audio visual devices for distribution to the public whether or not on sale but nothing herein will preclude performances of services by Artist not directly related to audio recordings or audio visual cassette devices intended primarily for home use.

5. All Sides and any Audio-Visual Recordings delivered hereunder and all Matrices and Derivatives manufactured therefrom, together with the performances embodied thereon, shall be entirely and forever the property of Company, free from any claims whatsoever by Artist of any Person deriving any rights or interests from Artist and Company shall have the right to copyright the Sides in Company's name as owner and author (as employer-for-hire, such relationship being solely for the purpose of applicable copyright law) and to secure any and all renewals of such copyright. Any claim to copyright that you or Artist may acquire in the Sides is hereby irrevocably assigned to Company, and you and Artist shall simultaneously with execution of this agreement execute the formal assignment of copyright annexed hereto as Exhibit "A" and made part hereof. The method, manner and extent of release, packaging, promotion, advertising, distribution and sales relating to reproductions of the Master Recordings recorded hereunder shall be within the sole discretion of Company unless otherwise herein specifically provided. Without limiting the generality of the foregoing, Company and/or its subsidiaries, affiliates and licensees shall have the exclusive and unlimited right to all the products of the services of Artist hereunder, including but not limited to the following, but subject to any express restrictions set forth herein:

(a) The sole and exclusive right of ownership of all performances recorded hereunder, and of all Sides embodying such performances, including the sole and exclusive right in all Matrices and other Derivatives of the Sides, irrespective of the method of such embodiment, whether electronic, magnetic, mechanical, or other method now or hereafter known;

(b) The sole and exclusive right to reproduce the Sides and the performances embodied thereon and to manufacture therefrom all forms of Derivatives and derivative works including Phonograph Records in any speed, size or format whatsoever, coupling any of the sides at Company's option with other Sides subject hereto and/or with Master Recordings not the subject hereof; provided however the option of coupling shall not be exercised sooner than nine (9) months following the release of the subject side and not more than (2) sides shall be couples in any contract year.

(c)   The sole and exclusive right to distribute reproductions of the sides and the performances embodied thereon by sale or other transfer, rental, lease, or lending, at any retail List Price or at any other base price and under any name, trademark or top line label which Company and/or its subsidiaries, affiliates and licensees may from time to time elect, provided, however, that the initial release of the Sides shall be on Company's "top line" label;

(d)   The sole and exclusive right to perform publicly the Sides and the reproductions thereof and to permit the public performance thereof by means of radio or television broadcast, or any other method now or hereafter known;

(e)   The sole and exclusive right, in the case of individual images of any Audio-Visual Recording subject hereto, to display the work publicly, except as provided for in paragraph 4 herein;

(f)   The right to add to, delete from, change, modify or amend the Sides by any and all means, provided, however, such additions, deletions, changes, modifications, or amendments to the Sides shall not be initiated or released without Artist's approval, which approval shall not be unreasonably withheld.

(g)   The sole and exclusive right with your prior consent, which will not be unreasonably withheld, to use and permit others to use the performances recorded hereunder in time synchronization with visual images;

(h)   The sole and exclusive right to use the names, photographs and biographical material of Artist in connection with the promotion, exploitation and sale of derivatives of the Sides subject hereto;

(i)   The sole and exclusive right to convey the rights set forth in the preceding paragraphs in whole or in part to third parties, whether by license or assignment, subject to paragraph 21 hereinafter set forth.

6.   (a)   You agree that Company shall have the exclusive right to utilize Artist's performances recorded hereunder in connection with Audio-Visual Recordings for release on Audio Visual Devices. You agree that Artist shall perform for said Recordings upon Company's written request, provided however, Artist shall not be required to perform in excess of two (2) videos per LP to maximum of ten (10) videos over the term of this agreement.

   (i)   Company shall pay for and produce promotional videos for Album number one and if applicable, Album number two. One-half of the cost of said videos shall be chargeable against and recoupable from royalties, payable hereunder, which costs shall be paid from the first monies received from use of said videos.

(b)   You agree that Artist shall be available from time to time at Company's reasonable request and expense, whenever the same will not unreasonably interfere with other professional activities of Artist, to perform for the purpose of recording by means of film, videotape, or other audio-visual media performances by Artist of Compositions embodied on the Sides for promotional purposes. All right, title and interest in and to such recorded performances shall from inception of their creation be entirely the property of Company or Company's designee in perpetuity throughout the territory, including, without limitation, the worldwide copyright therein and thereto. Artist's compensation therefore shall be limited to any minimum amounts required to be paid for such performances pursuant to any collective bargaining agreements pertaining thereto, provided, however, that Artist hereby waives any right to receive such compensation to the extent that such right may be waived in connection with any applicable collective bargaining agreement. Notwithstanding the foregoing, if Company shall receive any income from its promotional or commercial use of such film, videotape or other Audio-Visual Device it shall share such income with you in accordance with the provisions of paragraph 7 (q) below. Company shall not request Artist to perform for any video clip wherein the performance of another Artist shall be embodied, without first requesting your prior approval. In the event Company shall Commercially exploit the videos produced hereunder, there shall be a free goods limitation on said videos of no more than actual up to fifteen (15%) percent of total number of videos paid for and not returned. This agreement is subject to the GAMMA Rules and Regulations relating to manufacture and distribution of audio visual devices in Germany.

7.   Company shall credit to your account and shall pay you in accordance with the provisions of paragraph 9 below the following royalties for the sale of Phonograph Records derived from Sides against which all advances paid to or on behalf of you or Artist shall be chargeable against and Company shall recoup such sums from the following royalties:

(a)(i)   A royalty of ten (10%) percent of one hundred (100%) percent of the Retail List Price for all Singles sold by Company for distribution in the United States and Canada, and not returned.

(ii) A royalty of eleven (11%) percent of one hundred (100%) percent of the Retail List Price for all LP disk and tape albums sold by Company for distribution in the United States and Canada, and not returned.

(iii)   A royalty of seven and one-half (7 1/2%) percent of one hundred (100%) percent of the Retail List Price for all Singles and LP disk and tape Albums sold for distribution outside the United States and Canada by Company or other persons, corporations, or firms under leasing or licensing arrangements or agreements with Company, as to which Company receives payment or credit, or fifty (50%) percent of net receipts by Company, whichever is greater.

(iv)   The rate set forth in (i) above shall sometimes hereinafter be referred to as the "Base Rate for Singles"; the rate set forth in clause (ii) above shall sometimes hereinafter be referred to as the "Base Rate for Album", and collectively the said rates shall sometimes be referred to as the "Base Rate for Domestic Sales". The rate set forth in (iii) above shall sometimes hereinafter be referred to as "Base Rate for Overseas Sales". The foregoing rate shall collectively be referred to as "Base Rates". The foregoing provisions of paragraph 7 shall be subject to any modifications expressed or

(b)   Notwithstanding anything to the contrary contained herein implied in the following provisions of paragraph 7.

(i)   In the event the aggregate net sales through normal distribution channels in the United States and Canada of any particular LP or single (including disk and tape), computed separately single by single or LP by LP, embodying only newly recorded Masters hereunder shall exceed two hundred fifty thousand (250,000) units, then the royalty rate pursuant to 7 (a) (i) and 7 (a) (ii) hereof shall be increased by one (1%) percent only with respect to net sales through normal distribution channels in the United States and Canada of such LP or singles in excess of two hundred fifty thousand (250,000) units, but not in excess of five hundred thousand (500,000) units; and

(ii)   In the event the aggregate net sales through normal distribution channels in the United States and Canada of any particular LP or single (including disk and tape), computed separately single by single or LP by LP, embodying only newly recorded Masters hereunder shall exceed five hundred thousand (500,000) units, then the royalty rate pursuant to 7 (a) (i) and 7 (a) (ii) hereof shall be increased by two (2%) percent only with respect to net sales through normal distribution channels in the United States and Canada of such LP or singles in excess of five hundred thousand (500,000) units, but not in excess of seven hundred fifty thousand (750,000) units.

(iii)   In the event the aggregate net sales through normal distribution channels in the United States and Canada of any particular LP or single (including disk and tape), computed separately single by single or LP by LP, embodying only newly recorded Masters hereunder shall exceed seven hundred fifty thousand (750,000) units, then the royalty rate pursuant to 7 (a) (i) and 7 (a) (ii) hereof shall be increased by three (3%) percent only with respect to net sales through normal distribution channels in the United States and Canada of such LP or singles in excess of seven hundred fifty thousand (750,000) units.

(c) An increase in the royalty rate pursuant to paragraph 7(a) (ii) hereof by reason of the foregoing provisions of this paragraph shall result in the increase in any other royalty rates contained in paragraph 7. Accordingly, and without limiting the generality of the foregoing, for the purpose of computing any royalty rates pursuant to paragraph 7 which are based on the royalty rate contained in paragraph 7 (a) (i) and 7(a) (ii), the provisions of this paragraph shall be disregarded.

(d)(i) The royalty payable for Long Play Singles having a Retail List Price of less than Three and 50/100 ($3.50) Dollars shall be sixty-six and 2/3 (66 2/3%) percent of the amount credited to Artists royalty account for sales of an Album. The royalty payable for Long-Play Singles having a Retail List Price of Three and 50/100 ($3.50) Dollars or more but less than Seven ($7.00) Dollars shall be seventy-five (75%) of the royalty payable for an Album. The royalty payable for Long-Play Singles having a Retail List Price of seven ($7.00) Dollars or more shall be the royalty payable for Albums.

(ii) The royalty payable for EP Records shall be three quarters (3/4) of the otherwise applicable Base Rate for Albums.

(e)(i) As to Records derived from the Sides sold in the United States through Non-Affiliated Third Party record clubs or similar sales plans or devices, you shall receive a royalty equal to one-half (1/2) of the Base Rate or fifty (50%) percent of Company's net receipts, whichever is greater, for Overseas Sales.

(ii) As to records derived from the Sides sold for distribution outside the United States and Canada through record clubs or similar sales plans or devices, you shall receive a royalty equal to one-half (1/2) of the Base Rate or fifty (50%) percent of Company's net receipts, whichever is greater, for Overseas Sales.

(iii) No royalty shall be payable with respect to Records distributed to members of record clubs as "Bonus" or "Free" Records as a result of joining the club, and/or recommending that another join the club, and/or purchasing a required number of records, provided that Company shall pay royalties to you on all Records for which it receives payment, provided, however, that in the event more than fifty (50%) percent of the records distributed are bonus or free records, then, in that event, Company shall pay royalties on the excess over fifty percent.

(f) As to Records not consisting entirely of the Sides, your royalties otherwise payable hereunder shall be prorated, on the basis of the number of Sides which are on such records compared to the total number of Master Recordings on such Records.

(g) Royalties on Phonograph Records included in Albums, jackets, boxes or any other type of package or container (herein collectively referred to as "Containers") shall be based solely on the Retail List Price of such Phonograph Records in Containers less sales, excise or similar taxes and duties and also less a Container charge of: ten (10%) percent of the Retail List Price for a Long-Play Single: 10 (10%) percent of the Retail List Price for a single-fold disk Album in a standard jacket with no inserts (hereinafter referred to as the "Base Container Charge for Single-Fold Disk Album's"); fifteen (15%) percent of the Retail List Price for a double-fold Album in a standard jacket no inserts whether containing one or more LPs (hereinafter referred to as the "Base Container Charge for Double-fold Disk Albums"); and fifteen (15%) percent of the Retail List Price for a pre-recorded tape Album or compact disk. With respect to albums packaged in the non-standard jackets containing one or more inserts, the Base Container Charge for Single-fold Disk Albums shall be increased by the actual cost thereof.

(h)(i) Expressly, but without limitation of its rights elsewhere herein granted, Company shall have the right to license the Sides of Non-Affiliated Third Party for all methods of distribution, including, without limitations, the method known as "key outlet marketing" (distribution through retail fulfillment centers in conjunction with special advertisements on radio or television), direct mail, or mail order, or for "premium" use, or by any combination of the methods set forth above, and for sale on Budget Record lines. Unless otherwise provided from, Company shall credit your royalty account with fifty (50%) percent of Company's net royalty receipts for sales of Records containing such Sides in the United States and Canada in respect of each such license pertaining to the Sides.

(ii) As to sales of Records derived from the Sides by any of the methods set forth above outside the United States and Canada by affiliated licenses or Non-Affiliated Third Parties Company shall credit your royalty account with fifty (50%) percent of company's net royalty receipts with respect thereto.

(iii) With respect to sales of records on which the retail list price is at least twenty-five (25%) percent but not more than forty (40%) percent less than company's then current retail list price for "top-line" full priced LP's as initially released, the royalty rate shall be seventy-five (75%) percent of the applicable rate as determined in this paragraph 7 (a) (i), (ii), or (iii), provided that Company shall not sell in the United States and Canada any LP's at such price for a period of eighteen (18) months from the date of initial release of any LP without your written consent. With respect to sales of LP's on which the retail list price is at least forty (40%) percent less than Company's then current retail list price for "top-line" full priced LP's as initially released, the royalty rate shall be fifty (50%) percent of the United States and Canada records at such price for a period of eighteen (18) months from the date of initial release of any such LP without your written consent.

(iv) Company shall be entitled to use and publish and to license or permit others to use and publish, Artist's Identification with respect to the products and services in connection with premium Records provided that such use is not an endorsement of the product or service, provided however, Company shall obtain Artist's prior approval, which approval shall not be unreasonably withheld.

(i)(i)For record club purposes. Company shall have the right to include or to license some others to include any one or more of the Sides hereunder in sampler Records on which such Sides and other recordings are included, which sampler Records are designed for sale at twenty-five (25%) percent or less of the regular price of Company's full priced Records embodying the same number of discs, or the equivalent thereof, and such sampler Records shall be royalty-free provided that not more than two (2) sides hereunder shall be included on any one such Record, provided, further, that Company shall not include such sides in a sampler record more than one time in any contract year.

(ii) With respect to sampler Records as provided for above, but other than for record clubs, Company shall have the same rights as above except that in such case not more than two (2) sides may be included on any one such sampler Record.

(j) Company shall have the right, subject to your prior approval, which approval shall not be unreasonably withheld to license the Sides on a flat fee basis. Company shall credit Artist royalty account with fifty (50) percent of the net amount received by Company under such license.

(k) The royalty shall be payable for Records sold in Armed Forces Post Exchange shall be fifty (50%) percent of the otherwise applicable Base Rate.

(l) No royalty shall be payable for Records returned for credit by any buyer, for Records given away gratis or for Records distributed to disk jockeys, radio stations, television stations, motion picture companies, publishers, distributors, dealers, customers, or any others for publicity, advertising, or promotional purposes only; for Records sold as surplus, cutouts, or for Records sold as scrap at less than $1.25 per unit. Company shall not have the right to manufacture records solely for the sale of the deletes or cutouts without your prior approval and in the event of such approval you shall receive a royalty of fifty (50%) percent over a bottom line price of $1.25 per unit. In addition, you shall receive a royalty of fifty (50%) percent of the net proceeds from any unspecified use of the Sides. Furthermore:

(i) The extent that Records are sold subject to a special sales plan entailing a selling price for such Records reduced by a percentage discount from Company's Gross Price, the number of such Records deemed for royalty purposes to have been sold shall be determined by reducing the number of Records actually sold by the percentage of discount granted applicable to such sale, and

(ii) To the extent that free or bonus Records are given away for the promotion of this Artist only, together with Records sold for monetary consideration (being the form of sales plan known in the Record industry as the giving of "free goods"), such Free or Bonus Records shall not be included in the number of Records deemed for royalty purposes to have been sold, provided however that:

(iii) The aggregate number of Records deemed not sold for royalty purposes under clause (i) above and deemed not sold for royalty purposes under clause (ii) above in connection with the requirements of special sales plans, shall not exceed the actual number of such records up to twenty-five (25%) percent of the gross total of single records sold and, for LP disk and tape Albums, the actual number up to fifteen (15%) percent of the gross total sold.

(m)(i) Notwithstanding the foregoing, at company's election it may report as Records sold the number of records deemed pursuant to (l) (i) and (l) (ii) above not sold for royalty purposes, and instead reduce the per Record royalty payable hereunder proportionately as the number of such Records deemed not sold for royalty purposes bears to the gross total invoiced, paid for or credited to and no returned. For the purposes of this agreement in any case where any event is predicated upon the achievement of a particular sales volume level, the terms "net sales" and/or "net royalty-bearing sales" shall be the sales determined by the operation of the above clauses (l) (i), (l) (ii) and (l) (iii) and clause (o) below.

(ii) Intentionally Deleted.

(n) Company's "Gross Price" shall mean for purposes of this agreement the net selling price of Company or its distributor (in particular, but without limitation, in the United States, PolyGram Records, or its successors) to its highest volume customers (i.e. "best Price") net of standard discounts or free goods in lieu thereof but before any discounts given in connection with a Special Sales Plan.

(o) Without limitation of the generality of paragraph 7 above, Company shall have the right to deduct from the number of Records sold returns and credits of any nature, including without limitations those on account of any return or exchange provided that returns shall be payable hereunder and Records distributed on a so-called "no charge" or "free" basis which are intended for sale by the recipients thereof in the same proportion as all such phonograph records are initially invoiced. Company shall have the right to withhold a reserve to a maximum of fifty (50%) percent of the sales of singles in the period to which it relates, and thirty (30%) percent of the sales of Albums in the period to which it relates and further, such reserve shall be liquidated within three (3) accounting periods of the date first withheld, as follows:

16 2/3% for singles and 10% for Albums after first accounting period.

16 2/3% for singles and 10% for Albums after second accounting period.

16 2/3% for singles and 10% for Albums after third accounting period.

(p) Royalties for Phonograph Records sold for distribution outside the United States shall be computed in the same national currency as Company is accounted to by its licensees and as to sales made outside the United States, shall be subject to any taxes applicable to royalties remitted by or received from foreign sources, provided, however, that royalties on Phonograph Records sold outside the United States shall be due and payable by Company until payment has been received by Company in the United States in United States Dollars, or where monies due to company have been applied to reduce any amounts recoupable against Company's advance account by any of company's licensees, and provided further, that if Company shall not receive payment in the United States, or in United States Dollars, or in advance account is not credited as aforesaid, and shall be required to accept payment in foreign currency or in a foreign country, Company shall deposit to your credit (and at your expense) in such currency in a depository in the country in which Company is required to accept payment but selected by you, payments so received applicable to royalties hereunder and shall notify you promptly thereof. Deposit as aforesaid shall fulfill the obligations of Company as to Phonograph Record sales to which such royalty payments are applicable. In countries where Company's licensees in general do not account for returns, an allowance of fifteen (15%) percent of gross shipments may be granted or deducted by Company, provided, however, in the event Company's licensees have established a reserve account, Company shall not be entitled to maintain a similar reserve for the same shipment.

(q) Notwithstanding anything to the contrary contained herein, the royalty rate for Audio-Visual Recordings shall be negotiated between the parties in good faith. Such negotiations shall take into account, among other things, prevailing conditions at the time thereof as well as your royalty rate for sound recordings, and Artist's then current stature as a recording artist.

(r) If any Recordings made hereunder embody Artist's performances together with the performances of any other artist(s) to whom Company is obligated to pay royalties, then the royalties and non-returnable payments due hereunder for such joint performances shall be the royalties and non-returnable payments herein provided for divided by the number of artists participating therein including Artist.

(s) If Company receives income from any commercial usage of Sides not specifically provided for the foregoing, and if Company's receipts are not already net of a payment made directly to you or Artist, then Company agrees to pay you fifty (50%) percent of the net amount received of such income, provided always that such income is accounted to Company on an artist-by-artist or Master-by-Master basis.

(t) In the foregoing provisions of paragraph 7 the terms "net royalty receipts" and "net amount received" shall mean the gross amounts received by Company in connection with the subject matter thereof less any amounts which Company is obligated to pay to third parties (such as, without limitation, manufacturing costs, mechanical copyright payments, AFM and other union payments).

(u) For the purposes of this paragraph 7, Company shall be deemed to have been paid when and if Company's account has been credited in respect of such payment.

(v) Company shall pay you fifty (50%) percent of all public performance and broadcasting fees, if any, received by Company in respect of public performance of sound recordings embodying masters hereunder (as opposed to the musical compositions embodied thereon), unless you shall receive payment directly from a performing rights society or other person, firm or corporation collecting such payments on your behalf and if such fees are not computed and paid in direct relation to public performances and broadcast of such records in any country, such fees shall be computed for the purposes of this agreement by taking that proportion of any such fees paid to Company or Company's licensees in such country as the number of records embodied masters hereunder and sold in such country bears to the total number of records sold in such country by company or company's licensees.

8. (a) Accountings as to royalties payable hereunder shall be made by Company to you on or before September 30th for the period ending the preceding June 30th, and on or before March 31st for the period ending the preceding December 31st, or such other accounting periods as Company may in general adopt, but in no case less frequently than semi-annually, together with payment of acquired royalties, if any, earned by you during such preceding half-year subject to paragraph (b) below. All royalty statements and all other accounts rendered by Company to you shall be binding upon you and not subject to any objection you for any reason unless specific objection in writing, stating the basis thereof, is given to Company within two (2) years from the date rendered, and after such notice of objection, unless suit is instituted within one (1) year after date on which Company notifies you that it denies the validity of the objection. Failure to make specific objection within said time period shall be deemed approval of such statement.

(b) Notwithstanding anything to the contrary contained above, if your net royalty earnings at the end of a given accounting period are less than Twenty-Five ($25.00) Dollars, Company may, at its option, carry forward such earnings to the next accounting period.

(c) You shall have the right at your own expense to audit Company's books and records and the books and records of Company's licensees, to the extent that Company has the right to audit such licensees, as the same pertains to sales, returns, free goods, and returns under this agreement and make extracts and photocopies thereof once a year with respect to the statements relating to the Recordings hereunder pertaining to the two (2) accounting periods prior to said audit and Company agrees to make all necessary sales information, data and documents available for such purposes at Company's accounting offices at its address first mentioned herein. Such audit shall be conducted by Certified Public Accountant or the Canadian equivalent during normal business hours and on reasonable written notice. If any audit conducted by you or on your behalf reveals an error in excess or fifteen (15%) percent (excluding the cost of the audit) in your disfavor, then Company agrees to pay actual costs of the audit up to a maximum of Five Thousand ($5,000) Dollars, such costs to be payable within thirty (30) days by Company.

(d) Intentionally Deleted.

9. For the rights herein granted to Company and for the services to be rendered by Artist, and provided that you are at no time in material breach of this agreement, Company agrees that it shall make the following payments in connection with the Recording hereunder, all of which shall constitute advances to be charged against and to be recoupable from royalties due hereunder:

(a) Conditioned upon your and Artist's full and faithful performance of each and all of the terms hereof, Company shall pay to you the following non-returnable sums in advances against and recoupable from royalties due hereunder, payable one-half (1/2) within ten (10) days after notice of commencement of preparation for recording, which preparation shall not exceed thirty (30) days prior the actual recording date, and the balance within ten (10) days following delivery of applicable LP, together with all other information and items to be supplied by you, the Artist or the individual producer in connection therewith.

Album	Advances
First Album	$55,000
Second Album	$55,000; provided that, in the event the first Album sales reach 100,000 units, said amount shall be increased to $75,000
Third Album	$55,000; provided, that in the event the second Album sales reach 100,000 units said sum shall be increased to $100,000
Fourth Album	$55,000; provided, that in the event the third Album sales reach 100,000 units said sum shall be increased to $125,000
Fifth Album	$125,000

(b) All monies paid to you or on your behalf during the Term of this agreement at your request, other than royalties paid pursuant to paragraph 7 hereof, shall be deemed non-returnable advances against and recoupable from royalties due hereunder, unless Company shall have expressly agreed in writing by an authorized officer of Company that such monies shall not be deemed advances.

(c) One-half (1/2) of all monies paid by Company or its licensees for independent promotion in the United States only, i.e., promotion conducted by parties other than Company or its licensees of Phonograph Records derived from the Sides, shall be charged against and recoupable from royalties earned from sales in the United States only and payable hereunder.

(d) Intentionally Deleted.

(e) Intentionally Deleted.

(f) Union scale payments by Company to Artist in connection with the Sides shall be deducted from the foregoing approved budget payable hereunder.

10. During the term, you shall cause Artist and Artist shall become and remain a member in good standing of any labor unions with which Company may at any time have agreements lawfully requiring such union membership, including, but not limited to, the American Federation of Musicians and the American Federation of Television and Radio Artists.

(a) Company shall be responsible for all payments to the Music Performance Trust Fund and Special Payments Fund of the A F of M and any payments to similar union funds under agreements provided for Company to make payments with respect to records sold and any such payments shall be non-recoupable. To assist Company in making such payments, Artist shall indicate in conjunction with Artist's execution hereof, Artist's Social Security number and applicable union affiliation.

(b) Subject to paragraphs (c) through (f) below, Company shall be responsible for mechanical royalties payable in connection with Records sold. The free goods policy of Company, as such policy affects mechanical royalties payable hereunder, shall be based upon the applicable provision of the Harry Fox agreement.

(c) The following provision shall pertain to Controlled Compositions:

(i) Controlled Compositions shall be licensed to Company's copyright royalty equal to seventy-five (75%) percent of the minimum statutory rate prevailing at the time of release of the respective side, subject to the provisions of clauses (ii) and (iii) below.

(ii) With respect to Records sold and/or distributed through any record club, by the methods of mail order or "key outlet marketing", or at a Budget Price or Mid-Price, the royalty rate shall be three-fourths (3/4) of the rate set forth in clause (i) above.

(iii) No copyright royalties with respect to Controlled Composition shall be payable on Records not royalty-bearing pursuant to the provisions of paragraph 8 hereof: nor with respect to Compositions which go into the public domain in a particular country of the Territory with respect to such country on or after the date on which such material goes into the public domain; nor for non-musical materials.

(iv) Company shall account to you for mechanical royalties on a quarterly basis. Your right to audit Company's books and records as the same relate to copyright royalties for Controlled Composition shall be subject to terms and conditions set forth in paragraph 8 in connection with your audit rights.

(v) Arranged versions of Compositions in the public domain when furnished by anyone or more of persons described in the definition of a Controlled Composition above shall be free of copyright royalties provided, however, that if any such arranged version has a new title and entirely different lyrics or a substantial addition of melodic material then, notwithstanding anything to the contrary contained herein, such arranged version shall be licensed to Company at a Copyright royalty rate to be calculated by taking the rate applicable for original Controlled Composition above and multiplying such rate by the percentage used by the applicable performing rights society in determining the credits to be given by the publisher of such arranged version for public performances of such work; provided, however, that you shall furnish to Company a copy of the letter of the performing rights society setting forth the percentage of otherwise applicable credit which the publisher will receive for such public performances. If you fail to provide Company with such letter from performing rights society, Company shall not be obliged to pay any copyright royalty with respect to any such arranged version.

(vi) Any assignment made of this ownership or copyright in any Controlled Composition or in any arranged version of a Composition in the public domain shall be made subject to the provisions of this paragraph.

(d)(i) Notwithstanding anything to the contrary contained herein, you and Artist warrant, represent, and agree that Company shall have no obligation whatsoever to pay any aggregate copyright royalty rate in respect of any Record hereunder regardless of the number of Controlled Compositions and/or other Compositions contained thereon, in excess of the following sums:

A. In respect of any single-LP Album: seventy-five (75%) percent of the minimum statutory rate in effect on the date of release of such single-LP Album times the actual number of sides embodied in said Album.

B. In respect of any multiple LP Album: seventy-five (75%) percent of a minimum of fifteen (15) times the minimum statutory rate in effect on the date of release of such single-LP Album.

C. In respect of any multiple LP Album: seventy-five (75%) percent of two (2) times the minimum statutory rate in effect on the date of release of such single.

(ii) "Minimum statutory rate" as used in this paragraph shall be deemed to be five and 63/100 cents ($.0563) or such comparable rate provided in any modification of 17 U.S.C. 115 which is in effect on the date of release of any Side.

(iii) Without limitation of the generality of clause (i) above, if the aggregate copyright royalty rate in respect of any Recording hereunder is more than the applicable amounts set forth in clauses (i) (A), and (C) above, then, without limitation of Company's rights, Company shall have the right, at its election, if it elects to release such Recording:

A. To release such Record and reduce the aggregate copyright royalty payable with respect to Controlled Compositions on such Record so that the aggregate copyright royalty payable with respect to all Compositions on such Record does not exceed the applicable maximum amount, and/or

B. To release such Record and deduct from mechanical royalties due to you hereunder that amount of aggregate copyright royalty payable by Company with respect to such Record in excess of the applicable maximum amount, provided, however, this provision shall be subject to the approval of the Harry Fox Agency.

(e) The provisions of this paragraph shall constitute and are accepted by you, on your and Artist's own behalf and on behalf of any other owner of any Controlled Composition(s) or any rights therein, as full compliance by Company with all of its obligations under the compulsory license arising from any use by Company of Controlled Compositions as provided for herein.

(f) The provisions of this paragraph shall constitute an interim mechanical license until a formal mechanical license is executed.

11. (a) You agree that Artist will be available from time to time at Company's request and expense, whenever the same will not unreasonably interfere with other professional activities of Artist, to appear for photography, posters, and cover art, etc., under the direction of Company or its nominees and to appear for interviews with representatives of the communications media and Company's publicity personnel and to perform other reasonable services.

(b) You agree not to directly or indirectly place or authorize or direct anyone else to place any advertisement in any newspaper, trade journal, magazine, or in any other advertising medium covering or relating to any Phonograph Records or pre-recorded tapes embodying the Sides, unless you first obtain Company's written consent thereto.

12. You warrant and represent the following:

(a) There are now in existence no prior record performances by Artist unreleased within the United States, except as set forth on "Schedule A".

(b)   There are no restrictions with respect to Compositions Artist is legally able to perform for Company hereunder, except as set forth on "Schedule B".

(c)(i)   No contract or agreement of any kind entered into by Artist prior to the time of execution hereof will interfere in any manner with complete performance of the within agreement by Artist. Artist is under no disability, restriction or prohibition with respect to Artist's right to sign and perform this agreement.

(ii) You and Artist have no knowledge of any claim or purported claim which, if valid, would interfere with Company's rights hereunder or create any liability on the part of Company.

(d)   Artist has the right to use Artist's real names,

_____

and professional name,

_____a/k/a_____

and any other professional names used by Artist and grant to Company for the Territory the non-exclusive right to use and allow others to use likeness of Artist, for Phonograph Record and audio-visual purposes as provided for herein, during the Term, and the exclusive right to such use thereafter in connection with Records subject thereto. Company's use of such names in accordance with the terms hereof will not infringe upon the rights of any third party. Notwithstanding the foregoing, Company shall have no right or authorization to use your name or the name of the Artist or the individual names of the Artists for any advertising, including commercial endorsement, which is not related to you, the Artist, the individual members of Artist, Company or the recordings made under this agreement.

(e)   No materials supplied by you or Artist to Company in connection with the Sides or the performances embodied thereon, nor such performances themselves, nor any use thereof by Company or its grantees, licensees, or assigns pursuant to this agreement will violate or infringe upon the rights of any third party.

(f)   You and Artist and Company agree to and hereby indemnify, save and hold each other harmless of and from any and all loss and damage (including reasonable attorneys' fees) arising out of or connected with any finally adjudicated claim by any one or more third parties which is inconsistent with any of the material warranties or representations made by you or Artist or Company herein, and agree to reimburse each other on demand for any payment made by such party at any time after the date hereof with respect to any liability or claim to which the foregoing indemnity applies, which is reduced to judgment or settled. Pending the determination of any claim involving such alleged breach of failure, Company may withhold sums reasonably related to the claim which may be due you hereunder .

(g)   Company shall have the right to reprint on Album jackets and sleeves the lyrics of Controlled Compositions in connection with the rights granted to Company hereunder.

13.   (a)   Company reserves the right by written notice to you to suspend the operation of the Term for the duration of the following contingencies, if it is materially hampered in the recording, manufacture, distribution or sale of Records, or its normal business operations become commercially impracticable: labor disagreements, fire, catastrophe, shortage of materials, or any cause beyond Company's control. A number of days equal to the total of all such days of suspension shall be added to the period of the Term in which such contingency occurs and the Term, the dates for the Term shall be deemed extended six (6) months in any period of the Term shall be deemed extended accordingly. It is agreed that no such suspension shall exceed six (6) months in any period of the Term unless such contingency is industry-wide in which event Company shall have the right to suspend the applicable period of the Term for the duration of such contingency, not to exceed one (1) year.

(b)   If in respect of any period of the Term Company fails, except as set forth in paragraph 13 (a) herein, to allow Artist to fulfill the Minimum Recording Obligation for such period pursuant to paragraph 3 above, and if no later than thirty (30) days prior to the last day on which Artist would otherwise be obligated to record the Minimum Recording Obligation for the applicable period of the Term you notify Company in writing of Artist's desire to fulfill such Minimum Recording Obligation, then Company shall either allow Artist to record sufficient Sides to fulfill the Minimum Recording Obligation within sixty (60) days of receipt of such notice, or you shall have the right to terminate this agreement by notice to Company given within thirty days of the expiration of such sixty (60) day period; on receipt by Company of such notice the Term such as warranties, re-recording restrictions, and the obligation to pay royalties if earned, and Company shall pay you union scale for the Minimum Recording Obligation not yet fulfilled for the applicable period of the Term in full settlement of its obligations in connection therewith, which payment shall constitute an advance against and recoupable from royalties hereunder. If you shall fail to give notice to Company within the period specified therefore, Company shall be under no obligation for its failure to allow Artist to fulfill such Minimum Recording Obligation.

(c)(i) In the event of any material default or breach by you or Artist of any of your or Artist's obligations hereunder except failure to timely record and/or deliver Sides, which is not cured in accordance with paragraph 24 below, Company, by written notice to you, in addition to any other rights or remedies which it may have at law or otherwise, may (A) within five (5) days of the act of non-performance suspend its obligations hereunder for the duration of such default or breach and until the same has been cured, and may, at its election, extend the then current period of the Term for a period equal to all or part of the period of such default or breach, plus an additional period of ninety (90) days and the Term, the dates for exercise by Company of its options as set forth in paragraph 3 and the dates of commencement of subsequent periods of the Term shall be deemed extended accordingly; or (B) at any time after six (6) months from such default or breach and during the aforesaid ninety (90) day period terminate the Term without further obligations to hereunder, except for the obligation to pay royalties, if earned.

(ii) Notwithstanding the foregoing and what is provided in paragraph 3(g), in no event shall the Term hereunder be suspended and extended in excess of the maximum permitted under any statute, law or order of any authority having jurisdiction of the Term in accordance herewith Company shall be entitled to all its rights and remedies under law and equity for reasons of Artist's failure to fulfill its recording obligation hereunder including but not limited to damages sustained by Company.

14. Wherever in this agreement your approval or consent is required, Company may require you to formally give or withhold such approval or consent by giving you written notice requesting the same and by furnishing you with the information or material in respect of which such approval consent is sought. You shall give Company written notice approval or disapproval within five (5) business days after such notice is received by you. In the event of disapproval or no consent, the reasons shall be stated. Failure to give such notice to Company as aforesaid shall be deemed to be consent or approval.

15. You agree subject to the provisions of paragraph 4 (b) herein above that Artist will not record or authorize or knowingly permit to be recorded for any purpose any performances for third party without in each case taking reasonable measures to prevent the manufacture, distribution and sale at any time by any Person other than Company of Phonograph Records and other devices including without limitation Audio-Visual Devices embodying such performance for home use and/or jukebox use and/or use in or on means of transportation. Specifically, without limiting the generality of the foregoing, you agree that:

(i)   If, during the Term, Artist performs any Composition for the purpose of making transcriptions for radio or television or sound tracks for motion picture films, or

(ii)   If, during the period referred to in paragraph 4(b) hereof Artist performs for any such purpose any Composition which shall have been recorded pursuant to this agreement, Artist will do so only pursuant to a written contract containing an express provision that neither such performance nor any Recording thereof will be used, directly or indirectly for the purpose of making Phonograph Records or any other device including without limitation Audio-Visual Devices for home use and/or jukebox use and/or use on or in means of transportation. You will promptly furnish to Company a copy of the pertinent provision of each such contract and will cooperate fully with Company in any controversy which may arise or litigation which may be brought relating to the rights of Company under this paragraph.

16. You agree that in all of Artist's endeavors in the entertainment field in the Territory, Artist will exert best efforts to be billed, advertised and described as an exclusive recording artist of Company.

(a)   Company shall have the exclusive right to use and/or sublicense others to use Artist's name, logo, likeness and/or performance for merchandising and other commercial purposes solely through "flyers", "bouncebacks" and similar album inserts, of T-shirts and other clothing, posters, stickers and novelties. You shall have the right to approve in advance any such items of merchandise, which approval may be withheld for any reason whatsoever. Upon Company's request, you and Artist shall execute a license agreement, which license agreement shall contain terms and provisions determined by good faith negotiations between Company and you and customarily used in the licensing of name and likeness rights. You shall have the right to approve all photographs or other reproductions of Artist's likeness which Company desires to use for the purposes set forth in this paragraph 16 (a). You shall have five (5) calendar days after receipt of each such photograph or other reproduction within which to disapprove the use of such photograph or reproduction. All such photographs and reproductions not timely disapproved by you shall be deemed approved for use by Company. Company agrees to credit your royalty account with fifty (50%) percent of the net income derived by Company from merchandising and exploitation of artist's name and likeness. Company shall not recoup advances and other recoupable charges under this agreement from such fifty (50%) percent of such net income payable to you, and such income payable to you with respect to the merchandising and exploitation of Artist's name and likeness pursuant to this paragraph 16 (a) shall be treated as a separate accounting unit from the income payable to you with respect to the sale of records hereunder. For the purposes of this paragraph 16 (a), "net income" shall mean the gross income actually received by Company which is derived directly from such use of Artist's name, likeness, voice or sound effects, as herein provided, less direct expenses actually incurred by Company in connection with Company's exercise of the merchandising rights set forth in this paragraph 16 (a) and not theretofore deducted from gross income, including but not limited to (i) cost of collection, (ii) commissions and/or royalties payable to any third parties, (iii) manufacturing cost, (iv) cost of packing, shipping, postage and insurance, and (v) advertising and promotion expenses (including the cost of manufacturing the album inserts as well as direct labor cost actually incurred by Company to put the insert into the album package).

(b)   You recognize that the sale of Records is speculative and agree that the judgment of Company with regard to any matter affecting the sale, distribution and exploitation of such Records shall be binding and conclusive upon you and Artist. Nothing contained in this agreement shall obligate Company to make, sell, license, or distribute Records manufactured from the Sides other than as specifically provided for herein, or to have artist in fact record the minimum number of Sides specified.

17. You and Artist acknowledge that Artist's services in connection herewith are unique and extraordinary and that Company shall be entitled to seek injunctive relief to enforce the provisions of this agreement.

18. You and Artist hereby authorize and direct Company to withhold and/or from any monies due to you or Artist from Company any part thereof required by the United States Internal Revenue Service any other governmental authority withheld, and to pay same to the United States Internal Revenue Service and/or such other authority.

19. (a)   Company hereby agrees to release or cause the release of each LP recorded and delivered hereunder in the following territories within one hundred eighty (180) days following the initial release of such LP in the United States: Australia, New Zealand, France, Italy, Switzerland, Germany, Austria, Holland, Norway, Sweden, Denmark, Japan and the United Kingdom. If Company fails to release or cause the release of any such LP in any of the aforementioned territories, you shall have the right to notify Company in writing of such failure and Company shall have sixty (60) days following receipt of said notice to release or cause the release of any such LP in that particular territory. If Company fails to release or cause such release of any such LP, then in each such instance you shall have the right to enter into a separate licensing agreement for that territory only as to such unreleased LP only (this being your sole and exclusive remedy for such failure); provided further that you shall credit to Company twenty-five (25%) percent of your proceeds (including any advance and royalties) for the sale of such LP in such territory (which amount will only be collected by deducting from monies otherwise payable to you hereunder). In addition to the foregoing procedure, if Company fails to release two (2) or more consecutive LPs in any of the foregoing territories then you shall have the right to elect, upon written notice to Company, to terminate Company's right in and to such territory as to all future LPs hereunder, and you shall have the right to enter a separate licensing agreement for such territory with any third person selected by you, and shall promptly notify Company of any such licensee (this being your sole and exclusive remedy for such failure, it being agreed that if you terminate Company's right to any such territory and enter into a separate licensing agreement

for such territory as set forth herein, you shall not be required to credit Company with twenty-five (25%) percent of your proceeds under any such separate licensing agreement). If you enter into a separate licensing agreement(s) pursuant to this paragraph with regard to any LP hereunder (each such licensee to be herein called a "Third Party Licensee" and each such territory(s) licensed to a Third Party Licensee to be herein called a "Licensed Territory"), you hereby agree, represent and warrant:

(1)   Your agreement with each Third Party Licensee shall provide that such LP shall be sold or otherwise exploited only in the Licensed Territory and you shall use your reasonable efforts to prevent the distribution or sale of such LP outside of the Licensed Territory

(2)   You and/or each Third Party Licensee shall be solely responsible for and shall make any and all payments required to be made in connection with the manufacture, distribution and sale or other exploitation of such LP in Licensed Territory including, without limitation, all artists' royalties (including royalties payable to the Artist), producers' royalties, mechanical or copyright fees or royalties, contributions which may become due to the AFM Music Performance Trust Fund, the AFM Special Payments Fund, or any other union trust fund, and you hereby hold Company free and harmless from any and all claims in connection therewith. You and/or each Third Party Licensee shall, at Company's request, obtain from any person, firm or corporation which may be entitled to any such payments, any documents which Company requests that confirm that such person, firm or corporation will not look to Company for any such payments in connection with the manufacture, distribution and sale or other exploitation of any such LP in Licensed Territory.

(3) You and each Third Party Licensee shall indemnify and hold Company and its licensees harmless from any damages, liabilities, costs and expenses, including legal expenses and reasonable attorneys' fees, arising out of any and all uses of such LP by any Third Party Licensee or its successors, assigns or licensees.

(b) Notwithstanding the foregoing, in the event Company shall fail to release an album in any of the countries listed herein and said album has achieved a chart position of at least seventy-five (75) on the Billboard Hot 100 Chart, said LP shall revert to you and/or Artist and Company shall have no further interest or right or title to said LP.

20.   (a)   The word "Artist" as used in this contract refers individually and collectively to the members of the group (whether presently or hereafter signatories to or otherwise bound by the terms and provisions of this   contract)   professionally   known as_____

_____

(b)   In the event any individual member of the group shall, during the term hereof, cease to be an actively performing member of the group (any such individual being hereinafter sometimes referred to as "Leaving Member"), you shall promptly give us written notice thereof by certified or registered mail, return receipt requested. You shall designate a replacement member for Leaving Member. You shall cause any such individual so approved by us as a replacement member to be bound by all of the terms and provisions of this contract, and you shall, upon our request, cause such individual to execute and deliver to us such documents as we may deem necessary or expedient to evidence such individual's agreement to be so bound. Pending such individual's execution and delivery to us of any such documents, we shall have no obligation to pay you more than fifty (50%) percent of any amounts which would otherwise be payable to you hereunder.

(c)   Company shall have the irrevocable option to utilize the exclusive recording service of any Leaving Member. Such option may be exercised by us by written notice given to such Leaving Member at your address hereunder no later then ninety (90) days after the date upon which we shall have received the written notice required to be served by you pursuant to subparagraph (b). If we shall so exercise such option with respect to any such Leaving Member, such Leaving Member shall be deemed to have executed an exclusive recording services to us on the same terms and provisions specified herein with respect to you, except as hereinafter provided:

(i) the term of our exclusive recording contract with such Leaving Member shall be for an initial term of one (1) year, commencing as of our written notice to him pursuant to subparagraph (c) above, and we shall have such number of separate irrevocable options as equal the number of renewal options remaining hereunder pursuant to paragraph 2 above as of the date such individual shall become a Leaving Member, but in no event shall the number of options be less than two (2). Each option shall give us the right to renew such term for one (1) year. Such renewal terms shall run consecutively beginning at the expiration of such initial term, all upon the same terms and provisions applicable to such initial term. Each such renewal option may be exercised only by our giving such Leaving Member written notice (at your address hereunder or at such other address of which such Leaving Member shall have notified us in writing) at least thirty (30) days prior to the commencement of the renewal term for which such renewal option is exercised;

(ii)   during such initial term and each such renewal term, such Leaving Member shall record six (6) master recordings embodying his performances, plus, at our election, additional master recordings embodying his performances, but in no event shall such Leaving Member be required to record in excess of ten (10) master recordings during such initial term of any such renewal term;

(iii) the royalty rate pursuant to paragraph 7 (a) (i) hereof with respect to such Leaving Member shall be ten (10%) percent and the royalty rate pursuant to paragraph 7 (a) (ii) hereof with respect to such Leaving Member shall be eleven (11%) percent; and

(iv) paragraph 7 (b) (i), 7 (b) (ii), and 7 (b) (iii) hereof shall be deemed incorporated and in force and effect with respect to any such Leaving Member.

(d)   At our request, you shall cause any such Leaving Member to execute and deliver to us any and all documents as we may deem necessary or expedient to evidence the foregoing, including, without limitation, an exclusive recording contract with us relating to his recording services.

(e)   Notwithstanding any of the foregoing, in the event any member of the group shall be a Leaving Member or in the event the group shall completely disband, we shall have the right, at our election, in addition to all of our other rights or remedies which we may have in such event, to terminate this contract by written notice to you and shall thereby be relieved of any and all obligations hereunder except our obligations with respect to Masters recorded hereunder prior such termination. In the event we elect to so terminate this contract, subparagraph (c) above shall be deemed applicable to each member of the group as if each such member were a Leaving Member.

(f)   In the event any member of the group shall become a Leaving Member, such Leaving Member shall not have the right thereafter during the term hereof to use any professional name utilized by the group or any name similar thereto.

21. Company may, at its election, and upon prior written notice to you, assign this agreement, or any of its rights hereunder to any other division of Company, or to any subsidiary or licensee in which Company now has or may hereafter obtain a substantial interest, or to any Company that merges its assets with those of Company or whose assets are acquired by Company whether by purchase or otherwise or to any company that acquires all or substantially all of Company's assets, provided that any assignee executes an assumption agreement regarding this agreement.

22. If any clause, sentence, paragraph or part of this agreement or the application thereof to any Person, shall for any reason be adjusted by a court of competent jurisdiction to be invalid or determined to be in violation or contravention of any applicable statutory legislation, then such clause, sentence, paragraph or part of this agreement shall be deemed to be automatically amended only to the extent necessary to bring this agreement within said judgment or determination, as applicable, effective as of the date thereof, and such judgment or determination shall not affect the remainder of this agreement, which shall continue in full force and effect.

23. All notices hereunder required to be given to Company shall be sent to Company at its address mentioned herein and all royalties, statements and payments and any and all notices to you shall be sent to you at your address mentioned herein, or such other address as each party respectively may hereafter designate by notice in writing to the other. All such notices shall be in writing and, except for royalty statements, shall be sent by registered or certified mail, return receipt requested, and the date of the mailing of any such notice shall be deemed the date of the giving thereof. All notices to Company shall be served upon Company to the attention of the President with a copy to the Vice President, Legal and Business Affairs. Notwithstanding the foregoing, in the event of disruption of postal services, all notices given under the terms of this agreement shall be delivered

personally, or by telex, telegram or telecopy, with a confirming notice sent by mail in accordance with this paragraph.

24. (a) Except as provided in (b) below, neither party shall have the right to terminate this agreement as consequence of the other party's default or breach hereunder (including Company's failure to exercise the options set forth in paragraph 2 above) unless such default or breach is a "material" default or breach and unless the party seeking to terminate because of the other party's default or breach gives notice of such claim in writing by certified mail, return receipt requested, and unless the party against whom such default or breach is claimed shall fail to cure the same within forty-five (45) days after the receipt of such notice. If the default or breach is not fully cured within such forty-five (45) day cure period, the party claiming default or breach shall, without prejudicing its other rights and remedies, have the right to immediately terminate this agreement. In the event such breach is not capable of being fully cured within such forty-five (45) day period and the party against whom such default or breach is claimed commences to cure such breach within such forty-five (45) day period and proceeds with reasonable diligence to complete the curing of such breach, then such defaulting party shall have a reasonable period thereafter within which to cure said breach.

(b) The provisions of (a) above shall not add an additional requirement to the procedures set forth in paragraph 3 (g) for termination for failure to timely deliver the Sides, nor contravene Company's right pursuant to paragraph 17 to immediately seek injunctive or other equitable relief to enforce performance of the obligations of Artist pursuant to this agreement.

25. Notwithstanding anything to the contrary contained herein, Artist shall have the right to appear as a "sideman" on records embodying the performances of other recording artists provided; (i) Artist's name shall only appear on the back or the inside liner notes (and shall not appear on the record label, cover or any advertisement) in connection with any such record and shall not exceed the size and prominence of the credit to sideman; (ii) Artist shall be accompanied by the following credit:

" _____ appears courtesy of _____ "

26. During the term, Company shall not release through normal retail channels in the territory more than one (1) so-called "Greatest Hits" or "Best Of" album solely derived from masters delivered hereunder (a "Greatest Hits Album") provided that (a) such Greatest Hits album shall not be released earlier than three (3) months after actual date of delivery of the third LP delivered hereunder. If the Greatest Hits album is released hereunder, it shall not apply in diminution of your minimum recording obligation in respect of any period hereof. In the event a Greatest Hits album or Best Of album is released by Company, and, in the further event that yours and Artist's royalty accounts are in a fully recouped status, Company shall only pay you a sum of Fifty Thousand ($50,000) Dollars. Company shall be responsible for the payment of all recording cost in connection with said Greatest Hits or Best Of album.

27. This agreement is entered into in the State of Tennessee and shall be construed in accordance with the laws of said state applicable to contracts negotiated, executed and to be wholly performed therein. The parties hereto agree that any controversy arising under this agreement shall be adjudicated under the jurisdiction of a competent court within Tennessee. This agreement may not be modified except by an instrument in writing executed by the parties hereto. The invalidity or enforceability of any other provision hereof shall not affect the validity or enforceability of any other provision hereof.

28. This writing sets forth the entire understanding between the parties with respect to the subject matter hereof, and no modification, amendment, waiver, termination or discharge of this agreement shall be binding upon Company unless confirmed by a written instrument signed by an officer of Company. No waiver of any provision of or default under this agreement nor any failure to exercise its rights hereunder shall prejudice the rights of Company thereafter, nor shall it be a precedent for the future.

In witness whereof, the parties hereto have executed this agreement the day and year herein written.

By: _____ _____(title)

By: _____ _____(title)

Recent Issues in Recording Contracts

Allen Arrow and Jonas Herbsman

DIGITAL RIGHTS ISSUES IN RECORDING CONTRACTS

The digital explosion has resulted in a variety of new methods of delivery of music which not only weren't known a few years ago, but weren't even contemplated. Broader bandwidth, the growth of personal computers and the development of portable digital music devices has altered and promises to further alter the manner in which music is distributed and purchased by consumers. Equally significant is the impact these changes bring to the negotiation of a recording contract. While the artist or the artist's lawyer, manager or other representative must consider the effect of the digital age in all aspects of a recording contract, several areas require a greater degree of understanding.

1. Are Digital Rights Covered?

As noted above, paragraphs 1(d) and 1(e) of the artist contract are written broadly to encompass any delivery method which is now known or may be developed in the future. This language has now been supplemented in current recording agreements to specifically include the right to digital distribution, via downloading, streaming, satellite transmission, or such other methods as may be developed in the future. The addition of the specific language is meant to avoid the disputes which have arisen regarding older recording contracts entered into before such methods of distribution were contemplated. The older contracts frequently do not contain the broad granting language and certainly don't contain any reference to the granting of digital rights. Some older artists have begun to take the position that digital rights were unknown when their record contract was entered into and, therefore, the artist could not have intended to include digital rights in the package of rights granted to the record company.

2. Coupling/Compilations

New technology gives consumers greater freedom of choice. A consumer may purchase a custom compilation consisting of selections from different albums, whether by the same or different artists or a customer may choose to download or receive by wireless transmission one or more selections rather than purchase an entire album. Paragraph 5(b) of the artist contract contains a limitation on the coupling of recordings delivered pursuant to the contract with recordings by other artists. Depending on the extent of the "anti-coupling" provision in its artist contract, a record company may face significant limitations in its ability to offer an artist's recordings in the form of custom compilations. In terms of digital distribution, a record label may even be contractually hindered in attempting to sell individual downloads or wireless transmissions of an artist's recordings, e.g., if a consumer purchases more than one selection during a single on-line session, an artist may argue that the purchase of multiple individual selections constitutes a coupling of the artist's recordings in violation of the artist's contract.

3. Release Obligation

Paragraph 19 of the artist contract provides for a release obligation on the part of the record company. If the obligation is not satisfied, the artist may, by following certain procedures, require that the album be licensed to a third party or notify the record company that the ownership of the album has reverted to the artist. In a digital world, the definition of "release" may take on new meanings which differ from prior standards. Is a record released in every territory if it is available for sale or download on the record company's website or via satellite and the website or satellite delivery is accessible from any computer throughout the world? Artists will attempt to protect their interests by requiring that a release commitment must include the distribution and availability of physical product in the traditional retail outlets in each territory for as long as such traditional retail outlets are the principal, or even just a significant, method of record distribution.

4. Royalties

Digital distribution raises numerous royalty related issues:

(a) Normal Distribution Channels/New Media

As set forth in paragraph 7 of the artist contract, an artist's basic royalty is computed and paid based upon sales through "normal distribution channels." While this artist contract does not define "normal distribution channels," other artist contracts do provide that "normal distribution channels" exclude sales of recordings in new media or new technology configurations, which sales are then subject to a reduced royalty rate. Traditionally, record companies have attempted to impose this reduced royalty rate for new media or new technology uses, arguing that such uses are initially more expensive, as was the case with compact discs. By placing digital distribution in the "new media" category, an artist would be subject to this royalty rate reduction. An alternative is to limit the time period during which a "new media" reduction applies based on a number of months/years or based upon such media being a substantial stated percentage of total sales.

A similar issue arises with "direct to consumer" sales, such as via television, mail order or digital distribution, where an artist contract may provide for a reduced royalty rate. These channels of distribution may actually cost the record company less per sale than sales through traditional distribution methods. Therefore, a persuasive argument can be made for no royalty reduction for such sales, as the record company's profits have actually increased in such instances.

The categorization of digital distribution as a new media royalty may affect increases in royalty rates (paragraph 7(b)) and advances for subsequent albums (paragraph 9(a)), to the extent such items are based upon unit sales. In some instances, if a sale is not through "normal distribution channels," the sale is not considered in the royalty calculations. Additionally, mechanical royalty rates for new media category sales may be at a lower percentage of the otherwise applicable contractual rate.

(b) Packaging and Container

Paragraph 7 of the artist contract contains the standard reduction for packaging and container charges. These charges have long been the subject of complaints from artists and their representatives due to the fact that the charges greatly exceed the actual costs incurred by a record company for such items, essentially resulting in an artificial, percentage based reduction in royalties. Where delivery is by digital means, record companies continue to deduct packaging and container charges where there is no packaging and no container, utilizing a catch-all provision contained in most recording contracts allowing for deduction of the "artificial" packaging and container charge for compact discs and "all other configurations."

(c) Foreign Sales

The royalty provisions of paragraph 7(e) refer to reductions for foreign sales. The rationale for this reduction in the past was the lower profit associated with foreign distribution, particularly where the foreign distributor was unaffiliated with the record company. With digital distribution, where delivery is not by means of a physical sound carrier, the distribution costs incurred by the record company should be the same regardless of the territory in which the sale occurs, bringing into question the validity of the foreign sales royalty rate reduction.

5. Websites

While it is established practice that an artist retains ownership of the artist's individual or group name, it has become common for a record company to seek to control the artist's on-line presence by securing the ownership of domain names encompassing the artist's name and operating websites utilizing those domain names. Artists interested in controlling their on-line presence have refused to agree to these clauses. The potential for increased sales, sales of merchandise and direct interaction with an artist's fans promise to make this issue a significant one in future artist negotiations.

6. Marketing and Promotion

Previously, a record contract was necessary in order to provide an artist with the money necessary to record and distribution facilities to deliver the records into the hands of the purchasers. With the decrease in recording costs as a result of the new digital equipment available to artists, the barrier to entering the marketplace has fallen for artists attempting to distribute their music without a recording contract. It has been argued that this is leveling the playing field and allowing every artist to be his or her own record company. The problem is that the artist must have a method for getting through to the listening public. Why does a consumer choose to visit one artist's website instead of the other five million artist websites? How does the consumer even learn of the website's existence? The record company is the source of marketing and promotion, making the negotiation of guaranteed marketing and promotion budgets one of the key elements of artist contracts in the digital age.

The new methods of distribution and the new tools available to artists may result in a shift away from the traditional relationship of the record company as owner of the artist's product toward artist/record company partnerships with the record company acting as a marketer and distributor and not as an owner. The result may be, for the artist, a more equitable division of the income derived from the exploitation of the artist's recordings.

WORK FOR HIRE

Under the United States Copyright Act of 1909, an author was granted two (2) consecutive twenty-eight (28) year terms of copyright protection. The rationale for separate periods arose from the fact that the legislators realized that the value of a work is generally not known when initially created and an author, in need of income, may be in an unequal bargaining position with the assignees of the work. The separation of the duration of copyright into two separate terms was an attempt to remedy this disparity, but assignees simply required assignment of the renewal term at the time of the assignment of the initial term. The 1976 Copyright Act ended the concept of a renewal term for newly created works, instead adding a provision stating that any transfer, regardless of the terms of the transfer agreement between the parties, may be terminated by the author thirty-five (35) years after the date of the grant. Safeguards as to negotiation periods and service of notice on grantees were included in the 1976 Copyright Act in order to prevent an author from transferring the termination rights prematurely.

In an attempt to avoid the applicability of the termination right, record companies have included a "work for hire" provision in artist contracts, stating that sound recordings created pursuant to such contracts are "works for hire" made by the artist as an employee. This position, however, conflicts with court decisions holding that, to fit within the definition of "work for hire" under the Copyright Act, the work must specifically fit within one of nine categories set forth in the Copyright Act as works which can be commissioned as "work for hire." If subjected to a court challenge, record companies feared their position might not be substantiated.

On November 22, 1999, the Copyright Act was amended to add "sound recordings" to the definition of works considered "work for hire." This change in the Copyright Act was championed by the Recording Industry Association of America or RIAA (the record industry lobbying arm) as a clarification of the existing "work for hire" definition. The RIAA asserted that a sound recording had always been a "work for hire" under the Copyright Act, either as a compilation or a contribution to a collective work, both of which are within the nine (9) enumerated categories of "work for hire" set forth in the Copyright Act. The change was attacked by recording artists as a covert attempt by the RIAA to preclude recording artists from exercising their statutory termination rights. Only eleven months later, on October 27, 2000, the Work Made for Hire and Copyright Corrections Act of 2000 was adopted with the specific purpose of excluding sound recordings from the definition of a "work made for hire" under the Copyright Act.

The return of the "work for hire" definition to its prior state does not resolve the debate regarding the applicability of the termination rights set forth in the 1976 Copyright Act to sound recordings. It is possible that the issue will not be resolved until 2013, when the termination rights are first effective. If a sound recording is ultimately determined not to be a "work for hire," who will have the right to exercise the termination right? Does the termination right belong to the principal performer, the producer, the sound engineer, all of the musicians appearing on the recording or a combination of these parties? The "work for hire" issue has clearly not yet been settled and will likely be the subject of dispute for at least several years.

Updating the Recording Contract

Linda Mensch

Linda Mensch is a prominent entertainment lawyer based in Chicago, Illinois with over 30 years of experience in the music industry.

NEW TECHNOLOGY PROVISIONS IN RECORDING CONTRACTS

Not all Recording Agreements contain explicit clauses dealing with digital rights issues, which would include ownership and use of URL's, domain names and websites, the rights to control and own the content in the sites, linking rights, and marketing and promotional rights. In examining several agreements currently in use as of the date of publication, we decided to contrast the language of two major companies. These provisions, which have been modified, are used courtesy of CEMA and WEA.

1. Grant of Rights

Most current contracts include a provision on website maintenance which grants the Record Company this exclusive right for a stated period of time, defined as the "Website Term." Note that the Website Term extends for 3 months after the release of the last single in connection with the last album delivered during the term. (Would a BEST OF or GREATEST HITS CD which generates a new single extend this term?). This Website is the "official" website of the artist. The artist is permitted creative input on the initial site design and content. Note that in this Agreement, the content cannot include musical material unrelated to the artist's performance, or advertisements for other products or services, except for advertising for retail shops or browser frames. The Agreement allows the artist set up additional web sites related to goods and services unrelated to artist's recording, including fan club sites and merchandising/touring sites. A separate question is who should own and control the fan email lists, and how is that information shared?

In this Agreement, the Website stays with the label unless (and until) the artist notifies the Company that Artist wants it reassigned any time after 3 months after the release of the last Single in connection with the final album delivered during the term. After the expiration of this term, the Company has a nonexclusive right to continue to maintain a site of the Company's choice using artist's name or URL in order to distribute records and related products. The Company also reserves the right to establish links to and from its sites with other sites relating to the artist or that the artist would have an interest in; the artist is also allowed to establish links as long as the links are to "first class."

Here is a modified website provision: Company shall have the exclusive right throughout the universe during the Web Site Term: (i) to establish and maintain a website or its equivalent with content related to you/Artist (the

"Company-Artist Site") on the Internet having the address (i.e. Uniform Resource Locator, or "URL") "[Artist].com" which contains Artist's professional name (the "Artist URL") and to utilize Artist's professional name in connection with such Artist URL; (ii) to couple the Artist URL with any such other appropriate suffixes (e.g. top-level domains such as .com, .net, .co.uk, etc.), which Company determines in its sole discretion are necessary or desirable and to register the Artist URL and any such suffixes in Company's name in any and all territories with the appropriate entities and to secure any and all renewals and extensions thereof on your behalf, it being understood that you and Artist hereby appoint Company as your attorney-in-fact for such purposes; (iii) to refer to the Company-Artist Site as the "official" site relating to Artist; and (iv) to include the Artist URL on Records embodying any Recording or its equivalent and on any advertising and marketing materials used by Company or its licensees to promote the rights granted herein. Company shall be the sole and exclusive owner of the Company-Artist Site and its operation and content shall be controlled by Company. Notwithstanding the foregoing, during the Web Site Term: (A) at your request, Company shall consult with you or Artist regarding the initial design of the Company-Artist Site and shall give due consideration to any reasonable request made by you or Artist relating to the content of the Company-Artist Site; (B) unless you or Artist shall consent thereto, Company shall not include on the Company-Artist Site: (I) any musical material that does not embody Artist's performances; or (II) any advertisements or endorsements for products or services other than Recordings embodying Artist's performances or Artist's services (provided that Company shall have the right to place on the Company-Artist Site advertisements for any seller of Records designated by Company and/or advertising in or in connection with Company's browser frames which reside outside of the Company-Artist Site and which are common to one or more of Company's main web pages). Provided that you and Artist comply with the material terms and conditions of this paragraph 5(c), nothing set forth in this paragraph shall be construed to restrict you from establishing or maintaining (or authorizing other Persons to establish or maintain) additional web sites relating solely to goods and services other than Artist's Recordings or recording services (including fan club sites and sites relating to Artist's merchandising and touring activities). You may elect to terminate Company's exclusive right and license in the Artist URL by notice to Company at any time after the date which is three (3) months after the release of the last Single in connection with the final Album Delivered by you during the Term. (The period commencing on the date of this agreement and ending thirty (30) days following the date on which you provide such notice to Company is referred to in this agreement as the "Web Site Term.") After the expiration of the Web Site Term, Company shall have the non-exclusive right to continue to maintain one (1) site of Company's choice established or maintained by Company during the Web Site Term or to establish and maintain one (1) new site on the Internet, the URL of which may use Artist's professional name, in connection with Company's distribution of Records subject to this agreement. In this connection, Artist hereby grants to Company the exclusive right to an alternate URL embodying Artist's professional name (e.g. [Artist]cds.com) (the "Alternate URL"), which Alternate URL: (A) shall be chosen by Company in its sole discretion after consultation with you to ensure that the Alternate URL does not conflict with any URL you are then using; and (B) shall be owned in perpetuity by Company and used exclusively by Company, at Company's election, at any time during or after the Web Site Term. Company shall have the right to establish links to and from Company's sites with all other sites relating to Artist that you or Artist control, in which you or Artist have an interest or to which you or Artist have granted a Person the right to operate or administer, including fan club sites and sites relating to Artist's merchandising and touring activities. You shall have the right to establish links to and from the Company-Artist Site with all "first class" sites relating to Artist that you control; provided that, in Company's reasonable, good faith opinion, such other sites or material embodied on such sites do not constitute an invasion of any Person's rights (including copyright infringement, libel, or slander) and do not violate Company's standards of decency or any applicable rules, regulations, statutes or laws. You and Artist shall coordinate with Company with respect to the establishment of such links. Upon Company's reasonable request during the Web Site Term, you and/or Artist shall provide Company with information obtained about users of and/or visitors to any sites which you or Artist control, including e-mail lists obtained or derived from any such site; provided that, in no event shall you and/or Artist be required to provide any information you or Artist reasonably believes would violate any applicable rules, regulations, statutes or laws. At your reasonable request, Company shall provide you with information obtained about users of and/or visitors to the Company-Artist Site during the Web Site Term; provided that, in no event shall Company be required to provide any information which Company reasonably believes would violate any applicable rules, regulations, statutes or laws or the privacy policies, guidelines or practices of Company or any of its affiliates, subsidiaries or parents. Company shall be responsible for and pay all costs in connection with the establishment, registration and maintenance of the Artist URL at its non-recoupable expense.

The important point to note is that the record company wants to retain rights to the Internet domain name "artist.com."

Contrast this lengthy provision with the more common and shorter provision: Company shall have the right to register, in Company's name, Internet domain names incorporating Artist's name. Company acknowledges that Artist has previously registered "youartist.com".

2. Creative and Marketing Matters

In connection with these promotional appearance provisions, the traditional contractual language requires the artist to make personal appearances, appear on videos, TV, promotional events, photo shoots, provide biographical material, and meet other marketing requirements. Some recent additions require the artist to be available to appear for online "chats," webcasts and other online promotional activities in addition to on-camera interviews.

Modified provision: Artist shall be available upon Company's reasonable request to appear for exclusive on-camera interviews, so-called online "chats," webcasts and other promotional activities, and you shall provide Company with a reasonable amount of additional exclusive promotional material upon Company's request.

3. Royalties

Record companies tend to treat digital royalties (electronic transmissions) as they would the sale of a single record. The sales price set by the I-Tunes equivalent or ISP becomes the retail sales price, subject to packaging and other deductions and reductions. The artist royalty is then a percentage of this number. Most major label agreements contain a provision on new technology formats and royalty calculation. The clause is written to broadly include any new form of technology, known at present or not, and to determine when a new technology format has become widely distributed enough to calculate royalties on mainstream level. Although CDs have been around and are not "new technology", some agreements treat it as such. A common approach might state that for records produced in the widely distributed CD format, the royalty rate is 100% of what is otherwise set forth in the agreement. But for records produced in any other technology format, the royalty rate is 75% of otherwise applicable rate. However, if in any calendar year, once the revenues from the sale of records in a particular new technology format exceed 20% of total U.S. recorded music revenues, the format is no longer considered new and the royalty rates rise to 100% of the otherwise applicable royalty rate.

New Technology Royalties: Notwithstanding anything to the contrary contained herein, for sales by Company or a Principal Licensee of: (i) Records in now widely distributed compact disc forms including Enhanced CD and CD Extra formats, the royalty rate shall be one hundred percent (100%) of the otherwise applicable royalty rate set forth in this agreement; and (ii) Phono Records in any form, format or technology not herein described, which is now known but not widely distributed or which hereafter becomes known, including Super Audio CD and DVD Audio ("New Technology Formats"), the royalty rate shall be seventy-five percent (75%) of the otherwise applicable royalty rate set forth in this agreement; provided that, if in any calendar year the revenues generated from the sale of Records in a particular New Technology Format exceed twenty percent (20%) of total United States recorded music revenues (as reported in a reputable published industry source such as IFPI's *The Recording Industry in Numbers*), then, with respect to sales of Records hereunder in any subsequent calendar years, such particular New Technology Format shall no longer constitute a New Technology Format and the royalty rate with respect to such particular New Technology Format shall be one hundred percent (100%) of the otherwise applicable royalty rate set forth in this agreement rather than seventy-five percent (75%).

Electronic Transmissions: With respect to Electronic Transmissions, the royalty rate shall be one hundred percent (100%) of the otherwise applicable royalty rate set forth in this agreement.

Note: Recently, Cheap Trick and the Allman Brothers filed a class action suit against SONY/ BMG, claiming that digital royalties are really third party licenses, adding fuel to the debate over calculating royalties for electronically transmitted recordings. Should container charges apply?

Two main methods of calculating royalties have surfaced, and have similar results even though one does not deduct "container" fees and the other does. In "Retail Price Method," the Basic Rate is 15% and the Royalty Base Price is usually set at $18.98, but companies subtract a 25% container deduction to make the royalty base price $14.23. In the "Transparent Accounting Method," the basic rates and Royalty Base Price start off lower, at 12.25% and $12.00 respectively, and contain no container or CD reductions. Both methods take 5% of records shipped and reserve 25% for returns. However, both methods end up calculating similar royalty earnings because the Retail Price Method subtracts further discounts of records shipped, while the Transparent Accounting Method does   not.

The record companies who use the "Retail Price Method" are continuing to deduct container fees when their recordings are distributed electronically. Is this reasonable? When CDs are sold electronically, the record company does not have to spend money on physical containers or packages for the records. Record companies have not adapted, and have not changed their royalty calculation method. What are the arguments? Aren't labels still spending money to "package" and market artist's materials online? The solution is to change the method to the so-called Transparent Accounting Method, but, if labels "re-distribute" royalty percentages the royalty earnings are going to come out the same. Why? Almost every Agreement will contain a provision that allows the label to change their method of computation provided in the contract as long as the computation results in substantially the same new amount of royalties otherwise payable to the artist. And here it is:

"Company may elect from time to time to compute and pay you royalties hereunder on a royalty base different than the Royalty Base Price provided herein, as long as such computation results in substantially the same net amount of royalties otherwise payable to you at that time hereunder."

Note that in the language below, the rate is even LESS than the artist's CD royalty. The rate for a digital download is 85% of that rate.

Digital Royalties: The royalty rate on any Digital Record (excluded New Media Records generally but including Electronic Transmission Records) will be eighty-five percent (85%) of the otherwise applicable rate. The royalty rate on any New Media Record (other than Electronic Transmission Records) will be seventy percent (70%) of the rate that would otherwise be Digital Records. The royalty rate on any Electronic Transmission Record is in a Singles or in an Album format.

Note: Some recording contracts also have a specific provision for calculating royalties with respect to electronic transmissions sold through a "subscription" service. Unless the record company receives payment on a per-stream or per-download basis, royalties will be attributed to Masters using the following formula: (Total royalties received by the company from the applicable service for the relevant reporting period) x (actual number of streams and/or downloads for such period/total number of streams and/or downloads of all Masters reported to the record company for such period).

"On Masters licensed by Company or its Affiliates/Principal Licensees on a flat-fee or a royalty basis for the sale of other exploitations of Electronic Transmission Records, your royalty hereunder shall be an amount equal to the royalty rate set forth herein with respect to Electronic Transmission Records applied to Company's Net Receipts from such exploitation of the Masters."

4. Licenses For Musical Compositions

This language has not changed much from the older agreements, but will include broadcast and transmission language, refer to videos, website postings, and the right to reproduce, distribute and perform the controlled composition itself on websites.

Modified provision: Company shall provide appropriate copyright notices and writer and publisher credits with respect to such reprinted lyrics; provided that, Company's inadvertent failure to do so in any instance shall not constitute a breach of this agreement. You also grant to Company and Company's licensees an irrevocable license under copyright to reproduce each Controlled Composition in Videos and in advertisements for Recordings hereunder (including so-called EPKs) or Artist's recording services in any and all media (including television, radio and the Internet), to reproduce, distribute and perform those Videos and advertisements in any manner (including publicly and for profit, and including use of such Videos and advertisements in Records containing audiovisual material and in webcasts), to manufacture and distribute Audiovisual Records and other copies of those Videos, and to exploit such Videos and advertisements otherwise, by any method and in any form known now or in the future, in perpetuity and throughout the Territory, and to authorize others to do so. Company and Company's licensees shall not be required to make any payment in connection with those uses, and that license shall apply whether or not Company receives any payment in connection with any use of any Video or advertisement. If any exhibition of a Video and/or advertisement is also authorized under another license (such as a public performance license granted by ASCAP or BMI), that exhibition shall be deemed authorized by that license instead of this agreement. In all events, Company and Company's licensees shall have no liability by reason of any such exhibition. You also grant to Company and Company's licensees at no cost an irrevocable license under copyright to reproduce, distribute and perform each Controlled Composition or any portion thereof for promotional purposes on websites maintained by Company or its licensees or affiliates throughout the Territory.

5. Warranties and Representations

The re-recording restriction has been expanded to include new forms of media. The label still has to approve by written agreement recordings in other media. The language has been expanded so that Re-recording restrictions will state that performances cannot be recorded for digital broadcasts or other transmissions (including webcasts), nor can they be recorded for on-demand (repetitive broadcast enabling the consumer to approximate a time at which to access the recording), including transmission via television or internet.

Modified provision: During the term, Artist shall not perform for, and neither you nor Artist shall authorize or knowingly permit Artist's performances to be recorded and/or transmitted by, any Person for any purpose, without an express written agreement with such Person for Company's benefit that: (A) prohibits the use of such performance and/or Recording for: (I) making, promoting, or marketing Recordings or Records (provided that this paragraph shall not preclude Artist from performing for analog television broadcasts and no rights are granted with respect to such performances other than analog television broadcast rights); (II) digital broadcasts or other transmissions, distributions or other communications now or hereafter known, including webcasts; and (III) any form of transmission or broadcast of Recordings by any means which permits the consumer to access the Recording concerned (whether in isolation or with other Recordings) on demand or via repetitive broadcast enabling the consumer to choose the approximate time at which to access the Recording concerned, including television broadcast, cable transmission and/or transmission via the Internet; and (B) specifically provides that, if a Recording is made of Artist's performance, such Recording is made for the benefit, and is the exclusive property, of Company.

6. Definitions

Most older agreements will need to expand their definitions to include new technology formats. The following definitions are useful:

a. **Consumer compilation**: a compilation record embodying recordings that are individually selected and/or sequenced by the consumer (via systems such as I-tunes, myspace, and digital on-demand kiosks).

b. **Digital Record:** all records embodying, employing or otherwise utilizing any non-analog technology and shall include, without limitation, compact discs and "new media" records (including electronic transmission records).

c. **Electronic Transmissions:** Short Definition: Records sold by company or through company's distributors in the U.S. or by company, company's principal licensees or their distributors outside the U.S. other than as phono records including via telephone, satellite, cable, point-of-sale manufacturing, transmission over wire or through air, downloading and any other methods now or hereafter known. Or longer alternative definition: Records sold via the distribution, transmission or communication of such record over a communication medium (including but not limited to, wired and/or wireless systems, broadband, narrowband or other Internet, satellite, optic fiber, wire or cable), whether now known or hereafter devised, from one location to a remote location, in such a manner that the Record when received at the remote location is sufficiently permanent or stable to permit it to be perceived, reproduced, or otherwise communicated to the recipient at such remote location, without regard to whether the sound recording or audiovisual work embodied in the record is simultaneously performed in an audible fashion during such distribution, transmission or communication, and for the avoidance of doubt, shall be deemed to include transmission or communication of records by cybercast, webcast of any other type of so-called audio or audiovisual "streaming."

d. **Internet:** the wide area cooperative network of university, corporate, government, private computer networks, Internet Service and any current or future proprietary, private, subscription online networks or services communicating through Transmission Control Protocol/Internet Protocol (TCP/IP).

e. **New Media Records:** records in the following configurations: mini-discs, digital compact cassettes, digital audio tapes, laser discs, solid state memory devices, digital versatile discs (i.e. DVD's), compact discs capable of bearing visual images (including without limitation, Enhanced CD, CD-Plus and CD-ROM), records sold via "point of sale" manufacturing, Electronic Transmission records and any other configurations other than conventional vinyl records, cassette tapes, and audio-only compact discs, whether such records are interactive (i.e. where the user is able to access, select or manipulate the materials therein) or non-interactive, and whether now known or hereafter devised.

f. **On-Demand Usages:** licensed usages of records other than phono records as part of a service containing a functionality which permits a consumer to access a particular recording or recordings on a so-called "on-demand" basis including subscription.

g. **Online Store Compilation**: a compilation record embodying recordings that are individually selected and/or sequenced by an online retail store (such as amazon.com, i-tunes and similar stores).

h. **Record:** any form of reproduction, distribution, transmission or communication of recordings (whether or not in physical form) now or hereafter known (including reproductions of sound alone or together with visual images) which is manufactured, transmitted or communicated primarily for personal use, home use, institutional use, jukebox use, or use in means of transportation, including any computer-assisted media (e.g., CD ROM, DVD Audio, CD Extra, Enhanced CD) or use as a so-called "ring tone."

Given the growth of ringtones, and the application of technology terms to artist and label "content" we have also included some definitions from contracts that deal solely with electronic transmissions and digital downloading :

1. "Content File" shall mean each digitized and encoded electronic file containing a digitized Master, Video or other media property right, and which may contain any or all associated Artwork, parental advisory notices, copyright notices and/or Metadata.

2. "Digital Music Service" or "Digital Media Service" shall mean those Internet, Web-based, online and other electronic business-to-business, business-to-consumer and peer-to-peer services, owned and/or operated by third party Resellers, which are authorized pursuant to License agreements to sell, license, distribute and broadcast music, videos and other digital media in digital form via Permanent Downloads, Limited Downloads, Full length downloads of individual tracks, Mix tapes, Streams, Ring Tones, Compact Disc

Burns, Podcasts, Webcasts, Internet radio, TV, video games, ads, and other existing and future digital delivery methods, by any means now known or hereinafter devised, including, without limitation, delivery over the Internet, cable television infrastructure or wireless communications networks.

3. "Download" or "Downloading" (used as a verb or gerund) means the single, encrypted digital audio transmission of a Sound Recording (not a Stream) delivered from a Digital Music Service server via the Internet to Service Users accessing such Digital Music Service using a Playback Device. "Download" (as a noun) means the digital audio copy that results from the process of Downloading, which a Service User may access using a Playback Device

4. "Limited Download" means the encrypted digital copy that results from the process of downloading in which a Service User's use or access is limited in a certain defined way; i.e., to that period of time during which a Service User is actively subscribed to a Reseller's Digital Music Service. Limited Downloads will also include transmissions from sharing between Service Users made as so-called "file sharing", pre-loaded content on a Playback Device or included as a software bundle.

5. "Permanent Download" means a complete digital copy of one or more individual Sound Recordings that are encoded in one of the compression/decompression algorithm compressed formats.

6. "Ring Tones" mean sounds made by mobile phones to indicate an incoming or received outgoing call, triggered by receipt of a specific radio-frequency signal, including "Polyphonic Tones" (composed of multiple notes and MIDI sequences that can be played at the same time to recreate instrument sounds), "Real Tones" (aka "True Tones", composed of portions of Masters and typically contained in AAC, MP3, WMA, WAV, QCP, or AMR formats), and "Ringback Tones" (either Polyphonic or True Tones indicating that the recipient's phone has received an outgoing call).

7. "Sound Clip" shall mean a preview of a Master to be provided to or created by Resellers for purposes of allowing such Resellers to promote the sale of applicable Label Content, which may be in the form of a Stream, a Limited Download and/or a Permanent Download, generally no longer than sixty (60) seconds for Jazz or Classical Masters or thirty (30) seconds for all other music, as further detailed on the Reseller Term Sheet.

8. "Stream" shall mean an encrypted digital transmission of a Master, or any part thereof, whereby such transmission is substantially contemporaneous with a public performance and with the ability to see and/or hear the Master(s) embodied therein, and which does not produce a fixed file embodying such performance, but solely produces a temporary file in the form of a data buffer or cache copy.

Over the past few years we have seen Napster, Aimster and other sites challenge the music industry through piracy. We have also watched the growth and success of new models such as iTunes, MySpace, and ring/voice tones. The role of the music entrepreneur and the creative artist is to find and monetize content, expand its promotion, marketing and licensing opportunities. As these business models evolve, the agreements between the label and artist must be broad enough to incorporate technologies and methods that are not yet dreamed of and to insure that those rights are protected and can turn into royalties and income streams for the labels and the artists.

Artist-related sites:

- Twitter
- Myspace
- eMusic
- Rhapsody
- YouTube
- iTunes

- Napster
- yahoo! Music
- bittorrent
- garageband
- purevolume
- any mp3 posting sites

REVISING THE CONTRACT

If the recording contract in this book were to be updated, here is what needs to be done:

A. Terms that should be replaced:

1. ALBUM: all references to "LP" should be replaced with the term "Album." The definition should not contain any reference to phonograph records, and can be as specific as "a Record having no less than forty (40) minutes of playing time and which embodies at least eleven (11) Masters each containing a different Composition sold in a single package" (WEA), or could incorporate earlier terminology in a broader context: "an audio-only long-playing record which is not an EP, Single, or Long Play Single, and where the context requires, Master Recordings sufficient to constitute a long-playing audio-only Record" (CEMA).
2. All references to "Sides" should be replaced with the term "Masters" or "songs." MASTER should be defined more simply: "every form of recording or storage device, whether now known or unknown, embodying sound, or sound accompanied by visual images recorded during the Term or delivered to Company during Term.
3. Delete mention of LONG-PLAY SINGLES.
4. BUDGET RECORDS – can remain the same except that the retail price cut-off is around 66% instead of 75% of retail price. Probably doesn't make too much of a difference, but both WEA and CEMA have lower #s.
5. Speak in terms of ALBUMS or RECORDS, don't bother mentioning "PHONOGRAPH" records.

B. New Technology terminology (starred items SHOULD be added, the others are not necessarily standard, should simply be considered):

1. CONTENT FILE: digitized and encoded electronic file containing a digitized Master, Video or other media property right, and which may contain any or all associated Artwork, parental advisory notices, copyright notices and/or Metadata.

2. DIGITAL RECORD: All Records embodying, employing or otherwise utilizing any non-analog technology and shall include, without limitation, compact discs and New Media Records (including Electronic Transmission Records).

3. DIGITAL MUSIC SERVICE: those Internet, Web-based, online and other electronic business-to-business, business-to-consumer and peer-to-peer services, owned and/or operated by third party Resellers, which are authorized pursuant to License agreements to sell, license, distribute and broadcast music, videos and other digital media in digital form via Permanent Downloads, Limited Downloads, Full Length Downloads of individual tracks, Mix Tapes, Streams, Ring Tones, Compact Disc Burns, Podcasts, Webcasts, Internet radio, TV, video games, ads, and other existing and future digital delivery methods, by any means now known or hereinafter devised, including, without limitation, delivery over the Internet, cable television infrastructure or wireless communications networks.

4. DOWNLOAD (used as a verb) means the single, encrypted digital audio transmission of a Sound Recording (not a Stream) delivered from a Digital Music Service server via the Internet to Service Users accessing such Digital Music Service using a Playback Device. Download (as a noun) means the digital audio copy that results from the process of Downloading, which a Service User may access using a Playback Device.

5. ELECTRONIC TRANSMISSION*: Records sold by Company or through Company's distributors in the United States or by Company, Company's Principal Licensees or their distributors outside the United States other than as Phono Records including via telephone, satellite, cable, point-of-sale manufacturing, transmission over wire or through the air, downloading and any other methods now or hereafter known.

6. RING TONES mean sounds made by mobile phones to indicate an incoming or received outgoing call, triggered by receipt of a specific radio-frequency signal, including "Polyphonic Tones" (composed of multiple notes and MIDI sequences that can be played at the same time to recreate instrument sounds),

"Real Tones" (aka "True Tones", composed of portions of Masters and typically contained in AAC, MP3, WMA, WAV, QCP, or AMR formats), and "Ringback Tones" (either Polyphonic or True Tones that a caller in a telephone system hears after dialing a number, when the distant end of the circuit is receiving a ringing signal).

7. SOUND CLIP shall mean a preview of a Master to be provided to or created by Resellers for purposes of allowing such Resellers to promote the sale of applicable Label Content, which may be in the form of a Stream, a Limited Download and/or a Permanent Download, generally no longer than sixty (60) seconds for Jazz or Classical Masters or thirty (30) seconds for all other music.

8. You may to make reference to streams, podcasts, on-demand usage, or other new technology formats in sections where they become applicable – or at least discuss them in the post-contract section.

9. "Singles" should not be a major component of the contract. Leave provisions in, but delete unnecessary references.

C. Standard terms that should be added:

1. ARTWORK: all material embodied in, or supplied by you or Artist for use in, the packaging of Records (including any inserts or other special elements or materials), or created, commissioned or acquired by Company or supplied by you or Artist, for use in publicity, promotion or marketing or as part of Videos, EPK's, or any other Records, including all drawings, photographs, logos, calligraphy, images, paintings or other visual or audiovisual material;

2. AUDIOVISUAL RECORD: a Record which embodies, reproduces, transmits or communicates primarily audiovisual (as opposed to audio-only) material, including any Video. – You can also add more specific examples of formats, including CD-ROM, DVD, or other interactive audiovisual media not intended primarily for audio playback.

3. COMPILATION RECORD: a Record embodying Recordings hereunder together with other Recordings.

D. Royalties:

In the "DEFINITIONS" section, include a definition for "ROYALTY BASE PRICE", and define as follows (from CEMA): "Company's published price to dealers (p.p.d.) applicable to the price series of the unit concerned at the commencement of the accounting period in which the sale occurs, in the country of sale, less ten percent (10%) ("Gross Royalty Base"), and less discounts and all excise, sales, purchase value added, or similar taxes (included in the Royalty Base Price) and less the applicable Container Charge. Royalties will be calculated separately with respect to each price series in which units of a particular Record release are sold during the semi-annual accounting period concerned."

Delete all references to LP's; refer to as Albums, masters, or records.

Section 7(a)(i) is O.K. as is,; include digital downloads -- use same formula to calculate royalties for digital downloads.

Delete Section 7(d)(i) on Long-Play Singles.

Delete Section 7(f).

In Section 7(g): this should be revised to get rid of mention of Long-Play Singles, Single-Fold Disk Albums, double-fold Albums. Replace with percentages for CDs, double-CDs, compilation albums, etc.

Section 7(i): change this into a provision about Compilation records and/or promos. Add in information about digital distribution. You might do the bulk of the explaining in a "marketing" section and then just reference the royalty fees here to shorten up a bit.

Section 7(o): maybe don't need reserves for singles but DO for digital downloads.

Sections 7(q, r, s): Use an example of a formula for how these royalties might be calculated. Example (from CEMA): "In respect of any master Recording embodying Artist's performance s and those by another artists with respect to which Company is obligated to pay royalties, the royalty rate to be used in determining the royalties payable to you shall be computed by multiplying the royalty rate otherwise applicable by a fraction, the numerator of which shall be one (1) and the denominator of which shall be the total number of royalty artists whose performances are embodied on such recording."

In general: perhaps mention on-demand or digital subscription provisions, and how those royalties might be calculated. Not necessary, but it couldn't hurt.

E. Notes:

1. SECTION 4(b) – add in "Internet," replace "HBO, SHOWTIME" with "premium cable channels or on-demand usages."
2. Delete references to CASSETTE TAPES or VIDEOTAPE. Focus on CDs and DOWNLOADS as main products.
3. SECTION 11(a) include webchats, webcasts.
4. SECTION 12(g): delete "jackets and sleeves," replace with "packaging materials, whether physical, digital, or otherwise."
5. I might suggest for your post-contract section to do a little commentary on where the industry is headed, technology-wise and business-wise. I don't know if it is appropriate for a textbook, but it is probably important for students to understand that the biz is currently changing, quickly becoming technology-driven. You might discuss some directions that new technology formats and the Internet (peer2peer, streaming and podcasts, Apple, pay-per-download vs. subscription services – i.e., iTunes vs. Napster) are taking the industry – especially with respect to the way albums are being made, the decrease in popularity of the Single, the way records are being promoted and released (digital albums released first in some cases, albums are previewable on the Internet, MYSPACE), what's happening to the $18.98 CD, and what effects these will have, if any, on the way recording contracts are negotiated. These provisions may have to be revised too often to be included, but a general discussion would be a good idea, if not elsewhere in the book.

The Music Business in Action:

A 'New' Music Label Model

A couple of years ago, John Scher of Metropolitan Music introduced his new music label model. Essentially, his plan is to share, on a 50/50 basis, the remainder of all revenue and costs from each artist's activity, whether studio, publishing, touring, and sales digital or conventional retail.

On 22 July 2006, EMI announced the formation of a label which will follow this exact model. The yet to be named label will pay up front recording costs, but will not give traditional advances. This label will collect money from all revenue streams and treat as costs related to touring, merchandising, video production, recording costs, and indie promotion. The artist and the label will jointly own the masters. No management fees will be charged by EMI. Again, revenue minus related costs, when positive, will be shared 50/50.

What effect will this new model have on the recording and touring aspects of the music business? It is too soon to tell, but the hope would be that, without the necessity of paying large advances to untried groups, labels might be more open to giving a chance to artists who might otherwise have difficulty securing a recording contract or a manager. If it increases the variety or what is available to the listener, it is certainly a positive step.

Chapter 6

Reaching the Audience: Marketing

Harmon Greenblatt

Note: *Much of the information for the first version of this chapter came from an interview with Vic Faraci, former senior vice president, Warner Brothers Records. For the current version, additional information was provided by Justin Sinkovitch, New Media Manager, Touch and Go Records.*

INTRODUCTION

As with everything in the recording industry, marketing begins with the music. The music sets the tone for how that music is to be marketed. It is the marketer's job to find the "magical chord" in the consumer that will make large numbers of people part with the money to buy or download a CD. In order for marketing to be successful, a label needs to develop a team of knowledgeable professionals who can each take responsibility for whatever area of marketing he or she is involved in, and can decide what kind of marketing approach will work best for each release. The record company does not reinvent the wheel for each recording, but every release has its own special marketing campaign. With the number of releases from each label running into the hundreds yearly, coming up with successful original ideas is the main challenge of the marketing department.

Two seemingly contradictory aspects compose the marketer's approach to his job: first, practical experience, what has worked in the past on similar recordings; and second, the devising of a new twist, an angle, a hook, a new way to promote this record. Ideas are explored for each track on each album and a plan developed.

COMPONENTS OF THE MARKETING PLAN

Marketing in the recording industry consists of promotion, publicity, advertising, and merchandising, all of which are intended to result in record sales. At most companies, promotion is a separate department from marketing, but they work together very closely. The promotion people have the all-important job of getting the music played on radio and now, with video becoming increasingly important, on MTV and other video outlets as well. Though MTV and many of the other video stations have reduced their video programming and lessened the importance of their airplay, all of the sites on the web, such as Google video, Youtube, artist/label websites, and others, have made videos important again. Airplay for a single should begin anywhere from three to five weeks prior to the release date of an album to give the marketing people an indication of how the new music is being accepted.

Publicity

Publicity means informing the public and the trade about each new release. It differs from advertising in that advertising is paid for by the advertiser, publicity is not. Publicity for each song or CD usually begins by developing a press release that contains the pertinent information regarding the artist and the CD, including release date, producer, content, etc. The release is sent out to both the trade publications *(Billboard, Hits, Radio and Records)* and to consumer publications *(People, Rolling Stone)*. The publicity department is also responsible for creating media via reviews or features about the artist or the music in newspapers, magazines, fanzines, and other publications. The publicity department also plays a vital role in arranging interviews on television and radio and personal appearances for the artists.

Advertising

Like publicity, advertising is aimed both at the trade and the consumer. Ads are designed to inform the industry of an upcoming album and to create awareness at the consumer level that the release is available at retail. Advertising is done in four media: print, television, radio, and online. A common theme for each release runs through all ads.

A mix of both publicity and advertising is important to a successful marketing campaign. However, where budgets are limited, or when the marketing department is trying to get an extra push for an album, most of the time publicity will be chosen over advertising. The obvious reason is that there is no extra cost involved, but this is not the only reason. Equally important is the fact that publicity is more believable to the consumer than advertising and, therefore, has greater value in selling the product.

Online advertising has made big gains in recent years. It has several distinct advantages over other forms of advertising: It is much cheaper per impression than print advertising; it is possible to track the results by monitoring click-throughs and page views; and it allows the user to click right through for immediately get more information or make a purchase. (For more information on online marketing, see the Chapter 17: The Technology Manager)

Creative Services

The creative services department creates ads. This department, with the artist's input, develops the artwork for the album package and any other visual material to be used in the marketing campaign. (The artist's recording contract usually has a stipulation that gives the artist album cover approval.) In most instances, the images used on the album package will be the same as those used in the ads, so a consumer who sees the ad can relate it to the album cover. The goal is to create an image in the mind of the consumer so that when he or she walks in to a retail store and sees the CD, the consumer will recognize it because he or she has seen it before.

The art department in the creative services department develops the artwork for the ad, and the editorial department creates the copy. The copy is used in the print ad, and also in any audio and/or video ads. This is the message the label wants to give to the consumer and, combined with images and possibly some of the music, is reinforced through repetition on TV, radio and print.

REACHING THE CONSUMER

There are two ways to advertise to the consumer: the first is to run ads with dealers. This is called co-op advertising, but in the record business co-op means the retailer is cooperating with the label by running the ad. The label pays the entire cost of the ad. The second means of advertising is consumer ads with no dealer tagging, again wholly paid for by the label.

In most industries, retailers either contribute towards advertising costs or pay for ads themselves. But in the record industry, with new product being released every day, the record company is forced to support advertising to consumers in order to compete. If one label will not pay for advertising, there are plenty of others who will. The labels develop "minis" (also called ad slicks) to send to its accounts to be used in ads. Retailers have their own advertising departments and art departments, so all the label needs to do is supply the minis. The retailer develops the theme of the ad and includes the release information the record company wants to appear in the ad. In most cases, the ad will feature mixed records from many labels. A full page ad will generally feature from 5 to 20 selections. Such ads from the retailer are frequently seen in newspapers.

The advertising department also develops merchandising materials, particularly point-of-sale items such as posters and 12" x 12" flats, also called one by ones. One side shows the album cover graphic and the other side the name of the artist in bold letters. Flats are primarily used for wall displays but are also used in window displays. Other merchandising materials include full-sized stand-ups, smaller easel back stand-ups that go on counters, and a variety of other in-store merchandising pieces to remind the consumer that the recording is available. In some cases, as part of a merchandising plan, a label will run an in-store display contest, in which store personnel build a display in each retail store. The most creative displays win T-shirts, tickets to a concert, a trip to Los Angeles or New York, etc., as an incentive for the stores to develop strong visibility with the merchandising pieces the label has supplied.

The total marketing budget for a CD release from a major label can vary widely. If the label is predicting platinum (one million plus in sales), a marketing budget of $500,000 to $1,000,000 can be committed. Such a figure is standard only for a major artist. A new artist, however, can't be expected to sell that kind of volume, so the marketing budget is likely to be much smaller. The figure may be quite small for a first release, possibly in the $50,000 to $100,000 range, and then escalate as the increase in sales dictates. All marketing costs are recoupable against artist royalties.

THE SEQUENCE OF EVENTS IN MARKETING

Because the timing of events is so crucial to a successful recording project, it is important to examine how the project unfolds, and the sequence of events involved in marketing a CD, as marketing is involved even at the earliest stages.

The first step is usually a meeting between the artist, the A&R person, and the producer to discuss the kind of album they want to make, what songs are written, and which songs the artist wants to record. At this stage, there could be a person present from the label who is the company contact between the label and the creative team, and that person is the product manager. It is the product manager's job to shepherd the project, and he or she is involved in every aspect of developing and carrying out the plan.

While the artist is still in the studio, the product manager develops ideas on how to promote the finished album. The product manager has regular discussions with the people who are working on the project, including the artist, management, and the label production people. The product manager is responsible for making sure that nothing falls through the cracks. A product manager may be working on several different projects, each in a different stage, at the same time.

The next step is the release of the first single, which may happen immediately after the artist is finished recording in the studio. The first single is all important, because it is used to set up sales of the entire CD. It is usually the artist who selects the single to be released, but the promotion department, the producer, and the product manager all have input, and if the promotion department, for example, vehemently disagrees with the song selected for the first single, the department will try to direct the rest of the group to another cut. In cases of great disagreement, the nod will usually be given to the artist, but it is important for the promotion department to be enthusiastic about the song, because it has to convince radio stations to play it. Proven artists have more influence on the selection process than do lesser known artists, but the goal is to make everyone involved enthusiastic about the upcoming release.

With radio narrowcasting getting ever narrower, one of a label's most important jobs is to designate which radio format to pursue for any particular song. This decision is usually left to those who are in charge of promotion in the different formats. In most cases, when the promotion people listen to a record they can determine which format or formats will play the song and they will then release it to their staff to focus on that format. If the product is a

CHR (Contemporary Hits Radio) record that is not likely to be played on alternative radio, the alternative staff will not even service those stations. Although everyone wants his or her song to be played on as many formats as possible, it is important for the label to hone in on a specific area of music and make a strong promotional push in that area. Trying too many formats and spreading a song too thin can result in no station wanting to play the song. If the song hits in one format, then others may pick it up and add it to their playlists, especially if it's close enough to their own format. Initially, however, it is more important to choose a limited number of formats and work hard to get acceptance.

Once the single is chosen and a date is set for the release of that single, the next step is to get radio play. A number of activities are being carried out to support the release at the same time: the creative services department is writing the editorial releases, the merchandising materials are manufactured, the singles are pressed, the video is produced and promotional touring is arranged.

The single is normally released four to eight weeks in advance of the release of the CD to the street. The promotion staff takes promotional albums and singles to seek radio airplay, and publicity sends promo albums to publications to be reviewed. The goal is to have the reviews begin to appear in newspapers and magazines all over the country. The publicity department also sets up interviews with television shows and print reviewers. Shows like *The Tonight Show with Jay Leno* and *The Late Show with David Letterman* are the most valuable, but other interview shows work well, depending on the artist. The promotion department sets up a promotional radio tour with the artist, which includes visiting radio stations and on-air interviews.

Getting airplay for a song is the biggest challenge the promotion department faces. As stations are bombarded with hundreds of songs every week, and maybe have only two or three open slots on their playlists, obtaining airplay gets more difficult all the time. All stations, whether big or small, and whatever the format, want to play only the hits, because this brings in the largest audience. The established artists, such as Billy Joel, Mariah Carey, Madonna, and Paul Simon will be added automatically to the major radio stations. So how does a relatively unknown song by a relatively unknown artist succeed despite seemingly insurmountable odds?

The secret is to find breakout stations, ones that separate themselves from the also-rans, with music directors and program directors who have good "ears" and are willing to take chances. They can hear a song and decide that their listeners will respond to it even if it is by a brand new act. These stations will play new music, and "break" records.

Sometimes, a major station will add a song, and other, smaller, stations with the same format will add the record as well. At other times, it is a smaller station in a tertiary market that begins to play the record, has great success with it, and then the larger stations see this success and they add the song. It is not only the major stations that can break a song; big stations frequently look to smaller markets to find what the next hit is going to be.

Much of the marketing activity happens before the CDs actually hit the street and continues as long as is needed or as long as the artist is available. By the time the CD is shipped to the retail stores, some kind of demand for it should already exist. The displays are set up in the stores, and the retail clerks all over the country should know about the release. The artist is touring and making radio and TV appearances. The label invites radio and retail people to see the act perform, with the hope that they will get excited about what the label is trying to sell.

Increasing airplay is the best way to build excitement. The first week a single comes out, "x" number of stations play it. The second week, "x" plus whatever number of stations have added the song play it. If all goes well, stations continue to add the song every week. Unfortunately, however, many times this is not the case. If, after the fourth week, radio stations do not get feedback from their listening audience telling the stations that it's a song they want to continue to hear, the single stalls. When this happens, it usually means the end of the single, and the label prepares to release another single from the album.

It is important to know when a single isn't effective. To keep pushing a song that is not succeeding is not good marketing, and it is also not a good use of human and financial resources. Rather than use up the marketing budget on a single that is not making it, the label will save that money and use it for the next single, in the hope that the second release will break through. There is no set time for giving up on a song. The Nielsen BDS and SoundScan information help the marketers in the decision-making process, but some songs build quickly, while others take much longer to find their audience. The number one complaint that artists and their managers have with record companies is that the company gave up too early on a song, that the song would surely have become a hit if the label had more faith and pushed it a little harder or a little longer.

Video airplay is also an important factor in generating excitement for the release. Today, the video image the label promotes is just as important as radio airplay. To maximize sales potential, the song needs TV exposure. MTV is still the most important television channel for potential rock hits, but there are many others, such as VH1 for more adult tunes, TNN or CMT for Country, BET for Urban songs, as well as the many local and regional independent video programs on stations throughout the country. MTV, however, does play more than the hits. It has specific shows that play new videos, and a song that gets a strong response on these shows is then elevated as a "pick" and it gets played in much heavier rotation.

Just as there are independent promoters to help get songs radio airplay, there are independent video promoters who help a video get played. Independents can be helpful in getting play in all of the alternative areas, such as local TV stations, college stations, and clubs. For example, if a song is breaking in a smaller market, working on video play in that market can be invaluable to the song's success and eventual acceptance in larger markets.

Once the CD hits the street, the label focuses on airplay and sales. Usually the cycle of a hit single is 13 to 15 weeks, which means the time that elapses from release, to climbing the charts, hopefully to #1, and then dropping off the charts. Therefore, the record company has to be ready to react quickly to consumer demand. If, after the street date, airplay continues to increase and sales are strong, the label will continue to expand its marketing efforts, which means further penetration into the market. If, for example, the label budgeted $150,000 in marketing costs, the CD has sold 100,000 units, and the marketing indicators are strong, the label will take the product to the next plateau and invest another $50,000 to $100,000 to keep the excitement going and keep sales increasing.

Why would a label commit this extra expenditure? The answer is profit, pure and simple. The label has already spent the majority of its budget on the project. If the record is doing well, the company can slightly increase its expenditure and realize a hefty profit from the increased sales. For example, the extra investment of $50,000 mentioned in the previous example may increase the cost by $ .50 per unit, but if that extra expenditure results in an additional 500,000 units sold, there is obviously a great return on the additional investment.

It's also important to understand how stations add songs. As was mentioned, stations may have only a few spaces each week for new songs, but if one of the big, powerful stations in a major metropolitan area adds a song, smaller stations with the same format in tertiary areas will usually follow. The label wants to have extra marketing support on hand to maximize sales from the increase in stations playing the song.

The time of day when the song is played is also significant. Having the song played five times a day is important, but if a song is added to a station it is vital that at least some plays are in the all-important drive-times, when the largest number of people is listening.

If, after the initial push, however, the single is not doing well at radio, the label will release the second single. Parts of the marketing campaign will be different so as not to repeat the failure of the initial release. The label will probably not spend as much on the second single as on the first, but will try to keep the CD up front at the retail level, using ad bumps to induce retailers to give the CD a prime position in the store and many facings, so that the consumer in the store will see it. Otherwise, if the artist is not selling, the retailer will begin to return the CD to the record company.

SALES

The sales department is responsible for visiting retail stores, taking orders, and making sure that stores have sufficient supply of product. This chapter discussed what happens to a new release, but the record company salesperson's job encompasses much more than new releases. In addition to estimating how many of the latest hot release the store is going to need, the salesperson's responsibilities include sales for the entire catalog of the label and all the other labels that have distribution deals with the company. The salesperson must cover all genres the label carries, such as classical, jazz, and children's music, in addition to mainstream artists. The value of any label is its catalog. The company must keep each store supplied with sufficient catalog so that no customer will come into the store and find that the recording he or she wants to buy is out of stock.

New releases and catalog have a complementary relationship that works to the benefit of both, and the label as well. The steady income generated from the catalog helps to support the new releases. Developing hit records is important because it keeps the salesperson visiting the store regularly to keep catalog items replenished while checking on the progress of the hit CD.

With SoundScan and computerized inventorying, the salesperson's job is easier than it was in the past, because he or she knows the number of any CD that has been bought in a given week. He or she also knows which catalog items are selling at other stores and make recommendations accordingly. And he is also careful not to overload the store with merchandise that does not sell. Doing this will only lead to returns, bad feelings, and slow payment.

CONCLUSION

The marketing effort begins with outstanding, commercially unique music. Then, there needs to be an effective marketing effort to bring the music to the public. This effort depends on creating an effective image for that music, and coordinating all of the many aspects of publicity, advertising, promotion, and sales into a successful marketing campaign.

With the recent closing of large record retailers like Tower records and the figures released by the recording industry, it is no secret that sales of CD's are in decline. And though online and digital sales are increasing significantly, as yet they have not produced enough revenue to cover the loss decline of sales at the retail level. Future marketing plans will have to pay greater attention to new, less traditional areas of marketing in order to be successful in the digital age.

The Music Business in Action:

Merging Music and the Cell Phone

South Korea is regarded as the most digitally connected market on the planet. Thus, the Warner Music Group has chosen to mount an experiment there that will smooth the path for music to be available on cell phones. This will be done via a joint venture between Warner Music and SK Telecom of South Korea.

In an unprecedented move a communications network and a music company will employ the cell phone as a platform for buying, storing, and listening to music.

The Warner Group regards the cell phone as the heart of the music business of the future. Ultimately the cell phone will be the device to store, listen, pay for, and free file share, wirelessly, for most or all music. Korea will be the model for this cell phone/music merger. Sixty-two percent of Korea households receive broadband Internet service and can play MP3 music files via mobile phones.

Mobile phones are more tightly controlled than the Internet and thus less prone to file sharing. The Warner/SK merger is a significant moment in this process.

While the music and cell phone industries are drawing closer together, now the announcement has been made that movies and television shows will also be able to be delivered directly to cell phones. Despite the potential limitations of sound quality for music and the diminution of the visual image when watching a film on a tiny screen, the once humble cell phone is making a strong claim as the most convenient delivery device for all media.

Chapter 7

Record Distribution

Harmon Greenblatt

Note: Much of the information used in this chapter has been obtained from interviews with Henry Droz, former president of WEA and president of Universal Music and Video Distribution.

Note 2: This chapter concerns itself with the physical distribution of records. For more on electronic distribution, see the chapter 17: The Technology Manager.

INTRODUCTION

Physical distribution is simply getting recordings from the manufacturing plant and placing them in stores and retail outlets to be sold. But record distribution these days is much more than that: it is helping to make sure that those records in the stores are sold, it is accepting and dealing with returns, and it is using the latest technology to help do the job most efficiently.

DEFINITIONS

To understand this chapter, several terms will be used that may be unfamiliar to people not in the record business:

Rack jobber: Supplies and services racks in department stores, grocery stores, discount stores, drug stores, supermarkets, and other stores. The rack jobber services the location with fixtures, manages the inventory, and adds his costs and profit to his charge to the rental location.

One stop: Carries recordings of many labels. Buys from manufacturers and sells to stores, usually those stores which buy in quantities too small for the majors to bother with. Rather than go to many suppliers, which may not want to do business with him anyway, a retailer pays a little more to the one stop for his CD's and cassettes, but gets all the retailer needs at one location. One stops used to be strictly local operations, but with the advent of UPS and other overnight delivery services, one stop are able to cover a large territory. Several chains also use the one stop for fast fill-in service.

Retailer: Sells CD's, cassettes, etc. directly to the public. It can be a chain, a big box store, or a "Mom and Pop" store.

Mama and Papa (or Mom and Pop) Stores: Independently owned retail record stores.

Fulfillment: Filling orders for records, making sure customers have adequate supplies.

Street date: The date the product (recording) is to go on sale in every location in the U.S.

HOW PHYSICAL DISTRIBUTION WORKS

Today, there are five main methods of record distribution: the major distributors, independent distributors, one stop, rack jobbers, and licensees.

The Major Distributors

Each of the four major labels owns a gigantic distribution network that takes recordings from its various manufacturing plants and places them into warehouses and retail outlets. In addition to the major labels, all the major distributors handle many other labels. Some of these are label-owned companies, others are independents that the company has contracted to distribute their product for them.

How the Majors Handle a New Release

All of the majors have distribution outlets (also called fulfillment centers) strategically placed throughout the United States to facilitate efficient delivery of goods to stores, and what is seen as an efficient way of dividing up the country in terms of workload. WEA, for example, has four outlets in the U.S. The first step in handling a new release is to determine a suggested initial quantity. This number is based on how well the last record sold, or if it is a new artist, what volume similar artists achieved on a first release.

The representatives in the field then go to their major accounts and decide on a number they think should be ordered. For example, if the last release by a certain artist sold 700,000 in a particular area, the initial figure used will probably be around 350,000 to 400,000, and the company will begin to solicit specific orders. (This number can be affected by factors such as advance airplay and perceived commercial quality, but this is a reasonable "ball park" figure.) Even when dealing with a major artist, the record companies feel it is better to underestimate demand for a new recording, so as to not have a large number of returns, which could hurt the reputation of an artist. Retailers won't remember retail sales of 600,000, but they will definitely remember 300,000 in returns.

Field reps go to major chains, one stops, rack jobbers, and large indie stores prior to the street date. Several days before the street date, the orders are locked in and shipments prepared. The shipments are done with little lead time. Labels don't want any store or area getting a jump on any others, but they also don't want them to be delayed.

Once the street date has passed, the job of the distributor becomes one of making sure the stores have enough supply. Every retail chain has its own computerized inventory point-of-sale system. The computer tells the ordering department how much it has of each release, and how much has been sold in the last reporting period, a week, day, month, etc. With this information, the retailer can decide whether he has an adequate supply or needs to order more. This cuts down on returns and helps control inventory, but its greatest value may be to keep stores adequately supplied with fast-moving new releases.

Catalog

In addition to new releases, all of the major distributors carry a supply of catalog: everything else that is available besides new recordings. As demand tapers off, the companies still want to be able to supply everything to stores, not just the new releases. On slower moving material, such as classical music, with which there is no urgency to ship quickly, the company may have its entire inventory at just one fulfillment center and ship directly from there to the stores, rather than having inventory in all centers.

Which titles are maintained in the inventory after they have peaked? Each label has a guideline, but that guideline is different for each label. Some say 500 sales a year, others 1000; this decision is made by the financial and marketing departments, because there is financial impact in maintaining inventory. A label's marketing department may want to maintain one or two CDs for a key artist for a time even if sales fall below the guideline, particularly if there are other circumstances involved, such as the artist coming out with a new release shortly, which may stimulate sales for the older recordings.

This inventory selection is not only based on the Billboard charts. Billboard lists only 200 albums. But albums like Led Zeppelin 4 still sell 250,000 copies yearly and never chart on the Top 200. The Eagles, James Taylor, and Fleetwood Mac continue to sell regularly. And it has already been mentioned that the strength and the financial value of any record company is its catalog.

Distribution of Other Labels

All of the major distributors have a long list of independent labels that they distribute along with their own product. Some of these may be owned all or in part by the label; others may be totally independent but have contracted with the company for distribution of their recordings. The labels claim there is no favoritism: once a company agrees to distribute another company's product, there is no greater attention given to one artist, one release, or one label than any others. What gets the greatest attention is what sells. Whatever sells, whatever needs fulfillment, gets done.

In addition, people in distribution never have enough product. They always want more and can handle more. They would sooner buy, build or rent more space than miss out on what might be a money-making opportunity. The more product there is flowing through the pipeline, the more volume to support the staff of the company. The companies are aware that this is a business of peaks and valleys, and so they want to have as much product of different labels and different styles as they can, so that they will not be affected by changes in people's tastes.

Distribution of Other Products

In addition to the various forms of recordings, CD's, cassettes, and even vinyl in some cases, record distributors frequently handle other products as well. WEA, for example, distributes videocassettes for Warner Home Video. For them it is a natural relationship. The Warner studio is part of the same parent company, but more important is the fact that many of the distribution arm's record customers also carry video. Rather than have the video department set up a separate building, it makes good business sense to use the already existing distribution system.

Staffing a Fulfillment Center

To staff a fulfillment center for a major label, the minimum necessary positions include a credit department, financial department, operations department, warehouse staff, controller, sales manager, marketing positions, security, and data processing. Data processing is vital to keep control of the vast inventory in any fulfillment center. The credit department establishes credit and determines its quantity; the financial department keeps track of the money moving in and out. But marketing, how good and how successful that marketing is, determines the success of a distributing organization. The quality and training of the marketing staff is the backbone of any distribution outlet. For more on marketing, see the previous chapter, Chapter VI. It should be noted that, although a fulfillment center may need all of these individuals, there are more and more instances in which a fulfillment center stands alone and only fulfills (ships) product and handles returns. Other functions, such as credit, financial, and marketing take place in branch offices, regional offices, or home offices.

Also, merchandising is important. The merchandising people are the ones who make the displays and put up displays in stores. Furthermore, the people who determine what kind and how much advertising is done are vital, particularly now when companies have expanded the whole marketing area to give attention to all the different genres of music. One fulfillment center may have separate sales managers for rap, classical, jazz, video, country, etc. There are also specific people concerned only with going into the field and breaking new product. Staff people are needed to go into music stores, acquaint the clerks with new product, and hand them a sample. Distribution encompasses all of these things, and therefore entails much more than just getting the product in and shipping it out. Sales, marketing, and distribution are all under one roof, with all of these individuals in each center working with the staff at the headquarters in New York or Los Angeles.

Service from the warehouse is also an advantage of a large fulfillment center. The company can have an account executive who calls on one independent distributor, another who calls on a different independent distributor, and still another on each of the major chains. The company can also ship either to individual stores or to the retail warehouse. One may have three shipping points, three warehouses in the U.S., so it can receive its orders at each of the shipping points containing all of the recordings. If something hot broke yesterday and Walmart needs 50 of a particular release in each of its 1,000 stores tomorrow, the warehouse can do that, too. The retailer pays a little more for this, but to ship product to a retail warehouse and then to the stores may take a week. This way the retailer need not disappoint a single customer, and also profits from the sale.

Returns

Inevitably, in an enormous and volatile business like the recording industry, large distribution outlets have to deal with returns. Companies try to limit returns, and computerization of inventories has helped to give retailers better control over inventories. Each major label has a limit on returns that it will accept from each retailer or chain. WEA has a system of debits and credits for returned items, and tries to keep returns to about 20% of the dollar amount sold on returns. Nevertheless, there are times when buyers guess wrong and returns do occur. WEA has a center in Chicago whose sole purpose is to deal with returns. When possible, returns are shipped to a fulfillment center that needs them. If no centers need them, and there is no foreseeable demand, they are usually sold to dealers who specialize in returned records.

INDEPENDENT DISTRIBUTION

Before the major labels formed their own distribution systems, all labels sold their records to independent distributors, who sold the records to the retail stores. Today, the independent distributor handles only smaller labels, and most independents service only a limited region of the country. Until recently, the importance of the independent distributor had declined substantially from what it once was. But with the advent of a number of new genres of music in the marketplace, the independent has seen its influence reborn, so that now independents sell more than 20% of the recordings in the U.S. The share of all independents now exceeds all but one of the four major labels, and in some weeks the independents' share is greater than any of the majors.

The independent distributor is and is not competing with major label distributors. The aim of the indie is to sell to people to whom it can give increased personal service. Independent distribution is often better for product that does not have a huge audience. The independents know the stores that specialize in specific types of music (such as folk music, house music, dance music, etc.). Moreover, the independents can make a substantial profit from music that may not do enough volume to get the attention of the majors. But the independent distributor is competing with the majors in that indies sell to the same customers and compete for shelf space and representation.

The independents have another big advantage: they have had huge success with rap music, which is capable of selling quantities in the millions, but which was at first rejected by the major labels. The independents have the ability to move more quickly than the majors, and in rap music the demand seems to ebb and flow almost overnight. It can take months for a major to get product into the system and solicit orders, compared to a few weeks for the independent. It's not difficult to see that, for the kinds of music that need quick handling and special care, there can be a real advantage in being handled by an independent distributor. Today the rap music picture has changed. Just about all the majors now release rap music, which has grown substantially as a genre, and the time gap between majors and independents to get product through the system has narrowed considerably. But the impact has been enormous, and continues to be felt by the independents' ever-growing market share.

The majors have seen that there is profit to be made from independent companies and have acquired, in whole or in part, several of the independent distributors. Sony has bought into several companies, and most of the majors have followed Sony in buying into independent distributors. They do not become part of the major's distribution, but remain independent, staying close to "the street" so that they can continue to do their job well. The major may help the independent financially, either by supplying it with capital or by helping with financial controls (collections, etc.), but so far the contention of the majors is that they need the independents to help find the new material and make it successful.

A few of the independents are branching out and going into the retail record business. This sometimes occurs when the distributor has extended credit to a retail store and the store fails; the distributor then takes over operation of the store. The big advantage to the distributor is that in this case it is selling to itself. This kind of vertical integration has saved many of the independents from failing during tough economic times. It allows the company to have its own stores to cater to the demand for the specialty merchandise in which it excels.

In smaller markets where a major label does not have a branch office, an independent distributor may handle product for a major label. The indie may provide promotion services as well. While some independents are just order takers, others have staffs similar to the majors who do marketing, sales, and store displays, just as the majors do but on a smaller scale. For more on independent distribution, see the following chapter on independent labels and independent distribution.

ONE STOPS

One stops began in the 1940s, primarily to supply the new jukebox industry with recordings. Since jukeboxes stocked a variety of recordings from all labels, major and independent, it was easier for a jukebox operator to make one trip to a supplier where he could get all the product he needed quickly, rather than order from the companies and wait weeks for the product to arrive. Though the jukebox business is nowhere near what it once was, one stops still play an important role in the record business today. They continue to supply CD's to independent stores as well as whatever jukebox business there is. And with next-day delivery, one stops can service a much wider area than before. Further, one stops supply even the large retailers with specialized records from independents that they may not be able to get from the larger distribution outlets.

Like the rest of the record business, there is a consolidation taking place in the one stop business. One stops are being bought out by a few holding companies that control most of the one stop business in the country. This consolidation gives the one stops increased buying power, and helps it compete effectively with the other means of distribution available to retailers.

RACK JOBBERS

As described above, a rack jobber is a sub-distributor. At its peak, in the 1960s, rack jobbers accounted for 75% of all record sales in the United States. But as the '60s progressed, the retail record chains began to grow; Tower Records, Musicland, and Camelot all began to open more stores. By the end of the decade there were more and more rack jobber locations selling fewer and fewer records. Part of the problem was that the rack jobbers featured only the top-selling records, the top 100 or 200, depending on the amount of space, but the record chains were carrying a much larger selection of merchandise. A shopper might go into a department store and see something he wanted in the record rack and buy it, but that would account for only one sale. That same shopper could go into a record retail chain store and find that same record, plus an older record by the same artist, and maybe two or three other recordings he didn't know he wanted, and buy them all. So the new record retailer had a big advantage over the rack jobber. The rack jobber found his profits being squeezed to the point where, in many cases, he could not afford to stay in business.

Another problem rack jobbers had was returns. Rack jobbers mismanaged their inventory and the result was heavy returns, as well as the high cost of large inventory. This was, of course, before the days of computer inventory systems. The situation drove the poorly financed rack jobbers out of business or forced them to sell. During the '70's and '80's, the rack jobbers that remained became large, because they acquired the other rack jobbers who could not survive any longer. Today, there are only a couple of major rack jobbers and several relatively small independent rack jobbers.

LICENSEES

One of the fastest growing areas of income is the licensee business. Long considered the bargain basement of record sales, these television-advertised packages are now of the verge of respectability. With artist like Placido Domingo and John Denver doing television-advertised CD's, the market is expanding.

Such collections are sold via credit card on many cable TV channels. The packagers of these collections, such as Heartland Music and Time-Life, license the songs from the record companies that hold the copyrights. This allows packagers to manufacture and distribute records on their own labels rather than those of the original companies.

This arrangement is essential because CD collections like Super Hits of the '70's contain selections from many labels.

Perhaps the most important feature of this type of record distribution is that it has tapped into a new market: the person who prefers not to go to a record store, but to buy through the mail. This mostly older audience is the main target of these licensed recordings. The advertisement usually states that the record cannot be purchased in stores, but can only be ordered by phone and received through the mail.

This segment of the market has grown substantially in recent years, to the extent that the licensees are now licensing these collections to foreign countries for distribution. For more on licensing, see Chapter 9: Additional Income and Special Products.

CONCLUSION

Distribution is not just moving CD's from plants to warehouses to stores. It is essential to the efficient functioning of the company and to the consumer receiving the product. It is the scientific and yet visceral estimating and balancing to avoid over- or under-supply. Technological changes have affected record distribution in the past, and other changes will affect it in the future. PolyGram has recently announced a shift in its distribution that will target the retail buyer rather than the distributor or the buyer for the chain as the target of its distribution effort. With iTunes currently the number one music retailer in the U.S. needing no physical distribution, this shift in emphasis is having enormous effect on the way recordings reach customers.

Distribution is paying a growing role in artist development, making customers aware of new acts with in-store play, listening stations, and making store personnel aware of certain artists to enable them to recommend them to their customers.

Although distribution will change, it is doubtful that it will disappear as some have predicted. It is too much intertwined with the many other functions of the record company. As can be seen by the popularity of TV packages, delivery systems for recordings are changing. This doesn't mean that record stores are going to disappear, but it does mean that distributors need to be aware of the changes on the horizon and react to those changes. For other views on record distribution, see also Chapter 8: Independent Labels, Independent Distribution, and Chapter 16: Technology.

The Music Business in Action:

The Virtual Concert Tour

The Rock band "Widespread Panic" played to a sold out crowd at Atlanta's Fox Theatre. At the same time the band appeared on screens in Houston, Pittsburgh, and Denver. It was a simulcast in 100 movie theaters in the USA. Virtual concert going is changing the live music industry. This is redefining concert going for the Internet generation and at a lower cost per ticket.

In movie theaters during the summer of 2006, hard rock band KOM could be heard and seen for $20; and on the Internet Radiohead, free; and via mobile phone Mary J. Blige free to Verizon's V Cast subscribers; and through TV On Demand the Goo Goo Dolls for subscribers to digital cable.

Involved distributors and promoters face a "blur" of rights in seeking permission from artists, labels, publishers, and other interested parties. This kind of content distribution is at its beginnings but is, definitely, a gathering "stream."

And the classical music business is getting into the act as well. Under Peter Gelb's directorship, The Metropolitan Opera has simulcast several of its operas during recent seasons to audiences at movie theatres around the U.S. Audience response has been favorable. The classical music industry has been moribund for a long time. Possibly, simulcasting might be innovation that provides the impetus that will reawaken a new generation to classical music, as well as making concert performances of all genres available to a wider audience.

The Music Business in Action 2:

Retail Consolidation

In 2006, Transworld acquired the assets of the 400 Musicland stores. Retail has been going through a constant consolidation and one of the prime consolidators will be Transworld.

The big question is, as the consolidation continues and the number of retail stores declines, will Transworld be the last man standing?

With physical sales falling and online sales of music increasing, students of the music industry should be aware of the changing retail structure as it consolidates and seeks to come to a conclusion as to what is going to be the delivery system to the consumer in the future.

The Music Business in Action 3:

Two Crossroads: DRM and Big Box Retail

There is a real crisis in the record business concerning DRM (Digital Rights Management). An entire industry may be hanging in the balance. On one hand, DRM technology restricts users from transferring tracks to different devices. On the other hand, EMI's recent decision will offer for sale unprotected digital music via iTunes and other services. EMI chose to circumvent interoperability and related DRM restrictions by simply eliminating DRM.

Follow the money, and note investment is drying up in DRM. Can we then assume the music industry might never return to DRM? The direction could be that the world of music gives up control in exchange for income from advertising revenue. If so, then technology such as fingerprinting would come into play to assess and identify the revenue and its source. The risk takes place as control is exchanged for the described income.

In addition, the DRM crossroad occurs just as Big Box Retail (Wal Mart, etc.), where 65% of the reduced CD market prevails, becomes more restrictive in both what they are willing to "carry" as well as reducing square footage devoted to music.

It is no exaggeration to regard the music industry at risk as it makes decisions to deal with these two revenue stream matters.

Chapter 8

Independent Labels, Independent Distribution

Note: The original version of this chapter was written by Clay Pasternack. It was revised for this edition by Harmon Greenblatt.

INTRODUCTION: INDEPENDENT LABELS

Independent labels, or indies, once content with the leftovers from the major labels, have become big business. From a volume of 5% of the market just a few years ago, the indies' share of the pie has grown to more than 20%, making it a significant force in the music business in terms of total volume. What differentiates the indies from the major labels and how have they gained such strength in so short a time?

The biggest difference between the indies and the majors is in approach. The indie knows that the market share for any one release is going to be smaller than for a major. Therefore, the indie is going to have to define where it can find a style of music that is not being handled by the major record companies, or that is not being given sufficient attention.

The most recent example, and the way the indies got a foothold in the business, is through rap music. For nearly ten years, the majors didn't pay any attention to it, so the independents found a genre of music they could profit from. There was a demand for it from the public, but the independents were the ones at the street level who noticed the demand, recorded the music, and profited by it. Now the majors have caught up and every label has an entire rap department: rap sales, rap promotion, and rap marketing. But it is still the indies who are the ones to find new trends at the street level and take advantage of it before the majors can react.

The independent scene has always been a niche business, in which a smart record person can find something that is a little offbeat, but still mainstream enough that someone will want to go into a record store and buy it. Before rap there was dance and disco. The indies were the first on the street with the product, and much later the majors caught up.

There are also those people who refuse to buy a CD if it is released by a major label. If it is on an independent label, they will be glad to part with their money. Part of this comes from the belief that the person wants to discover something, which can't be done if the CD is released on a major, because everyone will know about it due to the publicity push. Another part of it may be that there is a belief that if it is released by a major, it must be directed to a mainstream audience and can't be good because it is aimed at the lowest common denominator of the record buying public. Whatever the reason, this core of devoted indie music buyers has become important to the survival of independent labels.

To many, the majors in today's marketplace are little more than distributors. They market and sell records, but they've become so large that they're not really in touch with what's going on at the street level. For example, if a small label is truly passionate about a certain type of music that the majors have decided is not sufficiently profitable for them, the indie can be successful. For example, Bruce Iglauer of Alligator Records has found a niche in blues. Similarly, there are labels that have a niche in other forms of music: folk music, jazz, and classical. Iglauer has been offered the opportunity to have his label be acquired by a major many times but never wanted to do that. He, as well as many of the other successful indies, is happy to keep his purity and independence.

Another major factor in the growth of indies in today's marketplace has been the influence of Nielsen BDS and SoundScan. In the past, indie releases have been underreported at both radio play and at retail sales. Now, these automatic systems track each individual song so that every sale and every play on the radio is reported. Retail stores see that there is a demand for these releases and are less resistant to carrying them. Radio stations see that indie releases selling and are being played, so are more willing to add them to their playlists. As a result, independent releases are getting more visibility in the market.

INDEPENDENT DISTRIBUTION IN THE 21st CENTURY

The playing field of independent distribution today is radically different than it was in previous decades. The first significant move into the nationalization of independent distribution was the creation of the holding company INDI (Independent National Distribution, Inc.) in 1990. Backed with significant funds to acquire existing regional distribution companies, INDI purchased Malverne Distribution of New York in 1990, Big State Distribution of Dallas in 199,1 and California Record Distribution in 1991.

The second significant event of the 1990s in independent distribution was the demise of Schwartz Bros., Inc. (SBI) of Latham, Maryland. One of the pioneer independent distributors, founded in 1947, SBI became a significant force in independent distribution in the late 1980s, covering much of the U.S. east of the Mississippi River. Upon SBI's bankruptcy in 1992, the assets of the company were purchased by INDI, but many labels that were financially dependent on SBI for a significant portion of their business were severely hurt. The move also forced many record labels to abandon regional distribution, and consider distribution with one independent company. Within six to nine months after the closing of SBI, national distribution companies such as REP and Distribution North America (DNA) were able to gain a significant foothold in the independent distribution market. Companies such as M.S. Distributing were also forced to grow from regional distributors to national distributors. At the same time, distribution companies such as Koch and Allegro began to expand their musical influences; both companies had previously been more genre-specific.

COMPETING WITH THE MAJORS

Independent distribution became nationally focused in the 1990's. A number of factors enabled the independent labels and distribution companies to increase their market share:

A New Breed of Independent Labels

A number of independent labels entered the business in the early and mid-1980's. Many of the successful indie labels were dance and urban labels based in the New York area, such as Sugar Hill, Profile, Sleeping Bag, Select, Tommy Boy, Sutra, Warlock, Next Plateau, and Streetwise. The majority of these labels were extremely successful in the 12" singles market. Other labels, such as Priority, Sub Pop, Caroline, Relativity, Combat, Luke Skywalker, and Pandisc were involved in other music genres. Over the course of the 1980's, many independent labels matured from 12" only product to full length albums, which increased their volume, and ultimately increased their market share.

Computer Technology

By the beginning of the 1990's, virtually all independent distributors had some level of computer sophistication. The computerization of the indies was yet another opportunity to obtain and analyze sales data, just as the majors were doing, for marketing, to implement inventory management and purchasing, and to enable fulfillment centers to handle order processing in a more expeditious manner.

Many of the retail chains and sub-wholesale operations (one stops) utilize the ability to transfer data electronically. The major labels were far ahead of the independents in this area for many years, but now with sophisticated computer systems, independent distribution companies are able to send and receive electronic data on a level equal to the majors.

Independent Radio Promotion

From the early 1980's to 1986, a network of independent radio promoters virtually dictated what was to be played at CHR (Contemporary Hits Radio, formerly known as "top 40"). The price that major record companies paid for promotion resulting in radio airplay became so exorbitant that independent labels were unable to compete financially for airplay. The first single release by New Edition was a good example. "Candy Girl" was a smash single on the Urban charts, but was unable to crack CHR radio because the cost of promotion of this single (estimated at the time to be in the area of $150,000) was more than the label (Streetwise) could afford.

In 1986, a federal investigation into the practices of independent radio promotion enabled independent labels to have a greater chance of success, as pop and urban/crossover product became more accepted by mainstream radio. When the major labels backed off using the independent promotion network, independent labels like Profile (Boys Don't Cry, Run D.M.C.), Next Plateau (Salt 'N' Pepa), Tommy Boy and others were able to gain crossover acceptance. As time passed, many of the acts on these labels began to have chart success with crossover releases. Word-of-mouth on many rap records helped them become crossover hits, as interest in and the success of many of these releases transcended racial boundaries.

The Changing Face of Retail

A major factor in the change in independent distribution over the past thirty years was the consolidation of retail. The "mom and pop" retail store that had been the staple of the music industry after World War II and into the 1950's began its decline in the '60's due to the discount department store. The free-standing retail store was reborn in the 1970's and the free-standing chain store and the shopping mall chain store location also grew. After unprecedented growth in the late 1980's and into the 1990's, retail growth slowed considerably. Coupled with this slowdown was the cannibalization of the small and medium-size regional and local retail chains. Store names that had become synonymous with their locality or region, such as Flipside, Turtles, Music Plus, Sound Warehouse, and many others, became victims of purchase by larger competitors or simply closed their doors.

Two new music retail marketing concepts emerged in the 1990's: the big box store concept and the book/music entertainment store. The big box store concept is utilized by Wal Mart, Best Buy, Circuit City, and others. The store is a super size retail location, offering books, video, and computer software in addition to music. Both Best Buy and Circuit City offer an array of hard goods (appliances) as well as electronic goods. Stores such as Borders and Barnes & Noble offer the bookstore/music store atmosphere, complete with cafes for coffee consumption and reading areas. Both areas offer a very large selection of recorded music with thousands of SKU's (stock keeping units); the Borders/Barnes & Noble stores stock very eclectic genres of music in greater depth than their mall/chain store counterparts. Both concepts enable independent labels and their distributors a much greater opportunity to sell a larger selection of their product. Greater visibility relates directly to greater sales, and greater market share.

Beating the Majors to the Marketplace

One of the advantages of the independent system, both on the label and distribution levels, is the ability to get to the marketplace faster than the major labels and their branch operations can. Virtually every music trend or new wave of music has its embryonic stage at the independent level. Many of the successful indie labels over the course of the industry's history have been entrepreneurial operations with very low overhead, often a one-person operation. These entrepreneurs find the talent, record the talent, have goods manufactured for sale, and often sell the goods themselves. These individuals do their own radio promotion, and collect their money. The street sense that the independent label owner often has gives him or her an edge in spotting a trend, finding the talent, recording the talent, and finding a way to get the music to the public. Because of layers of executives and decision-making processes, the major labels and their distribution companies usually cannot make such decisions as quickly.

There have been many instances over the years in which independent labels have sold a label or an act or made a distribution deal for a label or an act with a major label. In such a situation, if there are not sufficient goods in the distribution and retail pipelines to carry the record through the down time when the transition is made, the major label can lose a lot of sales. The time it takes the major label to prepare finished goods for sale may be such that momentum is lost on a release that was building at the retail level through independent distribution.

Nielsen SoundScan and BDS

Prior to 1991, the chart reporting system for trade magazines such as *Billboard* was an antiquated system subject to abuse by record companies. Free records, tickets to concerts, and other giveaways were used by record companies to influence the reporting of sales by retailers. In 1991, SoundScan was created to obtain legitimate reports of music product at retail. In that same year, SoundScan and *Billboard* teamed up to utilize SoundScan for *Billboard*'s retail charts. The first week of use of actual retail sales on the *Billboard* charts showed a dramatic change. However, once in place, the SoundScan system reflected an accurate account of retail sales in the marketplace, which greatly benefited the independent music community.

Previously, releases that had sold significantly large quantities were not necessarily reported to Billboard because sometimes the cost of influencing reporters was too expensive. However, labels such as Priority, Profile, Next Plateau, Fourth & Broad-way, Tommy Boy, Sub Pop, Caroline, and Relativity, now found their releases appearing on the top 200 of *Billboard* because they were legitimately selling in quantity, and Soundscan's accurate reporting process tracked their sales. The industry realized that independent labels were having hits, and indie releases had to be taken seriously by the merchandise buyers at retail.

Just as SoundScan legitimized reporting of retail sales, BDS (Broadcast Data System) upgraded the reporting of radio airplay. BDS was started in 1989, monitoring real airplay as opposed to verbal reporting that was subject to the same inaccuracies as the former retail reporting system. BDS utilized a monitoring system to track the identity and frequency of airplay by individual recording. While BDS does not have the impact on the independents that SoundScan has, it is a very important tool to measure actual airplay. It does help those labels who have country, urban, and pop records to more accurately report their airplay and develop their marketing and sales plans. For more on Nielsen Soundscan and BDS, see chapter 13 on The *Billboard* Charts.

Successful National Independent Distribution

The move of independent distributors to become national entities became the watchword of the independent marketplace in the 1990s. Well-planned and executed marketing and sales plans similar to those of the majors can result in unit sales similar to those of the majors. An excellent example of this scenario was the overwhelming success of Allison Krauss and Rounder Records/Distribution North America (DNA). According to label General Manager Duncan Browne, a great symbiosis occurred at the time of the release of the fourth Allison Krauss CD.

Rounder Records left the REP Distribution Group in early 1995 for Distribution North America. The Allison Krauss release represented the first major release handled nationally by DNA with Rounder. Browne stated that the third Krauss release shipped in the neighborhood of 300,000 units nationally, utilizing various independent distribution companies. By having total control over their distribution network, Rounder and DNA were able to formulate a concentrated national marketing and promotion campaign for the artist, similar to the kind that is done by a major branch distribution operation. The Rounder/DNA team was also able to capitalize on the promotion efforts of a major label entity (DNA, a subsidiary of BMG Distribution) to promote the first single from the album. Rounder/DNA additionally received the assistance of two major retailers, Anderson Entertainment/Wal-Mart and Best Buy which heard the record, understood the music, and believed in the release. Because these factors came together at the same time, the initial promotion of the release was substantial. Coupled with the cooperative promotion efforts of Rounder and DNA (including video exposure on CNN and other cable TV stations), the album was a runaway smash, and put Allison Krauss at a level rarely attainable by independent labels and distribution. As a result of the hit single and album, media exposure of Allison Krauss throughout the remainder of the year was extensive, including many talk shows and late night entertainment programs, culminating in the Country Music Association Awards program, where Krauss was a big winner.

THE MAJORS AND THE INDIES AS ALLIES

Although competition between the majors and the independent music community is very strong, there are significant instances of inter-relations between major labels and independent labels and/or distributors. In 2007, each of the four majors has indie labels that they either own or distribute. The secret for the majors is to not let the corporate bureaucracy affect the ability of the indie to move quickly in its ability to react and get product to the marketplace. If it can let the entrepreneurial spirit exist within the corporate culture, the major and the indie can have a successful relationship.

INDEPENDENTS AND THEIR CUSTOMERS

The customer base serviced by the independent distribution network is quite similar to that of the major branch operations. The majors require their direct accounts to maintain a specific sales volume to remain an active customer. Most independent distribution companies have more active accounts in their system than the majors, as the independents are more niche-market sensitive and genre-specific than the majors' branch operations. It is also apparent that many sub-wholesale accounts (one stops) do not always carry the in-depth catalog on lines that are the mainstays of a number of independent distribution operations. Many independent retailers will buy their hit product from these sub-wholesalers, but depend on independent distribution for deep catalog product.

The types of accounts serviced by independent distribution fall into the following categories:

Independent retail: Usually a single storefront, or a small chain of two to five stores. These stores carry virtually all types of music.

Retail Chain: Chains can range from five to six locations to the largest accounts, such as Transworld and Best Buy.

Rack jobbers: Service merchandisers that supply leased departments with merchandise. Kmart and Wal-Mart are two of the biggest accounts handled by rack jobbers.

One stops: Sub-wholesale operations that enable the retail entity to purchase all labels of product in one location, hence the term "one stop". Until the demise of vinyl, the one stop was the primary source of servicing of recorded product to the jukebox industry. A number of one stops around the country still sell vinyl for jukebox use, as well as compact discs for the jukebox.

Non-music locations: Many distribution companies listed in this chapter service non-music retail locations. Gift stores, drug stores, supermarkets, mail order companies, and other such entities fall under this category.

FUNCTIONS OF THE INDEPENDENT DISTRIBUTOR

Warehousing and fulfillment services: All independent distribution companies purchase finished goods from record companies for the purpose of resale to their customer base. Warehouse facilities exist for the purpose of receiving finished goods from the label, and fulfilling customer orders. The warehouse operations also function as the processing locale for customer returned goods, be they items that did not sell, or items that were defective. Since all product is sold on a 100% guaranteed sale basis, customers have the right to make returns on unsold goods at any time, unless otherwise specified by the distributor.

Marketing and merchandising: It is the responsibility of the distributor, often in conjunction with the record label, to formulate plans to secure retail shelf space for its products. In-store advertising, such as end cap/waterfall displays and listening stations, are sought by the distributor to maximize potential exposure. Media advertising of product by the distributor, in conjunction with both record labels and customers, is also a function of this area.

Collection and payment: The distributor is responsible for the collection of money from accounts for goods sold. Likewise, the distributor is also responsible for payment to the record label for goods sold at retail. Record companies often confuse "records sold" with "records shipped." It is conceivable that a distributor can ship 5,000 units of a particular item, but not sell 500 units to the end user, the retail customer. The record label has to realize in this instance that it has a liability to the distributor for the remaining 4,500 units in retail store locations and warehouses across the country (known as the retail "pipeline"), and that the record label will be paid only for the goods sold to the end user.

Sales and radio promotion: The distributor maintains a sales force, including field representatives who visit retail stores, corporate buying offices, wholesale buyers, or telemarketing people who contact accounts via telephone and fax. In addition, some distributors maintain a promotion staff who call on radio stations for airplay and who handle artist tour support.

Retail sales support: Many distributors employ account service representatives (ASR's) or junior sales representatives who inventory stores, provide stock replenishment on an in-store level, and set up displays and in-store appearances with retail.

NAIRD

In 1972, NAIRD (National Association of Independent Record Distributors) was created to foster an arena for the small, esoteric independent record distributor. Since that time, NAIRD has grown by leaps and bounds, so that it is now the primary organization dedicated to the growth, development, and survival of the independent music community. The name of the organization was changed in the 1980's to include distributors and manufacturers. However, NAIRD is more than a national organization: it now represents the independent spirit of labels and distributors throughout the world, and has actively pursued participation and membership in the American retail music community.

NAIRD's primary focus is to allow the independent music community an avenue for the exchange of ideas and interests, as well as the opportunity to educate people who are interested in entering the independent music community. This is done primarily through the annual NAIRD convention. NAIRD holds its convention each May on a rotating regional basis. There is something for everyone at the NAIRD convention: veteran music industry people are able to reinforce relationships and make new contacts for their business, and the "first-timers" session held on the Wednesday of the convention allows people new to the music industry to attend a series of seminars with music industry veterans. The NAIRD convention is different from most other music industry conventions as it is dedicated to the business of music. Unlike other conventions with very large numbers of attendees who are on the fringe of the music industry, or not in it at all, NAIRD provides a business atmosphere for the interaction of the independent music community.

THE FUTURE OF THE INDEPENDENT MUSIC COMMUNITY

There will always be people who want to be their own boss, who think that they can buck the system, and who feel that their creative ideas and destiny should be in their own hands, and so there will always be independent labels. If there are independent labels, they will need distribution to get their music to the marketplace. The independent distributors who are in business today have withstood virtually every possible hurdle to their success. With the market share of the indies over 20%, and the ability of the national distribution companies of independent labels to compete with the branch operations of major labels, the prognosis is very favorable. Indeed, the willingness of the majors to invest in the independents but leave them to manage their own affairs demonstrates the major's confidence in the permanence of indies in the recording community.

PRESENT DAY INDIES: THE PLAYERS

In its March 17, 2007, issue *Billboard* published three charts giving detailed information on the top titles and labels for the past 12 months, based on *Billboard's* Top Independent Albums Chart. These charts give an accurate, up-to-date look at what is going on in the world of indie labels.

Top Independent Albums Titles

(listed by Position, Title, Artist, Label)

1. *The Road to Here,* Little Big Town, Equity

2. *Jason Aldean,* Jason Aldean, Broken Bow

3. *Retaliation,* Dane Cook, Comedy Central

4. *If Only You Were Lonely,* Hawthorne Heights, Victory

5. *A Fever You Can't Sweat Out,* Panic! At the Disco, Decaydance/Fueled by Ramen

6. *Hustler's P.O.M.E. (Product of My Environment),* Jim Jones, Koch

7. *Whatever People Say I am, that's What I'm Not,* Arctic Monkeys, Domino

8. *Zombies! Aliens! Vampires! Dinosaurs!* Hellogoodbye, Drive-thru

9. *I Loved Her First,* Heartland, Lofton Creek

10. *The Eraser,* Thom Torke, XL/Beggars Group

11. *A Piece of My Passion,* Juanita Bynum, Flow

12. *Wincing the Night Away,* The Shins, Sub-Pop

13. *A Death-Grip on yesterday,* Atreyu, Victory

14. *You Can't Fix Stupid,* Ron White, Image

15. *Greatest Hits,* Bone Thugs-N-Harmony, Ruthless

16. *The Poison,* Bullet for My Valentine, Trustkill

17. *El Mariel,* Pitbull, Famous Artists/TVT

18. *The Heart of ta Streetz, Vol. 2 (I Am What I Am),* B.G., Choppa City/Koch

19. *Still Searching,* Senses Fall, Drive-thru/Vagrant

20. *Last Man Standing: The Duets,* Jerry Lee Lewis, Artists First/Shangri-La

21. *A Matter of Life and Death,* Iron Maiden, Sanctuary

22. *Listennn: The Album,* DJ Khaled, Terror Squad/Koch

23. *Vans Warped Tour 2006 Compilation,* Various Artists, SideOneDummy

24. *The Last Kiss,* Soundtrack, Lakeshore

25. *Karmacode,* Lacuna Coil, Century Media

26. *Fox Confessor Brings the Flood,* Neko Case, Anti-/Epitath

27. *Orphans, Brawlers, Bawlers & Bastards,* Tom Waits, Anti-/Epitath

28. *U.S.A. Still United,* Ying Yang Twins, ColliPark/TVT

29. *Undiscovered,* Brooke Hogan, SMC/Sobe

30. *Chemically Imbalanced,* Ying Yang Twins, ColliPark/TVT

Top Independent Albums Labels

(Listed by position, label (number of charted titles))

1. Koch (19)
2. Victory (17)
3. TVT (13)
4. Broken Bow (3)
5. Equity (1)
6. Comedy Central (5)
7. Epitaph (17)
8. Fueled by Ramen (7)
9. Image (5)
10. Madacy (24)

Top Independently Owned Labels

(Listed by position, label (number of charted titles))

1. Walt Disney (18)
2. Hollywood (22)
3. Curb (11)
4. Wind-Up (4)
5. Razor & Tie (12)
6. Show Dog Nashville (2)
7. Fueled by Ramen (4)
8. Koch (12)
9. Victory (9)
10. Equity (1)

Chapter 9

Additional Income: Special Products

Harmon Greenblatt

Note: Much of the information for this chapter was obtained through an interview with Mickey Kapp, founder and retired president of Warner Special Products.

INTRODUCTION

Special products, special projects, special markets, licensing, what do they mean? Different companies have different names for this department of a record company, but what it amounts to is asset management and additional income for the record company. For purposes of this chapter, we will use the term special products, but the other terms can be used interchangeably. Special products means using the company owned recordings in special albums and/or licensing the recordings owned by the company to various licensees. Such licensee could be a company releasing a compilation album, such as *Greatest Hits of the '70s,* a company making a movie or commercial, or a company producing a mystery show. In order for anybody to obtain the right to use the *recording* of any song in any of these areas, the record company must grant permission. Each of the Big 4 record companies, as well as many smaller companies, has a division devoted to managing the use of the recordings they control. Without major expenditures by the company, these divisions can contribute significantly to the company's bottom line.

Why do the labels need these departments? First, in order for anyone to use recorded songs, three permissions must be obtained: that of the copyright holder of the song, usually the music publisher; that of the holder of the copyright to the recorded version of the song, usually the record company; and that of the artist who recorded the song. Second, because the amount of payment that licensees need to pay to use the recordings is not mandated by law, the terms of the agreement must be negotiated. This is one of the responsibilities of the special products division, and can be a tricky business.

The user of the recording to be licensed needs to negotiate with both the music publisher and the record company, but the publisher has no right to negotiate for the record company, nor can the record company negotiate for the publisher. As a result, there are times when a recording won't be used in a film because the publisher, the artist, or the record company either said no or wanted too much money. Typically, most film studios will approach the music publisher first. If the record company declines, the licensee can pay the publisher's fee and re-record the song. Without the publisher's agreement, the song cannot be used at all.

Why is the artist's permission needed? The publisher holds the copyright to the song, and the record company to the recording, so where does the artist come in? The answer is in the artist's recording contract. There are two important clauses in the contract. First is the "no coupling" clause. This point was first included in Bing Crosby's recording contract long ago to prevent Decca Records from putting a recording by an unknown artist on the 'B' side of his 78 rpm record, thus forcing him to split the royalties with an unknown, even though it was Bing Crosby who was selling the record. This stipulation still exists in every record contract, and to this day there is no coupling without permission. Artists thus understand that when the special products department inquires about a project, if the special products people give permission and establish the rate, permission for coupling has been acquired from the artist.

Second is the clause regarding album cover approval. Usually, part of the marketing plan devised by the creative team in the marketing department includes the cover for the CD. The artist has the right to accept or reject the cover art. When there is a compilation album, for example, the special products department is not able to acquire permission from each artist for the cover, so the artist must relinquish the right to have approval over the compilation cover art. Artists who refuse to relinquish control are often excluded from compilation packages.

Many people might ask why an artist would ever reject a coupling project when it would seem like money in the bank. First, the artist might fear that the coupling project will lower sales for recordings of the song selling at full price. Since his additional income for the coupling project is a small fraction of that of a full-price CD, why should he take this tiny amount when it may kill off sales for the real moneymaker?

Second, egos come into play. All artists think they front the number one band in the world, no matter what the recent sales or airplay might be. An artist may not want to be coupled with artists who are not number one. What the artist considers is: 1) I don't want to be the only big artist in the compilation and have the CD sold based only on my name; and 2) is there anyone else on the CD of comparable stature? In many artists' opinion, there is nobody of comparable stature.

One other financial wrinkle in compilations is the deduction for packaging, often around 20%. This cost is shared pro-rata among all of the artists who are featured on the compilation. The deduction is taken from the suggested retail list price of the album, thereby creating a smaller dollar amount on which the artist's royalties are based.

FILM AND TV USAGE

Why do the makers of film and television insist on using an original recording when it would be more cost-effective to use a sound-alike? The original recording establishes a time and a mood. It is an effective shorthand way, done without dialogue or titles, of grounding the story. Furthermore, it is a way of understanding a person or group of people without endless dialogue explaining who they are. A scene at a party at which gangsta rap is playing would denote characters different in age and character from a party where Joni Mitchell is being played. Finally, TV producers frequently have a very short lead time between when they negotiate for the music and when they use it on the air. They need quick decisions, and they need the music immediately. Even if they could go into the studio and do the song more cheaply, the tight time restrictions won't allow it. A recorded song is a known quantity, and worth the extra expense for the convenience and for its effectiveness.

Based on the individual artist agreements, some artists must grant permission for their songs to be used in films or commercials. Others are contractually available for the record company to use without special permission. For commercials, the artist is paid a synchronization fee as well as a "per show" royalty, which is based on usage tracked via television transcripts.

HOW THE SPECIAL PRODUCTS DIVISION IS ORGANIZED

The Special Products Division at Warner's is an A&R oriented division of the Music Group, with a strong emphasis on understanding the repertoire and its uses. A large company such as Warner Special Products has three major sections: domestic, international, and synchronization for film and television, all of which report to the vice president of A&R in special products. A legal and business affairs department has several people just working on contracts and paper work. Everything in this part of the business is contracts, and with as many as 10 or 12 agreements needed for one CD, the result is an enormous amount of paper work.

The three sections have distinct responsibilities. Domestic covers any use in the United States except for TV and film. Synch is any use, worldwide, in TV or film. International is a bit more complicated. There is an incorrect assumption that all artists are signed by their recording companies to worldwide agreements, but this is not always true. There are artists who may be Warner artists in the U.S. but PolyGram artists in Europe, and with some other label in other countries. At Warner, if a foreign company wants to use an artist who has signed with Warner in the United States but not the rest of the world, it must get permission from Warner Special Products (WSP), which would provide the artist clearance for an album coming out in a foreign country. In general, the country in which an album is being released dictates who is responsible for clearances.

Price schedules are established based on the popularity of the song and the different kinds of uses, so that when people call asking for license fees, this information is readily available. This structure is built up with the agreement of the managers, artists, and attorneys with whom the company deals, and results in a price that is fair and reasonable for the user, the company and the artist.

One of the reasons that Warner Special Products is so successful is that it spends a great deal of time and effort soliciting business and establishing and building relationships with music supervisors. One of the biggest users of music on TV is episodic television, better known as soap operas. The music supervisors for these shows have very short deadlines and need to have permissions right away. The representative at the special products division knows which artists to turn to for quick approvals, and who is willing (or unwilling) to cooperate. In the case of needing quick approvals, there is very little time to waste, and doing a good job means not offending the music supervisor by demanding outrageous fees or making him or her wait, and also not insulting the artist or the artist's manager by asking for a ridiculously low price. Once a trust relationship has been forged between the supervisor and the special products person, when the supervisor asks for a song, he or she can usually assume that the price quoted is a fair price. Remember, these people are dealing with each other every day. The special products representative has a line of continuing business (and income) and is not about to jeopardize that by overcharging for a recording. He/She knows which recordings are available immediately, and has an approximate scale to charge for each one.

The type of use is an important aspect in determining the fee for a recording. If it is played in the background, it will be one price. If it figures more prominently, such as playing under the credits, there will be a higher rate charged. It is the job of the special products division to know what a reasonable fee to charge for varying uses is and for the user to understand the rationale for these charges.

COMMERICALS

The making of commercials is a far different world. There the time frame is much longer and usually the special products person works with an advertising agency. Ideas aren't usually pitched in this situation, because the agencies usually have their own ideas. If the client wants to use the original recording, he wants to use it for the mood, the timing and the authenticity. Frequently, however, the agency will re-record the song with its own lyrics for the product it is trying to sell. In this case, the agency will get the rights for the song from the music publisher and not use the recording at all.

However, there is a good reason for using the original recording in a commercial. Before the product can be sold, the commercial must get the listener's attention. A familiar song in a well-known recording will grab the attention of a listener in a way a sound-alike won't. A sound-alike will probably cost less, but it does not have the same impact as the original recording.

What an original song can't do is what commercial licensees frequently want, and that is to use the original recording but insert lyrics plugging their own product. An agency may want to use Aretha Franklin's "Respect" for a Cocoa Puffs commercial. But Aretha never sang about Cocoa Puffs and if she wanted to now, the agency wouldn't need the original song. In this case the agency would probably get the publisher's permission, re-record the song, and put in the words it desired.

When selecting an artist's song for a commercial, the record label must recognize the tacit association the artist will have with the product, and also that the audience may identify the product with the artist, not just the song. This often requires a sensitivity to the artist's reputation and beliefs by the special products department. The most obvious products to be concerned about are those containing alcohol or tobacco, but artists who are vegetarians, for example, may not wish to be associated with meat products, or even dairy products. The ideal special products person knows in advance what will fly and what will not fly with the artist and acts accordingly.

What a licensee gets with an original recording is authenticity. The song says the product is real because the recording is real. But it is difficult to sell this concept to the ad agency, because the agency is not as directly concerned with the product as the manufacturer is. The agency may not comprehend the correlation between the use of the original song and the authenticity of the product. Advertisers and their agencies need to understand the impact an original song may have on the sales of the product, because the original song's overall ability to attract people's attention may be much greater than if another recording is used.

FILM

With the film industry, the special products staff works with directors, producers, and music supervisors to try to convince them to use a recording that fits a scene in the movie. Frequently, a special products department receives scripts and is asked to make suggestions as to what songs are most appropriate for a particular film. The film producer then compares the suggestions from one company with those of the other companies that have made suggestions, and chooses which are most suitable.

A major part of the business of special products is being able to get approvals quickly. Knowing who wants to cooperate, who doesn't, and for how much makes the special products person's job much easier. For example, if someone calls and wants Madonna and has only ten dollars to spend, he is not going to get her music. Even if the person asks the company to try, the special products person won't do it because it needs to deal with Madonna's manager every day and doesn't want to insult the artist or the manager. Over time the special products department builds up a reputation and users trust the department. The department quotes the price, and the users have the option of using the song or not. There is not much room for haggling, which takes too much time and threatens the trust of other users.

On occasion, music and film work together to benefit both media. A few years ago, the combination of the movie *Ghost* and the song "Unchained Melody" led to the movie's being a smash hit and resurrected the career of the Righteous Brothers, whose recording was used. Still more successful was the use of Whitney Houston's song "I Will Always Love You" in the movie *The Bodyguard,* in which she also starred. The film and song worked together to further her acting career, the movie's grosses, and the song's sales. The song became the all time *Billboard* hit for most weeks at #1, spurred on at least in part by the film's success.

PACKAGES

A prime effort of the special products department is compiling packages for marketers. The special products staff works with a TV marketer, such as Heartland, Sessions, or Time-Life, to put together a concept for a CD and then acquire all of the rights to the recordings for the album from the copyright owners to use in the compilation. Heartland and the other TV marketers produce TV packages, such as the ones you see advertised on cable television, but there are also catalog and print packages, marketed by companies such as Reader's Digest, Good Music Record Company, and Publisher's Clearing House. A large company like Warner Special Products will not only be a licensor of its own recordings to companies that want to use them, but will also be a licensee from other owners of recorded copyrights. The company compiles the recordings, manufactures them, and sells the finished CDs, all payments made, to the end user, the marketer, who then markets it to the record-buying public. WSP, for example, created the "Rock & Roll Era" series for Time-Life, but it was up to Time-Life to buy the television time and market the product.

REISSUES

There are times when a special products department wants to reissue a recording that originally appeared on the company's major label. There may be renewed interest in a band, they may be getting together a reunion tour, or their music may have been used in a film and become popular again. To do this, the department needs permission from its own record label. For example, if the special products department wants to do a Best *of the Doobie Brothers,* it will approach Warner Brothers Records, who may say that they are already releasing a *Best of the Doobies,* so the special products department can't do it.

At other times, however, such a project can be done, and increasingly with well-known artists. *The Best of John Denver* is seen frequently on cable TV ads, and the extraordinary benefit from TV advertising is that when people see these ads they are getting a visual impression of the music, something unusual for recorded music. The result is not only sales of the CD through the mail, but also stimulated retail sales for the full price recordings of the artist. There is definitely a double benefit: reaching a new market of buyers who buy from TV but who may not go to stores to buy records, and increased sales at regular retail outlets.

PREMIUMS

The special products department is also in the premium business. Premiums exist when companies give away (or sell cheaply) a product when the customer buys something else. In the record business this is difficult because people's differing tastes are so important. For example, it is relatively easy to use a camera or a dozen golf balls as a premium, and every U.S. manufacturer seems to have a premium division. But on recordings, whose recording are you going to use as a premium?

There are other difficulties as well. Many artists may not want their music used as a premium. For example, does Rod Stewart want his recordings used as a premium? You don't know until you ask, and he may be outraged if you do. On the other hand, nobody wants a five year old CD by a has-been artist as a premium.

Classical music, which has a longer shelf life, is somewhat immune from the topicality of popular music, but it is a much smaller market and people still have a wide range of tastes. Classical music's big advantage is that the music is mostly in the public domain and in most cases, there are no major artists who will demand high royalties, so that getting permissions is much easier.

Nevertheless, there have been many successful premium promotions. Gasoline companies tend to be the leaders in these promotions, giving away a compilation cassette of oldies or country music with a 10-gallon purchase, for example. Banks will also use premiums frequently as holiday gifts. In this case it will usually be a recording that already exists or a collection of holiday songs with the bank's name stamped on it. One of the most successful of these promotions occurred when the cigarette company, Marlboro gave away about two million copies of each of three cassettes, giving away a cassette with the purchase of a carton of cigarettes. Victoria's Secret has a very successful promotion of a series of brief classical selections that began as a premium but became so popular that they continue to be sold in stores.

For example, Deutsche Grammophon (DG) and the Theater Development Fund (TDF) worked out a promotion at the TDF Half Price Ticket booth in New York City. Using DG crossover artists such as Bryn Terfel, the opera star, TDF gave away a sampler cassette of Terfel's *Something Wonderful* with every purchase at the booth on 47th Street.

Premiums are used for many different reasons: to stimulate sales, as a thank you, or as a holiday gift. It is fascinating that a product as differentiated as recordings can be used successfully in this area. But the battle for any special products division is that, because the product is being used as a giveaway, it is very price oriented. There is not much profit in giving music away, and the bidding can sometimes become so fierce that any company profit winds up being very minimal. But it does happen that these recordings do occasionally hit the jackpot, and even a 50 cent profit per CD on a 2 million seller comes out to be a million dollar profit.

It is important to note that the premium area has nothing to do with record clubs, which also give away records. Record clubs are a completely different business, which deals directly with the labels, not with the special products department.

RINGTONES

Is it possible that commercial ringtones are barely 10 years old? The first commercial ringtones were created and delivered in Finland in 1998 from a service called Harmonium. At that time it was possible for customers to create monophonic ringtones and also a mechanism to deliver tones to a handset. The charge was added to the customer's phone bill. The service spread quickly and has since become a multi-billion dollar industry. This quick increase created a need for high quality professional ringtones and commercial ringtone libraries.

How has this industry become so successful? Why do so many people pay money for ringtones when there are plenty of free ringtones available? Just as the cell phone has become part of its owner's personality, so has the ringtone. Phone personalization and customization are the watchwords, and with cell phones becoming increasingly sophisticated and soon with the iPhone's ability to perform even more tasks, the user sees the payment of a few dollars as an extension of his/her personality, as something important to his/her identity as a person.

While older telephones allowed for only a pair of bells for the ringer, modern ring tones are much more sophisticated. Rather than the former ring of older telephones that worked on an AC wave, mobile phones receive their ringing signal by a specific radio-frequency signal. This allows the consumer to have any combination of sounds he desires within a set time limit. Ringtone users may buy their tones from the web's many providers, create a melody of their own, or upload from music they already own from an MP3, CD, etc. If copyrighted music is being used, then it must be licensed from the copyright holder. At a major label, this is done through the Special Products Department

Companies that provide ringtones to consumers license music for use as ringtones the same way that they would for any other use. There are two choices, either an upfront fee, or a fee per user, or a combination of the two. If a company wants the exclusive license for a song, the upfront fee is generally higher than for a non-exclusive license. Just as with other uses, what the user gets with licensing a recording is authenticity, that this is the exact sound as heard on the CD. The user gets to equate the song with his/her own identity, and the label makes additional income for itself and the artist.

CONCLUSION

With all of these potential sources of income, it is important to remember that the special products department is not important in developing an artist's career. It is, as the title of this chapter suggests, a way to make additional income from recordings in the vault. That income can be substantial for the artist and the label, and that income is an important function of maximizing profits from the assets of the record company. With new technology making use of music in all sorts of ways never dreamed of in the past, the possibilities for Special Products just keep increasing.

The Music Business in Action:

Music and Podcasting

An interesting example of where the music industry is heading is Rock River Communications located in San Francisco and Brattleboro, VT. They were, in earlier years, known for licensing and making "mixed" CDs for Gap, Victoria's Secret, Pottery Barn, and others. In 2004, Rock River began creating radio stations for Volkswagen and Ford, streaming demographically chosen music to those car owners' hard-drives in association with specific information on those autos.

Now Rock River is helping to guide the music industry in podcasting. The industry has been hesitant because podcasting, in MP3 format, lacks software to prevent copying.

Rock River is creating for corporate clients, Chrysler and Ford, a series of promotional podcasts, utilizing, at first, music from Sony only. A flat fee will be paid to Sony for one year's use of a few specific artists such as in *Chrysler Music Legends* (Miles, Cash, Journey) and uses 30 second ads. The deal is for one year and stays on personal computers throughout the year permitting unlimited downloads. The music is well embedded within a long biographical program.

Rock River is in talks with other major labels regarding podcasting. The existing program can be found on Chrysler's home page and the iTunes podcasting section.

If separate podcast radio channels for specific clients become widespread, it can mean extra income for the labels involved. It also has the potential to further erode the listening audience for traditional radio.

Chapter 10

The International Opportunity

This chapter was originally written by Brian Sutnick. It has been updated in 2009 by Harmon Greenblatt.

INTRODUCTION

Success in the international marketplace is vital in today's global music industry, both for the growth of a recording artist's career and for the survival of the record label. As markets around the world grow and hone their marketing skills, there are increasingly more and more opportunities for an artist to break on a worldwide level. That said, the competition is fierce and a label must have a comprehensive international marketing plan to maximize the artist's exposure.

THE INTERNATIONAL MARKETPLACE

The international marketplace is generally viewed by continents and/or major countries. Thus, from the viewpoint of an individual marketing acts internationally from the U.S., the global music business can be broken down as follows: Canada, Japan, Australia, U.K., Continental Europe, Southeast Asia, Latin America and Eastern Europe. Generally, the western culture music business does not have operations in most of Africa and the Middle East. (In 1996, Africa and the Middle East collectively accounted for about 2% of the global market.) Labels will generally lock in exclusive label license deals with independent distribution companies in these smaller markets, which basically just sell products to stores with little promotion. These independent distributors may, in fact, be selling products from several major companies.

According to the IFPI (International Federation of the Phonographic Industry), the total value of units sold worldwide in 1996 (the last year for which this information was available) was $39.8 billion. This value is for the entire global music business in 77 countries. Of that total, 80% was generated in the top ten markets, listed below:

U.S.	$12.3 billion
Japan	6.8
Germany	3.2
U.K.	2.7
France	2.3
Brazil	1.4
Canada	.912
Australia	.815
Netherlands	.660
Italy	.637

These figures may be a bit misleading to someone marketing acts internationally from the U.S. All markets generate a large percentage of their revenue from local repertoire; however, markets such as Brazil and Italy are even more heavily influenced by local music. Although ranked as the sixth largest market in the world, Brazil would not be a good choice to aid in the initial development of a new rock act from the States.

The following chart lists the sales necessary to attain Gold and Platinum record status around the world:

	Gold	Platinum
United States	500,000	1,000,000
Argentina	30,000	60,000

Austria	25,000	50,000
Australia	35,000	70,000
Belgium	25,000	50,000
Brazil	100,000	250,000
Canada	50,000	100,000
Chile	15,000	25,000
Colombia	50,000	100,000
Denmark	25,000	50,000
Finland	25,000	50,000
France	100,000	300,000
Germany	250,000	500,000
Greece	30,000	60,000
Holland	50,000	100,000
Hong Kong	10,000	20,000
Indonesia	25,000	75,000
India	30,000	60,000
Ireland	10,000	15,000
Israel	20,000	40,000
Italy	50,000	100,000
Japan	100,000	200,000
Korea	50,000	100,000
Malaysia	15,000	25,000
Mexico	100,000	250,000
New Zealand	7,500	15,000
Norway	25,000	50,000
Philippines	20,000	40,000
Portugal	20,000	40,000
Singapore		20,000
Spain	50,000	100,000
South Africa	25,000	50,000
Sweden	50,000	100,000
Switzerland	25,000	50,000
Taiwan		20,000
Thailand	25,000	50,000
Turkey	50,000	100,000
U.K.	100,000	300,000
Venezuela	50,000	100,000

Obviously, the United States still reigns as the largest market in the world. However, as the international markets are growing at a much faster pace than the U.S., it is slowly losing ground in terms of its percentage of worldwide sales. In 1996, the U.S. was up 2% in total value of music sales. The combined sales of the developing markets of Latin America, Southeast Asia (excluding Japan), and Eastern Europe were up a combined 18%. As music sales in these international markets grow, so does the likelihood that more media outlets will spring up to take advantage of these new music fans. Having more media outlets increases a label's ability to promote artists in these regions. As we go to press, the best estimate is that the U.S. still accounts for about 30% of worldwide sales.

The combination of sales that can be attained outside of the U.S can be greater, even much greater, than within the U.S. One extreme example is U.S. recording artists Bon Jovi. They released their greatest hits album, *Cross Road*, in the fall of 1994 and sold an impressive 2.5 million in the U.S., not a bad total considering that the height of Bon Jovi's career in the U.S. was in the mid to late '80's. However, Bon Jovi's international career had been growing steadily at the same time it was declining in the U.S., and the greatest hits compilation sold a whopping 10.5 million outside of the U.S.

It would be very difficult to estimate what international sales should be relative to U.S. sales of a U.S. artist. There are many factors as to what makes a project successful in foreign markets. Obviously the type of music dictates its ability to generate sales. One would not expect great sales of Country music in Portugal, for example, although Country does quite well in Ireland. The availability of the artist in foreign markets plays a major role in how well the project performs. Also, a project's success in its home territory is vital to its breaking outside.

RELEASING AN ARTIST INTERNATIONALLY

Artists are released on a label in one of two ways. A label either signs a deal directly with an artist or it licenses repertoire owned by another label. When a label directly signs an artist to a recording contract, the label, in essence, owns the master tapes that the artist records. As the repertoire owner, the label will, whenever possible, secure the rights to exploit that repertoire around the world. All major labels and many of the independent labels maintain some sort of department that looks after the release of its repertoire internationally. This department is known as the International Marketing Department.

However, when a label licenses repertoire from an overseas label, it obtains the rights to release product that it has not directly signed. In some companies, the International Marketing Department will have the added responsibility of bringing international repertoire to the attention of the local company. As the staff of the International Department has relationships with music business professionals from around the world, they are likely to know which acts are breaking in foreign territories. They can then forward this new music to the relevant A&R staff for their consideration.

The licensing label will pay the repertoire owner a percentage of the wholesale price to cover the copyright and royalty for every unit sold. This international royalty is, most often, split 50/50 between the artist and repertoire owner. Generally, this percentage is roughly 30% of the wholesale price (or 15% of the retail price). For example, a label in Italy sells product on an artist that it has licensed from a U.S. label. If the Italian label sells the CD to the retailer for $10.00 (U.S. dollars), the U.S. repertoire owner will collect nearly $3.00 per unit. This $3.00 is split with the artist, with $1.50 going to the label and $1.50 towards the artist's royalty account. Of course, the artist royalty account will be in the red until enough royalties are earned to cover recoupable expenses.

One advantage of being part of a major label group is that the affiliates generally license repertoire to each other without advances on the copyright and royalty. A label that licenses repertoire from an unrelated label may have to pay not only this advance, but perhaps even a nonrecoupable licensing fee. Such arrangements are negotiable between the licensing label and repertoire owner. The extra costs are over and above what is required to break the artist in the market. That said, there is an excellent opportunity to generate income from licensed repertoire. After all, the licensee does not have the upfront expenses of creating the product, such as recording the album or making the videos.

The major labels, or at least those that are able to conduct business on an international level, have set up companies in almost every country in the world. This network of affiliated labels is all owned by the same multinational company, which enables it to set up an exchange of artists around the world. When considering whether to release a project owned by an affiliate, the potential licensing affiliate has the right of first refusal. This means that the affiliated label can decide whether or not it will release a product before any other label can be considered. It will have the luxury of time to analyze the repertoire to decide whether it is right for the market and to see how the product succeeds in its home country. If the affiliate opts not to release something, the repertoire owner can then go to another label within the major label group. If there are still no takers, the label can then look to release the product through a third party.

Because an independent in the position of repertoire owner will often have to deal with many different companies around the world, the independent record label staff is forced to build one new personal relationship after another. Majors, on the other hand, can work from one project to the next with the same people around the world. As personal relationships are so vital to a project's success, independent labels often aim to lock in an international distribution deal with a major label. Of course, this affiliated international network is very attractive to the independents as well.

INTERNATIONAL INCOME

Labels generate the majority of their international income in two major ways. One method is through licensing. When an artist records for a label, the master recordings, which are owned by the label, can be used over and over to make money for the label. If an old track is placed on a new soundtrack release, it can generate new income on a project that has long since been recouped. This was the case with the song "Unchained Melody" by the Righteous Brothers, when it was included on the soundtrack for the film Ghost.

Compilations

Often, international markets will request the use of a track to include on a compilation. This compilation could be anything from Disco Hits of the '70's to Reggae Classics of the '80's to a movie soundtrack recording. The approval process begins with an international affiliate contacting the business affairs department of the repertoire owner. That department's decision to approve the use of the track on an international compilation will be based purely on the contents of the label's recording contracts (i.e., has the artist allowed the label to use tracks on compilations?). However, after the track has cleared the business affairs department, the international marketing department head will base its approval on marketing potential. For example, it would not be wise to clear the use of a track that is a hit on a current album. If that track appeared on a new compilation, it would take potential sales away from the current album from which the track was taken.

As a compilation is put together by a label within a major record company, some of the tracks may come from other labels within the company. This is yet another benefit for the majors as they will most likely be able to negotiate the use of this track for a lower royalty rate. When compilations are put together in the United States, the label releasing the compilation will often have to pay an upfront advance of the royalty on the use of a recording licensed from another label. Internationally, compilations are so abundant that the use of a track will usually not require an advance on the royalty, although this is not the case if a label is requesting the use of a very popular song. The inclusion of a huge hit song that will help to drive the sales of the compilation will often cost the label an upfront advance on the royalty.

Career Development

Labels also generate income through developing an artist's career, breaking songs and selling product around the world. A label is most proud when it develops an artist into a career artist. Internationally, the task begins with growing awareness overseas that there is a new band signed, say, in the U.S. The International Marketing Department must begin to 'turn on' the affiliated labels that have the first rights to release the project. The band's biography and copies of press that has been collected by the U.S. division are essential tools, and the department must continually inform the affiliates of all the positive reactions regarding the development of this new artist. The more information to feed the affiliates, the better. Obviously the affiliates will need all of this information when they do decide to release the project. By continually promoting an artist, it shows the affiliates that this new artist is a priority to the repertoire owner.

Release Strategies

After the basic servicing is done and everyone in the international community has all of the music and information on a new act, the next stage is to set up a plan for an international release. Setting up an album release differs from one project to the next. If the artist is a rock band with an energetic live show, then that tool (the live show) is an important asset in promoting the release. The band will want to be seen in a rocking club. However, a beautiful solo artist (who may not be known for the most amazing live show) needs to be on TV. To really go after a release, the artist must go on the road internationally. This is not an easy task, as there are many people requiring the artist's presence at the same time. The International Marketing Department must therefore fight for access to the artist to bring him or her overseas.

With a new artist, it would be rare to release an album overseas simultaneously with the U.S release. Usually it is after the U.S. has had some success that the international marketing department is able to obtain access to the artist to give him or her time to develop overseas and to fight for attention of the project from the overseas affiliates.

With an established artist, a worldwide simultaneous release is critical, and necessary to fight parallel imports, which occur when product from one country is selling on the shelves of another country. One will usually notice in U.S record stores that imports from Japan or the U.K., for example, are much more expensive than the domestic product. However, imports in other countries can often be cheaper than domestic product.

Parallel imports occur for several reasons. One is the ideology of retail around the world. CD's are viewed as more of a luxury overseas than they are in the States, so they are priced higher. The United States is notorious for selling product at very low cost, and not just in the music business, but for many products. From denim jeans to designer underwear, the American consumer is spoiled by low priced goods. Because the U.S. sells its products more cheaply than almost any other Western country does, its products will often end up on shelves around the world. For example, Japan sells CD's for about 2500 yen (currently around $22 U.S.). CD's in Australia sell for about $30 Australian (roughly $24 U.S.). Even the developing artist price of 22 Euros in France (roughly $17 U.S.) is much higher than a typical developing artist price of $10 in America.

Even if one market prices products similarly to another, the fluctuation of currencies can also lead to imports. For example, the relatively weak British pound in 1996 made the U.K. a cheap source of finished product for Continental Europe. An importer in Germany can bring product in from the U.K., paying shipping costs and custom taxes, and still sell it to retail outlets for less than the local German label can.

When imports come into a country, they greatly jeopardize the local label's ability to compete. The local label will be spending marketing dollars to promote an artist by buying advertising, bringing the artist into its territory for promotion, and printing posters. However, a record store may be buying the product from an independent business that is importing finished product from another country and selling it at a cheaper price. With an established artist, one for whom there is a foreseeable market, it is vital that the International Marketing Department do its job of setting up the release for overseas affiliates.

First and foremost, this requires securing the production parts so that affiliates can manufacture product for international simultaneous release. A delay of even one week can cost the affiliate a large percentage of its overall sales on a superstar act. If an importer can set up in the territory with imported product, he can, in essence, rob the affiliate, who has spent untold amounts of money setting up a major release, of unrealized sales. Labels will try to compete with a lower priced imported product by making the more expensive local product more attractive to the consumer, usually by adding bonus tracks or printing a larger package.

Many times a major will set up its own importing division, following the adage, "if you can't beat them, join them." By setting up an import division, a major label can compete with importers. In Japan, where imports are most sensitive, imports can count for 40%, even as much as 50%, of the overall sales of a project. Not just established acts can be exported, as sometimes the genre of music is such that the international retailers are very tuned in to what is happening. In such a case, a simultaneous release is necessary.

INTERNATIONAL DEPARTMENT ORGANIZATION

A basic international marketing department may include the following personnel: a department head, an international product manager, an international publicist, and an international production manager.

Department Head

The head of the department reports directly to the label's president, and will set the department's priorities. Certainly these will very often be the same as those of the label in general. However, there are times when the international marketing department is working projects well before or well after the U.S. division's involvement. Sometimes projects are created specifically for international markets. The head will approve the licensing of recordings to be used in international compilations, approve the price level that a project is sold at internationally, and determine whether or not a catalog title's price level should be changed. (i.e. should a catalog title that has declined in sales for an extended period of time be made available to consumers for a lower price, moving, say, from top price to mid price?)

Ultimately, it is the head's responsibility to generate income to meet the department's budgets and profit projections. This income can come from international sales of product created by the label, from licensing individual tracks for compilations around the world, or, perhaps, even by creating a compilation purely for the international markets. Along the way, he is responsible for developing new artists from the label's repertoire outside of its borders and maximizing international sales on the label's established artists.

International Product Manager

The international product manager is responsible for the implementation of the international release of specific projects. This includes setting a plan for the release date of the album and singles that will give the project the best opportunity for exposure. The product manager supplies information to all affiliates and licensees on the progress of projects both in the originating territory and around the world. He or she will make the necessary tools available to the international territories to enable them to properly promote the project and artist in their territories. Such tools can range from small items, such as a sticker of the artist's name, to T-shirts, to posters, to very large marketing endeavors such as bringing an artist into a territory for promotion.

International Publicist

The international publicist is responsible for organizing all international media opportunities. While the local publicity departments in each country pursue the local media for opportunities for an artist, the international publicist is concerned about how an artist is perceived in a country. The international publicist thus lends direction to the local publicists on which media should be targeted. The international publicist controls the distribution of the necessary publicity tools, such as photos and artist biographies.

Specifically, the international publicist works with publicists and product managers around the world to arrange contact between media and the artist. The publicist accomplishes this in two ways: the first, the phone interview, is a useful way to begin the process of obtaining publicity. However, the second method, the in-person interview, is almost always a more rewarding experience for both the artist and the journalist, and usually results in a better story. The international publicist creates daily schedules of promotional and marketing activities while an artist is outside of the U.S., either on a promotional tour or for a performance. The in-person promotional activities consist of face-to-face interviews, photo sessions, on-air interviews, and performances at a radio station, live in-store performances, and television performances.

The daily schedules prepared by the publicist may also include activities such as visiting retail outlets to meet some of the retail staff who buy product in quantity from the label, walking through the local label's office to shake hands with the staff, or even having dinner with a local radio programmer. Although these activities are not really considered promotional as they do not directly affect the media, it is vital to make friends along the way. The staff of a record label in Austria, for instance, cares more for an artist they have met and maybe even shared a drink with than for one they have never met. Such events help a licensing label treat a project as one of their own, and improve the chances of breaking that artist in that territory. A retail buyer in Zurich who met the artist for five minutes one afternoon may buy just a few extra units of that new artist's CD and position it conspicuously in his or her store. Little gestures like these can go a long way, so it is important to include them in an artist's schedule.

While the artist is appearing in foreign markets, the local companies use the opportunity to either release the full length project (the album) or a new single. The release of a new product will generally coincide either with the time when the highest profile quality media exposure hits, or, at least when the highest quantity of exposure hits. For example, if an artist performs on a nationally televised program, it is essential that the product is available, at the latest, immediately after the TV appearance airs. If an artist does not have sufficient stature to obtain a TV appearance but does accomplish many interviews with journalists, it is just as essential that the product be available when these articles hit the streets. Having a product available when there is exposure of the artist through media is vital to a record label's purpose.

International Production Manager

The international production manager is responsible for supplying all of the parts required to physically manufacture product locally. If a foreign affiliate is going to manufacture an album locally, it will need an audio master tape of that album as well as the computer graphics necessary to create the printing films for the CD booklet. It may also require the graphics necessary to produce a poster. The affiliated label will also require legal information, such as the names of the songwriters and the song publishers. The international production manager works directly with mastering studios, graphic designers, and the label's A&R department to insure that all parts needed for manufacture are delivered to the international affiliates.

As international marketing departments expand, labels generally add more product managers or publicists to handle more and more of the label's artists. For example, some labels may have three product managers and two publicists. With an increase in management level staff, there will also be more assistants.

The positions and duties described above are the theoretical responsibilities within an international marketing department. In practice, however, responsibilities are often shared among the staff. For instance, the department head often takes on the product management duties for some of the major artists on the label. The product manager often works with the international publicist in organizing press activities.

A responsibility shared by everyone in the department is motivating the international affiliates to promote their artists. Within a major entertainment company, overseas affiliates are most likely working repertoire from many, if not all, of the labels or repertoire centers within the major. As major entertainment companies have many major artists recording for their labels, a label manager in Norway, for example, may have little time to work on a developing artist. The same situation is also likely for an independent that is working many different labels' repertoires simultaneously. In addition, more and more local repertoire is being developed within each country. The international marketing department must show the affiliates that the department is their ally and is there to aid them in breaking a new artist and maximizing the potential of their established artists.

THE INTERNATIONAL OPPORTUNITY

Although there are increasingly more opportunities internationally to expose an artist to the consumer, there are many artists vying for those coveted opportunities. The international marketing department must fight with the licensing affiliates for those opportunities, even at the expense of other artists signed to labels within the same major label group. Artists signed to different labels within the same label group compete with each other internally long before they compete in the marketplace.

Affiliates generally license repertoire to each other at no cost. This may be an advantage in terms of money, but the very fact that the label does not have to pay for the rights upfront can work against a project. If a major acquires a project at no cost, along with many other free projects, it often chases those projects that receive the most immediate response, which can be very damaging to artist development. If the label doesn't spend any money in the marketing of a release, it can generate income from the first record sold.

Money is a major motivator. A company naturally wants to see a return on its investment. If an independent pays an upfront sum of $100,000 for the rights to release a project, that independent label is likely to be committed to the project and development of the artist in its market. Just because a project is a priority to the repertoire owner in the United States, for instance, doesn't necessarily make it a priority to the affiliate in the U.K. An international marketing department must do its job of fighting for its project and proving that it is worth the affiliate's investment. The more money an affiliate puts behind the project, the more committed the affiliate is to the project.

A repertoire owner may supply a master tape of a promotional video that may have cost $100,000 to produce to an affiliate for a nominal fee of $40, for example, to cover duplication costs. On the other hand, an independent may charge its licensees thousands of dollars, in effect, recouping the cost of video production, for the video. The independent that pays thousands of dollars for the video master will be more committed to getting that video played, while the major, who received the video for $40, may not feel as much pressure to get the video played unless many other factors are already working in favor of the artist.

There are advantages and disadvantages of both the major label arrangement and the independent label situation. The majors have an open exchange of artists from one affiliate to the next. As all of the affiliates are owned by the same company, the label artists are available to each affiliate without an upfront advance or licensing fee. However, this "free" exchange of repertoire can hurt projects, as many will not be given the time to develop in certain markets. That is, after all, the competitive nature of the music business. This disadvantage is countered by the fact that the major labels do have deep pockets when they want to. When they do embrace an artist, which is usually after there has been some early response by the media and/or consumers in their markets, they are able to inject money into a project to directly increase sales. For example, an independent just may not have the money to fly a band from America to Australia and cover the costs for a week. The product released by an independent, therefore, will generally not receive nearly as much coverage in the media as a product released by a major.

TECHNOLOGY AND THE INTERNATIONAL MARKETPLACE

As with so much in the music industry, the International Departments are facing sweeping changes. Technology which makes it possible to order music over the Web also makes it possible to receive music internationally. There is a big question whether labels in foreign countries will pay advances for artists if they fear that the number of CD's they will sell will be reduced by users getting their music through iTunes, Napster or any of the other providers now competing with the physical distributors.

This is not an idle speculation. iTunes already has representatives worldwide, in Japan, Australia, Europe, Canada, and has set up its own worldwide distribution network. Napster has set up a similar system, and the others are just getting into foreign territories. Rates need to be settled between the label and iTunes (or any other provider) for each song in each territory. But once the terms have been settled, iTunes has the right to sell that product over the Web. If iTunes chooses to feature that song, it can make a big difference for that song and artist in the territory.

This can be an opportunity for smaller, independent labels that lack the marketing budgets to get international exposure for their artists in a relatively low-cost way. Artists who may not have enough sales potential for a major international label may find success online. And other forms of music, jazz, classical, blues, may find opportunities to get their music heard where they couldn't do so in the past.

But will the increased exposure mean greater presence and greater physical sales in addition to online sales, or will the online sales reduce the market for physical sales? There is no answer yet, but it looks like there will major changes on the international scene in the near future.

CONCLUSION

The importance of developing repertoire in international markets cannot be denied. As international markets expand, they are, collectively, becoming a larger player in the potential profits for an artist and label. Even the more remote regions of Latin America and Eastern Europe are developing at record paces. Although the U.S. is still the largest market in the world, its share in the global business is decreasing. More and more media opportunities are being created in the foreign markets. The more opportunities to expose an artist to the public, the greater potential there is for sales (and income). As technology grows, the world continues to move towards one global culture. A label and an artist who work together to commit effort to development outside of the artist's own borders will have the opportunity to become part of this global culture. As technology changes, international departments will meet greater challenges and come up with creative solutions for artists to develop an international following.

Chapter 11

Business Affairs

Bill Stafford

BUSINESS AFFAIRS DEPARTMENT STRUCTURE

A record company's business affairs department is structured in much the same way as the corporate divisions of other industries. Company-wide, everyone reports to the President, who may or may not also be the chief executive officer. Next in the line of command may be the company chairman, or even the chief financial officer (CFO), depending on the particular structure of the company. After the CFO, the business affairs department begins with its own hierarchy, usually headed by the senior vice president, followed by any number of vice presidents, directors, managers and supervisors. Non-managerial positions within the business affairs department include administrators, coordinators, and administrative assistants, as well as numerous interns and temporary workers who help with inordinately large projects or during the absence of an employee.

The business affairs department works closely with the legal department, and many times they are combined as one operating unit within the company. Common areas of coverage include artist contracts, producer deals, publishing agreements, online deals including the accompanying security, trademark and patent issues, and legal claims. Most business affairs departments are composed of the following divisions: A&R administration, copyright, rights and clearances, and contract administration. These employees, as well as the legal staff, work closely with the technology division to support online music sales, ensure compliance with online regulations, and enforce cyber security for the online catalog and the company websites. The recent shift to artist branding and advertising opportunities has led to the creation of departments such as "brand partnerships and commercial licensing" at some record companies. Non-traditional revenue sources will likely spawn the creation of additional innovative departments as record companies look to offset the losses from the decrease in traditional retail sales. Employee titles and department names may vary among different record companies, but the basic responsibilities and company interactions of a business affairs department are similar, since they are influenced by the available technology, consumer demand, and copyright and other laws.

DEPARTMENT FUNCTIONS

A&R Administration

Although the term A&R (artist and repertoire) is included in the name of this department, it should not be confused with the A&R department which is responsible for scouting and signing the artists. The A&R administration department handles the expenses involved with the artists and the recording process, operating within the business affairs department of the company.

The recording process begins once the label president or senior A&R executive receives the approval from the company president and has consulted with the finance department regarding a recording budget. The maximum and minimum recording fund limits are usually outlined in the artist's agreement. Prior to signing the recording agreement, the only recording funds made available to the artist may have been through a demo deal. Record company demo deals, also known as development deals, provide the artist with the opportunity to professionally record some of his or her songs at the record company's expense. Demo deals are fewer in number due to the accessibility of affordable, quality digital recording equipment and software. Most artists come equipped with their own recordings, some of which are recorded and mastered to the level of being ready for commercial distribution.

Whether newly-signed or fulfilling their next recording option, an artist has a recording budget negotiated between the artist's attorney or manager and a senior executive at the record company. The amount of the recording budget is often governed by the record company's policies according to the artist's stature. The average recording budget for a beginning rock artist at a major label is $150,000. This amount is paid and tracked by the A&R administration department, and is usually recoupable against what the artist earns.

If the recording costs end up going over the allotted budget and the artist demonstrates considerable potential, the A&R administration department usually works with the label president to approve a re-forecast budget to accommodate the costs. Interestingly, new technology has kept even major label recording costs down for years. Many major studios have had to close their doors in the past few years due to the availability of digital recording packages such as Pro Tools and Logic.

Major record companies establish accounts with third-party vendors and authorize services through a purchase order. This guarantees that the record company will pay for the expenses incurred. The most common expenses include: equipment rental and cartage, travel and living, engineers, studio and tape costs, mastering expenses, digital encoding and watermarking fees, producer royalties, guest artist (sideman) payments and the fees involved with using samples of others' music in a recording.

Aside from the aforementioned expenses, an artist may require money for less conventional circumstances such as to pay for damages to a hotel room, settlement for infringement claims, or even to post bail following an arrest. Issuing "rush" checks to cover emergency situations is a common practice within most A&R administration departments. In addition, union payments required by the American Federation of Musicians (AFM) for instrumentalists and the American Federation of Television and Radio Artists (AFTRA) for vocalists are initiated and tracked by the A&R administration department.

Copyright

As the album nears the mastering stage and the A&R and production departments have an established track listing of songs and timings, the copyright department begins the process of securing the various licenses required by the publishers who own or control the compositions. A mechanical license sets forth the terms and conditions by which record companies pay the publishers for using their music. Each song is paid per use, per recording, in accordance with the Copyright Act. Mechanical royalties were first acknowledged by the 1909 Copyright Law, which referred to devices "mechanically reproducing sound," such as the perforated rolls used in player pianos. New technology has given rise to additional types of licenses that are required when record companies or other music licensees plan to release music for sale to the public. Digital phonorecord deliveries, or DPDs, are recordings that are downloaded from various online sites such as iTunes, Rhapsody, Musicmatch, and Napster. Licensing a DPD is similar to the mechanical licensing of a CD, except that the full statutory rate is in effect for all downloaded compositions subject to contracts after June 22nd, 1995, irrespective of the terms in a recording agreement. Mechanical licensing rates for physical sound carriers such as CDs can range from the controlled compositions that are subject to the language in the artist's recording agreement if he or she is also the songwriter, to the current statutory rate, which is 9.1 cents per song under five minutes. Songs over five minutes in duration are currently calculated at a rate of 1.75 cents per minute (or fraction thereof, rounded up) of playing time based on the "long song" statutory rate formula. This rate will be in effect until December 31st, 2012. Ringtones, the downloaded recordings that play when a cell phone rings, as well as ring back or so-called "answer" tones, are licensed by either the copyright department at a record company, or directly by a third party mobile aggregator or provider such as Verizon, AT&T, Sprint, T-Mobile, Cingular, or Nextel. The business affairs department at a record company is also involved in the licensing of their master recordings when the ringtones are processed through a third party company. A ringtone license for the composition is also similar to a physical mechanical license, however a recent ruling has set the royalty rate for ringtones at 24 cents per copy. For songs that a consumer enjoys through a limited download (temporary, "times-out", or has a set number of listenings), or as an on-demand stream (like a radio station whereby the consumer controls the playlist), the royalty rates are 8.5% of the retail price for usages prior to December 31st, 2007, and 10.5% for all usages thereafter. To begin the mechanical licensing process, it is necessary to clear the publishing information on each song of the album. This clearance involves securing ownership information from the publishers, or permission to use a song on a recording for the first time. Major record companies often have a separate division within the copyright department to do this research, prepare the label copy from which a CD's liner notes are based, and provide the technology department with any song information that they need to assign an ISRC number (an international recording code, similar to the ISBN code in books), apply digital watermarking security, or format into MP3 of other codecs for digital distribution and archiving In addition to ascertaining the proper publishing credit and percentage of ownership, it is also necessary to clear any samples which have been included in the recording. Sampling is the use of a song within another song, often mixed into a recording as a phrase or bass-line in the new composition. This type of usage requires the permission of the publisher for the song rights, and of the record company for the master recording rights The majority of artists who use samples retain the services of a sample clearing agency to approach the publishers and other record companies for permission, and to obtain the most favorable rate considerations when licensing their music. The use of a sample almost always involves paying an advance to the publisher. Publishers also work with the copyright department to ensure that their sampled song is licensed either as a new work based on the song using the sample (copyright participation), or separately as the previously existing work (income participation).

In instances in which the artist performs the melody of another song without using the original recording, the usage is called an interpolation. This would be licensed in the same manner as a sample without the necessity of clearing the master recording rights.

Mechanical licenses can come in many forms: those issued by the record company, the publisher's own license, or a license from the publisher's licensing agent such as the Harry Fox Agency. An artist who also writes his or her own songs would usually be licensed via his or her artist agreement with the record company. Most artist agreements contain information which controls the amount an artist/writer can be paid on mechanical royalties well as language stating that the agreement constitutes a mechanical license. The average amount paid to a recording artist/songwriter is 68 cents per album for mechanical royalties, which would be expressed in the recording agreement as 75% of the statutory rate per song with a ten song cap. Although negotiable, this cap alludes to the idea that ten is the average number of songs recorded on a compact disk. This rate is calculated based on the current statutory rate of ($.091) reduced to 75% of the amount ($.0682) multiplied by a ten song allowance cap ($.682). Variations to this rate exist depending on the circumstances of each negotiated artist agreement. For some, it is advantageous to publish their songs with the record company's affiliated publishing company. A higher mechanical royalty rate is typically offered by the record company as an inducement to do this.

Another provision of the artist agreement, which is administered by the copyright department, is the right to reduce mechanical royalties for albums which have been re-positioned to a different sales category. The copyright department is contacted by the sales department several times during the year to inform them of the albums which have been repositioned from top line to budget at the retailers. The budget albums are often called "cut-outs" since the package has been altered to deter retail sales at the full price, and they are often placed in a different location within the record store. The copyright department researches the mechanical royalty rates for these budget albums, and lowers the amount on controlled songs written and performed by the artist in accordance with the recording agreement.

The language in the recording agreement usually states that the record company may pay 3/4 of the current mechanical royalty rate on controlled compositions (written and performed by the artist) when an album is moved to the budget category. The rationale is that the album is now sold for less money, therefore the copyright expense to the record company should be adjusted down from the rate fixed at the time of release.

Major record companies owning a large number of master recordings often put together compilation recordings, re-issues, and anthologies to further exploit their back catalog of music. Since most of these projects are extremely budget-sensitive, the copyright department must make all efforts to secure reduced rates from the publishers whose songs are used, while the rights and clearances department works on licensing the master rights.

Copyright royalty rate considerations are usually only granted in the following situations: budget-priced releases, a large ownership percentage of the album by one publisher, samples or medley usages, or a charity album whereby the profits are donated.

The copyright department is also responsible for negotiating synchronization licenses for the music used on all commercial videos. The synchronization license is usually contingent upon an advance or "fixing fee" paid to the publisher. Most licenses expire after seven years, and are paid based on a negotiated rate (usually 10 to 12 cents per song) as opposed to the statutory rate. Unlike the era of VHS tapes, today's synchronization licenses for DVDs are often combined with quote options for free and cable TV, video-on-demand, and mobile video, and may include provisions for multiple song uses in menus and chapter stops, online streaming, and promotional trailers,

The U.S. Library of Congress requires all record manufacturers to deposit with it two copies of the best edition of each album within three months after the date of publication. The deposit is usually sent when registering the copyright of the sound recording with the Copyright Office. This process is assumed by the business affairs department of a record company, most often by the copyright department.

Rights and Clearances

The division of business affairs most often referred to as rights and clearances has many responsibilities directly affecting how a record company uses the sound recordings of others, as well as how they exploit their own catalog. Generally, the rights and clearances department handles the issues involved with the licensing of master sound recordings, while the copyright department is responsible for the licenses relating to the publishing ownership of each composition used on a sound recording. The rights and clearances department may be involved with projects ranging from researching the provisions of a contract for the licensing requests of their company's foreign affiliates, to retaining the services of the video production companies who produce promotional videos.

Market research and sales histories show that some recordings sell better abroad than in the United States. When an international division of a major record company wants to release an album by an artist who signed his or her recording contract in the United States, the rights and clearances department is contacted to research the specifics regarding foreign exploitation. Sometimes the record company requesting clearance is unrelated to the U.S. repertoire owner, which could happen when a compilation album is being created or an anthology is considered for an artist who has changed recording labels over the years.

Promotional videos, which are destined for online streaming or music television channels such as MTV or VH1, are created by the artists working with a video production company, which is contracted by the rights and clearances department. The scheduling of the video shoot is initiated by the marketing department, which works to create the most effective media "buzz" in conjunction with an album's release date. The expenses associated with promotional videos are usually shared evenly by the artist and record company, as stated in the artist's recording agreement. Additional licensing is secured for the use of promotional video clips on television shows. For example, a guest artist might show a music video clip as part of his or her appearance on a late-night talk show. The rights and clearances department will have granted a license, usually gratis (without a fee), to the broadcasting company prior to the air date.

The making of a compilation album such as *The Best of the 70's,* or a soundtrack to a movie may require the use or "licensing in" of other record companies' masters. Similar to the handling of requests of a company's foreign affiliates, the rights and clearances department has to detail the music usage in their request for domestic releases, working with the department releasing the compilation to determine if the quotes fit within the recording budget. It is not uncommon to have last minute substitutions for songs that are prohibitively expensive to use.

Agreements involving guest artists from another record company appearing on an album are also handled by the rights and clearances department. These agreements, called side-man clearances, are standard in the record industry and are usually conditioned upon the guest artist and her record company receiving the proper courtesy credits.

As previously mentioned, albums with failing sales are often repositioned into the "midline" or "budget" category. Although many departments are affected by such a change, it is the rights and clearances department that first researched the record company's right to do so in response to a recommendation from the sales department.

Archived and "re-discovered" master recordings, as well as other repertoire used on various compilations, lend themselves to unique licensing terms which are not always governed by a standard agreement. Albums being considered for repositioning may have waning sales due to their age, and may be subject to artist agreements which have since been amended. For these reasons, the rights and clearances department undertakes considerable research to interpret the provisions of past and present contracts for physical audio and video releases, as well as existing rights or the need for a contract amendment covering digital rights.

The licensing out of a record company's catalog represents an income source and is generally administered by a division called special products. Although not a part of the business affairs department, special products may work with the rights and clearances department to conduct business with other record companies.

Examples of situations covered by special products include the use of a recording in a film, on another record company's compilation album, or as an enhancement to a business meeting or seminar. The scope of usage for a special products project could range from a college student film to a major motion picture or multi-platinum compilation album. Price quotes to use a song can range from gratis (free) to many thousands of dollars, depending on the type, size, and frequency of use. For a detailed discussion of special products, see Chapter IX.

Record clubs are also major repertoire users who buy the rights to successful albums for re-release at a discount through mail-order channels. Record clubs may purchase finished products or manufacture their own using the masters and films from various record companies to reproduce the audio and artwork. Interestingly, the two major record clubs in the United States, Columbia House and BMG Direct, have merged into one company called Song BMG Direct. Regarding royalty rates, the historic position that record clubs sales are discount products that warrant reduced mechanical and artist royalties continues today for many successful releases.

Most major record companies will not grant record clubs the right to release their albums within three months of the original release to reduce the impact the record clubs might have on their retail sales. Some singles are even offered as digital downloads through companies like iTunes prior to their physical release. Certain artists have negotiated a provision in their recording agreement which denies record clubs the right to release their recordings at all. Such agreements require careful research and tracking, especially when dealing with hundreds of releases each year.

Contract Administration

As record companies sign and drop new artists, the need to follow the options and other provisions within their recording agreements becomes increasingly complicated. In addition to timely and accurate record keeping, the archiving and maintenance of files is an important process carried out by the contract administration department.

One key role of a contract administrator is to maintain and update a roster of artists currently active on each label within a record company. This important roster is circulated to all of the executives who have dealings with the artists. The roster also identifies who the record company has recently signed, as well as which artists have been released from their agreement. Most artists who have been dropped receive some money for their departure based on a "pay or play" provision of their recording agreement.

The contract administration department must also track all of the option periods of the recording artists and appraise the appropriate department heads when a business decision must be made. Most new artist deals commit to only one album at a time, but give the record company the right to at least eight optional albums, at its election, as the artist's career progresses. Artists generally receive royalty rate escalations (typically .5 to 1%) for each optional album, as well as an increase based upon certain sales plateaus. The points at which a record sells 500,000 units (gold) and 1,000,000 units (platinum) are the most common plateaus at which an artist realizes a royalty rate increase. The decision whether or not to continue releasing an artist's works is usually made by the label president, as a result of careful evaluations made in conjunction with the sales, finance and business affairs departments.

When a dispute, inquiry, or amendment is being negotiated, the first item to be researched is the original underlying agreement which contains the signatures of the parties involved. The ability to retrieve such information is crucial to the business being conducted within all record companies. The contract administration department archives and updates the agreements with two objectives in mind: ease of retrieval and preservation.

The ability to find information quickly within a vast archive of files is especially challenging for large record companies that have offices at numerous locations. The same major cities that are key music industry hubs are also notoriously short of storage space. Therefore, many record companies ship files to off-site storage facilities that are leased to help ease overcrowding. Regarding preservation, paper files are destined to deteriorate, especially older acid stock papers and thermal faxes. To address this problem, most contract administrators use computer software that allows them to scan and search documents. While additional security issues may arise, the information that is electronically stored is also able to be saved onto digital disks such as DVD, CD-R, and CD-ROM, and is often backed up on the company's computer server. The backbone of the company's information about its recording deals is maintained by the contract administration department.

Legal

The legal department works closely with the business affairs and technology departments to help draft agreements and address any claims which are levied against the company. Some record companies combine legal and business affairs into one department, due to the extent of involvement of the legal department with business proceedings. The projects handled by the legal department can be very diverse and often involve time-sensitive issues responding to legal claims. To keep track of each lawyer's projects, a confidential legal status report is maintained and distributed internally to employees who may benefit from such information.

Virtually every deal made within the record company involves the legal department in some way. Typically, the vice president(s) of legal or business affairs negotiate under the direction of the senior vice president who handles all of the deals, sometimes in conjunction with an outside law form. As deals are being negotiated, the legal department prepares the drafts, negotiates the changes, and ultimately follows through on securing fully-executed agreements. The department is also consulted for advice regarding matters not easily covered by the company's standard boiler-plate language, as well as all situations which may involve a lawsuit.

The legal department has a structure similar to most business affairs departments: a senior vice president supervising vice presidents and staff lawyers, who may be assisted by paralegals, assistants, and legal interns. In addition to in-house personnel, the outside law firms hired to assist with litigation and federal compliance matters are often kept on a retainer by the company.

The responsibilities of a record company's legal department include: litigation which is not assigned to outside counsel; drafting recording and video agreements; copyright infringement claims (including the publishing and master use issues involved with sampling); distribution deals; third party licensing; merchandising; digital rights, cases involving antitrust issues; trademark and patent issues; asset purchase agreements; employee labor agreements; audit settlements; and compliance with federal and state laws, such as the requirements by the Federal Trade Commission. Other projects may be included as well, especially from the larger record companies whose size allows them the opportunity to negotiate certain service agreements. For example, the legal department may review the cash management agreement with the company's bank, or negotiate a better calling plan with their long distance telephone carrier. Even the computer software used within the company is subject to a site-license that may have required a negotiation to best fit the needs of the licensor and licensee.

Record companies often have different regional divisions located across the United States and abroad. As such, the laws governing each location affect the way in which business is conducted, as well as the guidelines for forming and maintaining corporations. The legal department often assists with the articles of incorporation for new companies and renews existing corporate charters as needed. The department may also work with the finance department on issues involving taxation.

It would be difficult for a record company, whether it is a small independent or one of the four majors, to conduct business without creating a legal department or contracting the outside services of a lawyer. The impact of some business decisions can affect a record company for many years. Having the legal expertise upon which to base those decisions can make the difference between a failing business and holding a successful market share within the industry.

Business affairs may not be the department people think of when they see the high-profile lifestyles of record company executives as portrayed by the media. In fact, it may not occur to everyone that the business affairs department acts essentially as a hub from which most of the record company operates. The importance of this department is clear, as it finalizes the agreements for all of the recording artists signed to the record label. In addition, this department deals with a wide range of other company projects. For a major record company, the issues addressed by the business affairs department on a regular basis include those listed for the legal department, as well as recording budgets, branded advertising deals, record club deals, artist/writer co-publishing inducement deals, union negotiations, joint venture deals with other labels, foreign licensees, and inter-company operations and policies. Being involved with a broad spectrum of negotiations and contracts, business affairs executives are generally in the business of deciding what to hold and what to release. Record companies rely on their business affairs departments for decisions leading to the growth and maintenance of their business in an ever-changing industry.

Chapter 12

Radio 2009

Max Horowitz

Max Horowitz is President of Crossover Media, Inc., a promotions and marketing company serving record labels, production companies, and individual music artists, and is a Peabody award-winning radio producer.

INTRODUCTION

Unlike the objective images we get from the various forms of visual media, radio is unique in that it provides subjective images for each individual. By listening and not watching, the mind creates its own distinct images in what one famous DJ called the: 'theatre of the mind.' The term 'Broadcasting' was originally used in the field of agriculture and farming, referring to the scattering of seeds. Later used to describe radio and television as 'the transmission of airborne electromagnetic waves from antenna to antenna,' today broadcasting extends to various forms of transmission delivered to users via antenna, cable, or satellite. Furthermore, today's online music experience has arguably changed the very definition of radio to now include all media choices via web and mobile devices. This chapter presents an historical chronology of radio in the U.S., and includes a brief overview of the vast radio landscape in today's multimedia environment.

From 1920 to the mid-1950's, network radio was the dominant form of home entertainment in the U.S. The introduction of television in the mid-1950's was an enormous threat to radio, as television could offer sound and pictures compared to sound only on the radio. Radio managed to survive the introduction of television, and then once again thrive. Due in large part to localism and format narrowcasting, but even more so to portability via pre-installed automobile radios and the transistor, radio had advantages over television. Each decade provided new financial impetus and incentives for the medium whether it was Top 40 and Rock and Roll in the 1960's, the mass introduction of FM in the 70's, or 'broadcast deregulation' and narrowcasting in the 80's which created the group radio boom of the 90's. Post 2000, terrestrial (on-air) radio advertising has leveled off with more media choices than ever competing for both traditional and online dollars.

Traditional terrestrial radio stations fall into one of two categories. Either, AM (amplitude modulation) or FM (frequency modulation), commercial or non-commercial, and local or network.

An AM radio transmission is produced by varying the amplitude (strength) of the signal broadcast while its frequency (repeated wave cycles) remains constant. This method is good for broadcasting long distances but produces a sonically unsophisticated signal. Conversely with FM, it is the frequency that is varied producing a signal which does not travel as far as with AM, but has a superior sound quality. Commercial radio, which began in the 1920's, used AM. Although FM was invented in the 1930's, it was not fully implemented until decades later. The business or funding model for a terrestrial commercial radio station is to sell advertising. Non-commercial stations rely on public money primarily in the form of listener contributions collected during fund drives to generate revenue. Non-comm's also raise cash by selling underwriting announcements, the public radio variation on advertising. Unlike commercials, underwriting spots omit any 'call to action,' to purchase, and some public stations also receive financial support via government and foundation grants.

Local stations serve one market, community or region, whereas a 'Radio Network' provides programming and services for a group of local stations.

THE HISTORY OF RADIO

There are 3 fundamental forces in nature that all other forces are derived from: the 'electromagnetic force,' the 'nuclear force,' and the 'gravitational force.' Scientists in the early 19th century such as the German physicist Heinrich Hertz proposed that electricity and magnetism were linked, and by modulating (changing) radio wave properties such as amplitude and frequency, demonstrated that a transmission can be propagated. For this accomplishment, the International System of Units labeled the standard measurement of frequency as 'hertz.' 1 hertz (Hz) = one wave cycle per second, and measurements in multiples such as Kilohertz (kHz), megahertz (MHz), and gigahertz (GHz) accordingly are at a higher frequency (pitch) and sound higher.

There are multiple claims as to who the inventor of radio really is. Guglielmo Marconi the 1909 Nobel Prize winner who accepts credit for the invention. However others such as Nikola Tesla, who contributed to the fields of robotics, ballistics, computer science, nuclear and theoretical physics, and was the first to patent a means to reliably produce radio frequencies, was also essential to the invention. Additionally, scientists such as Thomas Edison, 'The Wizard of Menlo Park,' credited with the development of voice transmission, and Lee De Forest, the father of the electronic age, and inventor the 'Audion amplifier' were also integral to the process.

Wireless Telegraphy

The history of Radio includes 4 distinct periods: Wireless Telegraphy, The Golden Age of Radio, Post-TV/Pre-Internet, and Streaming. Hertz's discovery led to Samuel Morse's wired telegraph in the 1830s, which eventually became the worldwide standard for distributing up-to-the-minute news and sports reporting. The device evolved into early wireless. Developed by Marconi into the world's first transatlantic radio service, he refused to communicate with non-Marconi equipped ships and eventually created the first radio monopoly by acquiring the United Wireless Telegraph Company, dramatically increasing his number of land stations and ship installations.

Early radio firsts include: the transmission of human speech, which was made on Christmas Eve in 1900, the first broadcast of voice and music heard together in 1906, and the first weather broadcasts made by The U.S. Agriculture Department in 1912. Also in 1912, wireless communications helped save lives during the tragedy that befell the S.S. Titanic. During the disaster in which the luxury passenger liner hit an iceberg and sunk in the North Atlantic, nearby ships equipped with wireless radio sets were able to rescue passengers, and conversely the lack of onboard radio operations on other ships in the area were rendered powerless to help in the rescue resulting in unnecessary deaths. From that point forward, all ships would maintain radio operators at all times, and the U.S. Navy began to equip their entire fleet with transmitters, and set up an extensive chain of land based coastal stations for ships to communicate with.

The earliest radio transmitters were 'spark-gap.' Hertz was the first to use it in 1888, but spark gap was the product of Marconi, Tesla, and others. Simple, low power devices, Marconi created a monopoly providing communications and nightly news summaries on both sides of the Atlantic, via spark-gap. Spark-gap was eventually replaced by 'continuous wave,' transmitters which improved transmission by using mechanical alternators, and later the high frequency oscillating vacuum-tube. In those days, a radio oscillator was a two-electrode circuit that produced repetitive signals to flow through a filament called a 'diode.' In 1907, Lee De Forest developed a three-electrode circuit triode called the 'Audion.' Not strictly a vacuum tube, it was the first electrical amplification device, and in 1920, the London based Chelmsford Marconi factory transmitted the first entertainment radio broadcasts in the United Kingdom using a vacuum-tube transmitter. Although Tesla and Edison were critical of the early vacuum-tube technology, it's development led to the commercialization of radio, television, radar, hi-fi sound, telephone, and the computer. Eventually, the vacuum-tube set was replaced with transistors for amplification.

The Golden Age of Radio

'The Golden Age of Radio' refers to the period in radio history between 1920 and the mid 1950's, and prior to 1920 most broadcasting was experimental and happened in the laboratory. In 1920, KDKA Pittsburgh aired the first commercial radio broadcast, and later that year covered the presidential election returns from a shack located on the roof of the Westinghouse building in East Pittsburgh. Founded in 1886 as an 'air brake' company making braking systems for railroad trains, Westinghouse obtained the first patent for AC (alternating-current) transmission from their staff engineer Nikola Tesla. With the help of the General Electric (GE) Company and the United Fruit Company, Westinghouse co-founded Radio Corporation of America (RCA) in 1919. Originally just a logo, RCA became one of the largest holding companies in the world owning broadcast equipment and properties. Led by General Manager David Sarnoff, in many ways the story of RCA is the story of Sarnoff, whose drive, ambition, and business acumen led to RCA's dominance.

During the same period, the American Telephone and Telegraph (AT&T) Corporation, which manufactured transmitters and antennas, was developing voice and music transmissions for a group of interconnected radio stations. Anchored by their flagship WEAF in New York City, AT&T established the first national radio network in the U.S. between 1922-1926, and among other important events broadcast the opening of 1923 Congress and 1924 Democratic National Convention. GE, Westinghouse, and RCA responded by forming their own network but, unable to match AT&T, bought out AT&T's network operations and formed the National Broadcasting Company (NBC) and a monopoly of the radio industry.

With 50% owned by RCA, 30% by GE and 20% by Westinghouse, NBC's two networks, 'Red' (sponsored entertainment and music) and 'Blue' (non-sponsored news and cultural programs) were the pinnacle of American radio. Home to many of the most popular programs of the day, NBC appealed to families during the depression, emphasizing optimism and traditional values. With their 40 million listeners, NBC was responsible for dramatically increasing their sponsors' revenue using on-air advertising, as NBC stars such as Al Jolson, Bob Hope, Jack Benny, Edgar Bergen, and Fred Allen, were faithfully listened to nation-wide. This, of course, all came to an abrupt end during the 1950's, as stars left radio for the new medium of television.

In 1927, Arthur Judson, then manager of the New York Philharmonic and Philadelphia Orchestra, had also created a 16-station radio network called United Independent Broadcasters. In 1928, Judson teamed with William Paley to create CBS (Columbia Broadcasting System). Growing to 47 stations including a New York affiliate, they were the first to give affiliate stations free programs in exchange for ad time during their broadcast day, which he then sold to national advertisers. The other significant network of the day, the Mutual Broadcasting System included flagship stations: WOR in New York, WGN in Chicago, WLW in Cincinnati, and WXYZ in Detroit, as well as a large number of affiliate stations in rural markets. Like NBC and CBS, Mutual carried popular programs of the day such as the Lone Ranger, and The Green Hornet, but unlike the other two larger networks, did not own and operate their stations, nor did they have any production studios or centralized corporate owners.

Before radio advertising took hold, stations were either owned by electronics manufacturers who made radios, department stores who sold radios, or by newspapers that used radio as a way of expressing their opinions. The first 'radio commercial spot' was broadcast in 1922, and paid for by the Queensboro Corp. of New York who spent $100 for a 10-minute message promoting the sale of apartments on Long Island.

Headquartered in Washington, D.C., the NAB (National Association of Broadcasters) is a U.S. trade association that advocates on behalf of over 8,300 radio and television stations and networks before Congress, the FCC and the Courts. Formed in 1922 to work for favorable spectrum allocation (the distribution of frequencies), the NAB's efforts led to the Radio Act of 1927 creating legislation for station licensing and frequency allotment. Early on, NAB founders also focused broadcaster licensing and in working out these details with ASCAP and other licensing organizations, they eventually became the chief business representative and governmental lobby representing the broadcasting industry. Today, the NAB follows FCC activities and legislation, as well as economic, legal, and social trends that might affect the industry.

Radio grew by leaps and bounds during the 1920's and '30's, so much so that The Associated Press, fearing the threat that broadcasts posed to newspaper sales, greatly restricted it's use of radio reports between 1922 to 1939 in what became known as the 'Press-Radio War.'

The FCC (Federal Communications Commission) established by the U.S. Communications Act of 1934 was the successor to the Federal Radio Commission. Composed of a Chairman and 4 additional Commissioners appointed by the President and confirmed for five-year terms by the Senate, only three of the five may be of the same political party, and commissioners cannot have a financial interest in any FCC related business. Charged with regulating radio and television broadcasting, they also oversee all interstate wire, satellite and cable communications, as well as all international communications that originate or terminate in the U.S.

Although the 1930's brought the introduction of FM, the technology was not fully implemented until the 1960's as RCA lobbied the FCC to prevent the implementation of FM radios. FM, which spaces channels 20 times further apart than AM, requires a wider frequency range therefore producing a stronger signal to interference ratio and better tuning. Invented by Edwin H. Armstrong as a way of overcoming static problems present on AM, the original service began in the early 1940s, but RCA and Sarnoff, Armstrong's employer at the time, scuttled the effort by getting the FCC to move FM's spectrum from 42-50 MHz, to 88-108 MHz. RCA wanted to utilize the spectrum for their new television channels, and the decision rendered all Armstrong-era FM sets useless overnight. By doing so, the FCC protected RCA's AM-radio stranglehold, and set FM back by decades. Adding insult to injury, RCA sought and won the patent fight for the invention of FM in court against Armstrong, who was then unable to claim any royalties on his own invention.

From its inception the FCC had studied the monopolistic effects of the radio industry and put new limitations on the networks including a limit on the amount of network time local affiliates were required to air, as the networks could demand as much airtime as it wanted from an affiliate. They also limited the network practice of serving as both agent and employer for their radio artists, which was a clear conflict of interest. With respect to NBC, the FCC found that the company, along with their owned-and-operated stations, so dominated radio audiences, affiliates, and advertising dollars that they needed to divest themselves of one of the networks. After some legal battling, RCA was forced to sell their Blue network to Lifesavers magnate Edward J. Noble in 1943, which was then resold and eventually became ABC (American Broadcasting Company) in 1944.

By 1940, with the rise of the movie industry, radio shifted from music and local talk programs adopting a more sophisticated 'audio theater' format. With a network lineup which included adventure, comedy, drama, horror, mystery, musical variety, and romance serials, the period is most vividly remembered for its famous fragments and highlighted by legendary broadcast moments such as Orson Welles's *The War of the Worlds* broadcast, the Dragnet theme, and the "Hi-Yo, Silver!" call of the Lone Ranger.

Local Top 40

The idea of 'Top 40' was originally a response to the mid 1950's 'audience crisis.' As listeners were switching over from radio to television in droves, the loss in audience and sponsors prompted radio owners to offer something not available on television: short form programming. 1950's television programs consisted of long form dramas and soap operas, and Top 40 was thought to be the logical way to compete. With 3-minute songs and the first generation of star disk jockeys, Top 40 connected with listeners and 'hit parade' music marketing was born. According to legend, Todd Storz created Top 40 in Omaha in 1955. After observing customers at a bar jukebox playing the same handful of songs over and over again, Storz got the idea for a radio 'playlist,' and like a jukebox would ensure that listeners always hear the most popular songs regardless of what time of the day they tuned in.

Back then jukebox selections ranged anywhere from country & western, to pop, rock & roll, instrumentals, and novelty songs, with no emphasis on genre or artist, just the top 40 songs that people wanted to hear.

Many credit Top 40 DJ Alan Freed for coining and popularizing the term 'Rock and Roll,' as well as being a pioneer for racial integration during a period of intense racial strife in America. In the 1956 film 'Rock Rock Rock,' Freed unwittingly described Top 40 radio when he says in the film that: "rock and roll is a river of music that has absorbed many streams: rhythm and blues, jazz, rag time, cowboy songs, country songs, and folk songs. All have contributed to the Big Beat." Freed is also significant and relevant still today as his career was abruptly ended amidst accusations of accepting "payola," money paid by a label or distributor to a station DJ or executive to play specific records. Though payola was not illegal and somewhat commonplace during this period, Freed was singled out and fired from WINS in New York. In 1960 payola was made illegal, but by no means did that stop the practice which continues to this day.

One could say that 1960's Top 40 radio and the 'Transistor Radio' were equally dependant on each other's success. The evolution of the vacuum tube amplifier to the transistor, allowed for a truly portable radio that could fit into the listeners pocket, and required nothing more than flashlight batteries to operate. Before the transistor, the typical vacuum tube radio of the fifties was the size of a lunchbox and contained several heavy batteries. The transistor on the other hand weighed less than half a pound, and before earphones came with the radio, listeners often held the device with the speaker directly against their ear, to minimize the tinny sound. In 1954 with a cost of about $50, roughly $500 in today's dollars, about 150,000 units were sold in the U.S., but the transistor did not achieve mass popularity until the mid 1960's as radios flooded in from Hong Kong. After a remarkable run, sales have dramatically declined due to today's variety of digital listening devices. But transistor radios are still used for news radio and emergency information.

The 1960's Top 40 sound was characterized by three minute songs spun by nervous sounding DJ's. Developed by Gordon McLendon, the first DJ to air jingles on the radio, Top 40 was developed as an open, promotion driven format, stressing music and very little talk. The first Top 40 station can be traced back to 1956 when, due to weak ratings, KHJ/930AM/Boss Top 40 Radio was born in Los Angeles. The legendary RKO property flipped from it's then easy listening format and quickly went from being a failure to the #1 station in Los Angeles and the first real 'rock and roll station' in America. The format continued to build through the late 50's and in 1959 the Musicradio 77 (WABC, New York) era began which further elevated and legitimized this new format. Committed to a full-time Top 40 schedule and upbeat personalities, DJ's spun current pop records and mixed in some MOR (middle of the road), jazz, novelty songs and show tunes. Although its early days were humble ones, WABC became the #1 radio station in New York by late 1962. Their dominance was due in part to the timing of Top 40, in part to the station's 50,000-watt signal, which reached a huge chunk of New York City's suburban population, but most of the credit goes to their Program Director, Radio Hall of Famer Rick Sklar. One of Top 40's pioneering architects, Sklar is famous for programming the shortest playlist in history with the number one song heard almost every hour, all introduced by WABC superstar DJ's. Top 40 grew throughout the 1960's, as stations around the country starting cloning the format, and as network affiliate stations started becoming more reluctant to break from their local programming.

FM

As discussed earlier, FM, which was invented in the 1930's, had a much better sound compared to AM, but was suppressed by RCA during the development of television, and relegated to audio enthusiasts until the 1960's. Eventually broadcasts of classical music and educational programming in large cities started to pop up, and the more prosperous AM stations also acquired FM licenses so they could simulcast their AM signals on FM. By the late 60s, FM got an unexpected break as the FCC began prohibiting simulcasting, and stations needed to quickly fill the vacated programming. The freeform FM 'Progressive' format was there to fill the void as desperate station owners now developed original programming with longer songs that were not limited to hits. Newer, more adventurous artists normally not heard were now featured along with deep album cuts in an eclectic format where stations played everything from folk to hard rock, with a bit of Jazz fusion thrown in the mix. As progressive expanded through the 70s stations began to specialize more eventually becoming the new AOR (Album Oriented Radio). The eclectic or progressive format has never completely died, and today it is most closely exemplified 'online' and in certain 'college' radio formats.

AOR

By the mid 1970's music radio reflected the growth in album sales over singles, but it wasn't until 1978 that listenership exceeded AM. Virtually all this growth on FM was due to AOR's commercial rock format, which showcased artists such as Rush, AC/DC, Tom Petty, and Van Halen. As more people acquired FM radios and station market share and advertising rates increased, the occasional folk, jazz, and blues selections became more rare, and most black artists were eliminated from playlists. The success created new pressures to make more and more revenue and new implementations such as the 'clock' format (ratio of music to commercial spots each hour) and 'song rotation' (number of times a song is played per day or week) were adopted.

Disco

The name 'Disco' evolved out of the dance club scene of the 1960's known as discothèques, which means disc library. The disco radio format grew out of the R&B, funk, and soul influences spawned from the Motown sound and FM Progressive radio, where artists such as Stevie Wonder, War, and Sly Stone were championed. The city of Philadelphia is credited with creating the 'post-Motown soul' sound which later became known as disco. Typified by percussion, lavish orchestration, syncopated bass and drum parts, electronic keyboards, wah-wah and phased guitar, backing vocals, and string and horn instrumental fills, and with a great beat for dancing, the groove was supported by the prominent 'open and close' hi-hat style of drumming.

The first real disco radio hit came in 1973-74 with the Hues Corporation million-seller 'Rock The Boat,' rising to #1 on U.S. sales and radio charts. Barry White's 'Love's Theme' by the Love Unlimited Orchestra followed soon after as a chart-topper, and artists such as Gloria Gaynor, The Jackson 5, Van McCoy, and Donna Summer all contributed to bringing disco to mainstream radio. Popularity dramatically grew around 1977 with the release and aftermath of the groundbreaking movie: 'Saturday Night Fever.' Starring John Travolta, the film significantly raised disco's profile around the world, and made Travolta a huge movie star. Brilliantly showcasing not only the music and dancing, but also the disco subculture, clothing, and sexual promiscuity, the score, which features several songs by the Bee Gees, was a total departure for the group, who until that time recorded mainly soft-pop songs. The soundtrack became the best selling ever, and was one of the first instances of a soundtrack single being used to promote a film on the radio prior to its release. At its height, disco became so pervasive that it inspired parodies on U.S radio. One notable example was the song: 'Disco Duck,' conceived by radio DJ Rick Dees, who was forbidden to play this odd song on the air by his station management citing a conflict of interest. Later fired on-the-spot for talking about it on air, Disco Duck still went on to sell over two million copies and reached number 1 on Billboard's Hot 100 chart in the Fall of 1976. Interestingly, although the song was heard in the 'Saturday Night Fever' film, it was not included in the soundtrack, depriving Dees of any revenue and the Grammy award. The formats peak came around 1978 when WKTU in New York abruptly dropped its adult contemporary format in favor of the dance format, unseating #1 WABC practically overnight by gaining 11% additional market share.

The official end of disco was played out in an ugly 1979 display called: 'Disco Demolition Night,' as WLUP radio personality Steve Dahl who, after destroying disco records on his show, created and promoted this event during a twilight doubleheader baseball game at Comiskey Park. Also known also as 'Disco Sucks Night,' the stunt turned into total mayhem as the promotion drew non-baseball fans, and White Sox management hoping to draw an additional 5,000 people for the game, instead got 50,000. People were climbing the walls and fences to get into the stadium before the first game started. Mike Veeck, son of then-White Sox owner Bill Veeck recalled the scent of marijuana in the stands, spectators dumping beer and throwing lit firecrackers on each other. Spectators were flinging their disco LP's (long playing records) like Frisbees often striking people, and as planned in between games, Dahl along with bodyguards came out to center field with a box of disco records rigged to a mock bomb for demolition. When it exploded, the bomb ripped a hole in the outfield grass and thousands of fans ran onto the field in a mini-riot. The batting cage was destroyed, bases and chunks of the field were stolen, and after police cleared the stadium in riot gear, Detroit Tiger manager Sparky Anderson refused to field his team for the 2nd game citing safety concerns.

The evolution of disco radio in the 80's led to various 'Urban' formats, such as CHR (Contemporary Hit Radio) and 'Rhythmic Top 40.'

Group Radio

The onset of the 1980's and the Reagan administration marked a major shift in U.S. domestic policy, which included a more permissive shift favoring broadcasters. Starting with the relaxing of FCC monopoly regulations and restrictions to laws being downright ignored and not properly enforced, the mood eventually lead to a repeal of the Fairness Doctrine in 1987, a regulation which required broadcasters to present issues of public importance. According to the FCC, during this period radio and TV station ownership levels in U.S. cities were deemed local in reach (how big an area the market covers) and they thereby concluded that any local market is underserved by having only a limited number of broadcast stations. This decision allowed for the concentration of ownership in television, radio and on cable, similar to large-scale newspaper ownership. The environment fueled massive buying and selling of stations as broadcasters could purchase properties based on nothing more than a desire to do so in any particular market, as opposed to whether there was any community need, balance, or fairness. As a result, the number of U.S. radio properties swelled to 12,000 during the decade with almost half of all operating stations changing hands. Station consolidation followed, with significant changes that focused on cost cutting including voice tracked automation replacing live DJ's, as well as less news and public affairs programming which provide a community service but don't generate any revenue.

Earlier in this book the concept of oligopoly was discussed, which can be defined as a persistent market situation with only a few providers. Today, with little competition, the seven media conglomerates (Disney, CBS, Time Warner, News Corp, Bertelsmann, Viacom, General Electric) together own more than 90% of the total U.S. media market, creating an oligopoly in the media industry. After the Telecommunications Act of 1996 passed the U.S. Congress, concentration of media ownership only increased and large broadcast companies such as Clear Channel, Cumulus, and CBS Radio have fully saturated the country. At it's peak, Clear Channel had acquired over 1,200 radio stations, 30 television stations, and 9 XM Satellite channels, as well as a lucrative concert promotion and fixed advertising business in the U.S., among other international properties. Cumulus Media today owns toughly over 300 radio stations in 60 U.S. markets, and CBS Radio, formerly known as Infinity Broadcasting, owns just under 200 radio stations in over 20 states.

FORMATS

In the post-deregulation euphoria of the 1990's, competition for advertising dollars became particularly fierce and new formats started to super-serve listeners in a more focused and niche way. Stations now needed to pay closer attention and implement smart strategies in order to attain more market share. Aggressive music testing, focus groups, and call-out surveys, led to a new Top 40 with a more upbeat on air style, slick production, more station promotions, and an active morning show. Narrowcasting increased as new versions of AC (Adult Contemporary), Urban, Rock, and Country popped up with names like Hot, Main, Lite, Rhythmic, Alternative, Triple A, Americana, Modern, and Smooth Jazz.

AC

Presenting primarily established artists and songs, today's Adult Contemporary radio formats have a variety of sub genres including: Main, Hot, Light, Urban, Modern, and even Christian. Urban and Modern AC are genre based with Urban focusing on Hip Hop and R&B, and Modern on Rock. Main, Hot, and Light formats traditionally cater to the 25-54 listener demographic with Main and Hot playing primarily current songs while Light presents a mix of soft hits from the past. As the label indicates, Hot AC stations will spin more upbeat songs in a more active rotation as compared with Main, which generally takes longer to 'add' a song. Introducing new artists slowly, it can sometimes take weeks or months before Main AC will embrace a new song and give it enough airplay to really make a difference in record sales. 'Light' AC formats will spin their GOLD tracks in a low to moderate rotation.

Alternative Rock

AOR was king in the rock radio of the 1980's breaking bands like Rush, AC/DC, Tom Petty, and Van Halen, but after Nirvana, Pearl Jam and other similar bands broke a new rock format called 'Alternative' emerged. Born out of the 'rock and roll primitivism capital of the world,' Seattle, alternative, like the punk movement a decade before, started out as a rebellious idea committed to fighting the corporation and speaking truth to power. KISW was the radio station that broke AC/DC, and people like Chris Cornell, and Kurt Cobain, grew up listening to their raw aggression during the 80's. As the format grew sub genres called New Rock & Active Rock were narrowcast. New Rock stations played a format which included bands such as Metallica, Alice in Chains, Stone Temple Pilots, Guns 'N Roses, Soundgarden and Bush, and Active Rock skewed harder with Korn, Pantera, and Rage Against the Machine as examples. Both included some AOR gold staples like Led Zeppelin, Pink Floyd, and Jimi Hendrix in the mix. With huge record sales and radio play throughout the decade, the format eventually became what it had rebelled against, a business as usual mainstream format attached to its own success, competing for market share.

Commercial Triple A

Triple A (Adult Album Alternative) is a also a spin off from the AOR format of the late 70's and 1980's but closer to Modern AC than Alternative in sound. Early on it was more of an on the fringe and off of the mainstream format with a programming philosophy that mixed new rock artists with even some singer-songwriter and blues songs. This elevated status lead certain Triple A stations to bill themselves with slogans such as: 'World Class Rock,' 'Quality Rock', 'Finest Rock' etc., promoting the idea that the music is king. Generally speaking the song rotation is less active compared to Modern AC, and a successful Triple A artist may never make the Billboard sales chart, or get as much airplay as their pop counterparts with more of a focus on showcasing new artists that can eventually cross over.

Smooth Jazz

From the late 1960s until 1987, 94.7 in Los Angeles was the home of KMET, a very popular AOR station that broadcast to the greater Los Angeles, Orange County, and Riverside-San Bernardino areas. Sagging ratings during the 80's however prompted KMET's owner 'Metromedia' to flip the format in favor of an experimental format consisting of New Age and Contemporary Jazz music, called NAC (New Adult Contemporary). The new call letters were KTWV and the station soon became known as 'The Wave.' Focusing on new age instrumentals, they initially excluded vocals, but as the format grew across the U.S., the NAC sound eventually moved further away from its new age roots embracing contemporary jazz artists that had previously received only little attention on Jazz radio. Produced in a more commercial way as compared with straight ahead jazz, these artists found a home at NAC, which eventually renamed the format 'Smooth Jazz & Vocals,' then shortened to Smooth Jazz. Today, with a mix of smooth instrumentals and soft Urban AC leaning vocal tracks, the format is well represented in the major and secondary U.S. markets with 'The Wave' being perhaps the best known along with CD 101.9 in New York, KKSF in San Francisco, and WNUA in Chicago. For over a decade now, the company 'Broadcast Architecture' has been consulting with many of the Smooth Jazz stations providing research and strategies, as they have become an important part of the format.

Non-Commercial Radio

The FM dial positions between 88 and 92 were designated by the FCC for non-commercial radio which present programming not found on commercial stations, and the non-comm. revenue model relies not on advertising but on listener contributions, underwriting from corporations and small businesses, and on grant money. Presenting both news and music formats, stations are either owned by universities, foundations, or religious or community organizations, generally attracting a smaller audience as compared to commercial radio.

Dependant on their listeners rather than commercial advertisers, stations offer their communities more substance over style, and in particular markets have risen to become among the top rated in their market.
Non-comm. music formats include: Triple A, Americana, Blues, Folk, Jazz, World, and Classical music and generally include some news and information programming as well as specialty shows covering an eclectic mix of underrepresented music genres.

Non-Comm. Triple A also has a more community focused approach as compared with its commercial counterpart, presenting a more diverse sound that includes deeper album cuts, new artists, and more genre specialty shows primarily focused on singer songwriters, folk, blues, and world music. On Americana formats, 'twang is a good thang' and alternative country, folk, bluegrass and blues artists are showcased. With roots that date back to Elvis Presley's musical marriage of hillbilly and R&B, Americana's eclectic sound is reminiscent of old-time radio, and like Triple A, really took off during the 90s as a reaction to the highly polished sound of the mainstream rock, AC, and country formats of the 1980's.

With respect to Classical and Jazz radio, in the U.S. today there are under 20 commercial classical stations left, the rest being non-comms, and Jazz is now 100% non-commercial.

Today, there are over 500 College radio stations operating in the U.S., many of which are quite active and vibrant presenting an additional alternative to adult non-comms. The format has come a long way from it's humble beginnings in the 1960's, born out of the FCC issuing of class D licenses for ten-watt radio stations, a move intended to further the development of the then-new FM band. However, with the rise of FM in the 1970's and competition for channels intensifying, class D licenses ceased to be issued and college radio remained a 2nd class citizen until a dramatic change came in the mid 1980's with the AOR format. College stations led the way with AOR presenting new and creative programming, and proving to be the primary influence for alternative. Today, most college stations have been significantly upgraded in power. While many utilize faculty advisers to oversee programming, operations, and aspects involving the wider community, others are exclusively run by students. College programming generally offers the most eclectic and diversified music mix heard on terrestrial radio often paired with campus news and sports. College genres focus primarily on Rock, Hip-Hop, and RPM (Electronica), but stations now include Triple A, Americana, Blues, Folk, Jazz, World, and Classical programming in their mix and include plenty of specialty shows. The mission at college has always been to be on the cutting edge of exposing emerging artists and trends, but many stations today follow a very commercial approach with a strict music rotation, while others maintain a 'cacophony of randomness' strategy.

Arbitron

It is important to discuss Arbitron before we get to the section on Spanish Language Radio, because it pertains to audience demographics. From the beginning of commercial radio in the 1920's and 30's, advertising revenue has been its business model, and traditional advertising wisdom has always held that the price of a commercial radio spot is based on market size, ratings, daypart, length, and inventory. Arbitron is a U.S. radio audience research company that collects data for this purpose tracking consumer listening habits by ethnicity, economics, and lifestyle. Now owned by Nielsen Media Research, which collects data for television, Arbitron has measured audience patterns in local markets by selecting people and households at random, age 12 and older, to fill out diary surveys outlining their listening habits. Broken down into four key ratings periods roughly corresponding with the seasons, Arbitron collects listening information tracked from 6am-midnight Monday through Friday, and provides this information to radio stations, networks, cable companies, advertisers, ad agencies, and online marketing firms. Ratings categories include: total audience (Cume) and the average number of people listening every 15 minutes, known as average quarter hour listening (AQH).

Spanish Language Radio

As the Hispanic population in the U.S. has grown by leaps and bounds over the last decade, Arbitron and other firms have begun tracking the listening habits of 'Hispanic Radio.' With over 13,000 radio stations currently broadcasting in the U.S., today over 600 stations now program in one of the Hispanic formats which include: Latin Pop, Latin Rhythm, Regional Mexican, Tropical and Tejano. The number of Hispanic people listening to radio on a weekly basis is fairly consistent for men and women between the ages of 18-64, and in many ways mirrors the demographics reflected by the overall radio landscape. Data shows that Hispanic men 18 and older tune in just slightly more than women, and as no surprise Teens 12-17 strongly prefer listening to one of the 'current' Hispanic formats rooted in one of the Urban or Rock formats. Preferences for both men and women over 35 change to AC, Country, Smooth Jazz, Oldies, and Religious music radio in that order, and the 55-64 demographic show a solid interest in Adult Standards, and News/Talk formats.

Station Staffing and Operations

Today, cost cutbacks have significantly reduced overall staff at local commercial and public radio, but most stations still maintain a minimum number of employees utilizing DJ's & announcers to voice their on-air programming. Most stations also retain a General Manager, Program Director, Music Director, Sales, Promotions, and Production as well as support staff, which includes producers, engineering, traffic, and accounting, among other jobs.

Canned Radio

Over the years, Muzak, the first background music distribution service in the U.S., has come to mean, 'elevator music.' Founded in 1934, the service held a virtual monopoly through the 1990's for music distribution to the retail and business community. However, with lower priced, commercial-free competition from Satellite (XM, Sirius) and Cable (DMX, Music Choice) distributors, Muzak has lost considerable market share and subscribers.

Terrestrial Performance Rights

Today, multiple streams in various physical and electronic media performed in live, semi-live, and pre-recorded settings are subject to payment of Performance Royalties, and broadcast, cable television, radio and online, as well as concerts, nightclubs, and restaurants etc, must obtain a license to use copyrighted music and compensate the author and publisher. ASCAP (The American Society of Composers, Authors, and Publishers), BMI (Broadcast Music Incorporated), and SESAC (Society of European Stage Authors and Composers) compete for the collection and distribution of composer and publisher royalties. ASCAP and BMI are both not-for-profit collection agencies and protect their members by monitoring performances via broadcast or live performance. SESAC however, the smallest of the three retains an undisclosed amount of performance income as profit.

Digital Radio

Digital, like the digits on one's hand refers to counting, and unlike an analog, electrical system which uses a spectrum of values to represent voltage, frequency, current, and charge, digital processing is represented either as numbers or as keyboard symbols. Analog signals which are converted into 'on and off' pulses can be digitally encoded for storage, transmission and display.

Terrestrial radio has historically broadcast on either the AM or FM band via frequencies that listeners can tune into on their radio. This method uses a comparatively large amount of spectrum for the relatively small number of stations as compared with Digital radio, which can combine multiple audio streams on a single frequency using multiplexing and compression. Audio compression is designed to reduce the size of audio files by describing the data using pattern recognition. The difference is dramatic. For example, if one CD can fit 1 hour of music on it, a compressed music CD can fit twice that amount, and music compressed in the MP3 format can store 7 hours of music.

With the invention of the integrated circuit in the 1960s and the microprocessor in the 1970s, digital broadcasting has shown that it can increase frequency and channel space on the sidebands of terrestrial FM stations. Today, the UK is one of the most successful DAB (Digital Audio Broadcasting), markets with 40% projected saturation in UK homes by 2009, and although DAB has not yet been a financial success, 2006 statistics show 500 million people worldwide are in a DAB broadcast coverage area operating on over 1,000 stations. Later introduced in the U.S. as HD Radio (Hybrid Digital), this method can carry multiple audio streams and was selected by the FCC as the broadcasting standard in the U.S. Often mistaken to mean 'High Definition,' HD Provides higher fidelity and less interference as compared with FM. Many stations today use HD as a second on air channel to compliment and augment their programming, and can even put their content on several additional side channels. This type of service can only be accessed with an HD radio and can be purchased from $100 on up.

Satellite

Unlike terrestrial radio, which transmits signals from antenna to antenna, Satellite radio transmits down from above the earth to a wide geographical range and requires that there are no major obstructions between the Satellite and receiver. Listeners pay a subscription fee for a wide menu of news, talk, entertainment, sports, and several music channels. The two primary providers in the U.S. and Canada are XM & Sirius. Now that XM and Sirius have merged, this creates a single network of about 14 million subscribers, and reduces operating, licensing and hardware costs for both companies. This also includes savings on expensive satellites currently in orbit (4 XM and 3 Sirius + 1 ground spare each). Worldspace is the European and Asian counterpart to Sirius and XM.

Cable

Music Choice programs and produces music and music-related content for cable TV systems and cell phones around the country, and the service is available in over 99% of digital cable homes nationwide. DMX provides over 100 channels of digital music to consumers and businesses in the U.S. and is delivered via cable, satellite, and on-premise installation.

Online

Online radio has opened up a new world for musicians and listeners alike. It has brought millions of otherwise disconnected music-lovers back to music radio and has opened up tremendous access and promotion for thousands of musicians, artists and bands. Streaming has changed the very idea of radio both in terms of delivery and audience. Where terrestrial radio is expensive to operate and it's audience reach finite, streaming is the

cheapest, fastest, and most efficient way to distribute media and interactive tools worldwide.
According to Bridge Ratings & Research, in 2006 internet radio usage skyrocketed to 72 million users per month, up from 45 million at the end of 2005, and the survey concluded that the vast majority of internet radio consumers are listening to internet-only broadcasts as opposed to simulcasts by terrestrial stations.

During the 1990's, improvements in compression, storage and transmission along with greater bandwidth in the last mile increased the webcasters ability to stream. Prior to that, notable beginnings for online radio included the first news broadcast online in 1994 by Voice of America, the first webcast by a terrestrial radio station (WXYC, 89.3FM in Chapel Hill NC), the first full-time Internet station 'Radio HK,' began operation in 1995. In 1999, the 'MyCaster,' a MP3 player which eventually succumbed to the dot com bust in 2001, was a forerunner for portals such as Live 365, giving users their first chance to program their own stations.

A digital stream contains the source, the server (which repeats the source), and the playback (which receives the repeated source). Streams can be 'Live' (real time) or 'On Demand' (available at the user's request) and storage size is calculated by its bandwidth length and media type. Radio bandwidth in analog systems is typically measured in Hertz (units), whereby the bandwidth is the 'range of frequencies' generated by the sound wave (e.g. the more bandwidth the wider the range). In digital audio, bandwidth refers to the amount of data (bits) that can be transferred by the server. Streams accessed at lower bitrates (number of bits transferred per second) can be accessed more quickly, and are accessible to more users (e.g. slower connection speeds, dialup etc.), but contain a lower audio/video quality as compared with files accessed through higher bitrates.

Data 'compression' is the process of encoding information by using fewer bits than it's un-encoded representation. For example, the word compression could be encoded as 'comp,' which requires fewer bits for storage and transmission, and then de-coded back as the full word compression, for reading and editing. A 'codec' is the software that does the encoding and compressing of streams for transmission, storage and encryption, and then the decoding and decompressing for listening, viewing and editing. Codecs are designed to save space by representing only certain aspects of the media. For instance, an MP3 file is compressed audio that maximizes available space by discarding the less audible aspects of the recording by efficiently organizing the information.

Popular compression standards include 'MPEG', which is an acronym for 'The Moving Picture Experts Group.' Charged with developing video and audio encoding standards, MPEG standardized MP3, as well as developed MPEG-2, which delivered broadcast & digital television standards, MPEG-4 which supports object based 3D content, and DRM (Digital Rights Management), and MPEG-7 for multimedia.

The raw encoded audio and/or video stream also contains metadata (data about data), which tags information and allows for synchronization all within a multimedia 'container.' Well known containers include: MOV (QuickTime / RealAudio), which is a compressed format, and WAV (Waveform) & AIFF (Audio Interchange File Format), which is uncompressed. Metadata is structured encoded data that describes, identifies, and manages data characteristics. Sometimes critical, sometimes not, but always providing more description, context, and abstraction than the data that it is describing, metadata can cover all aspects of a particular system, and depending on the hierarchy and context can have it's own metadata. A simple example to illustrate metadata might be, "when considering the geography of London, if 'E83BJ' is the main data, then 'Post Code' could be a piece of it's metadata." Metadata is also used to speed up searching by filtering. For example, if a search engine knows that 'Van Gogh' was a 'Dutch painter', it can answer a search query on 'Dutch painters' even though the exact words were not searched.

iTunes is loaded into all Apple computers and comes with it's own radio service which offers both terrestrial radio streams and content from independent producers. From the hobbyist and music aficionado to terrestrial radio stations simulcasting their on air broadcasts, online radio networks have given thousands of users the ability to create their own streaming niche music channels. Live 365, as of 2007, had approximately 7,000 active users. Y! Music, formally Yahoo Music, selects their users playlist based on the ratings users provide and then makes recommendations to the user based on similar songs in the system. Both of these networks are supported by a subscription or advertising business model. RadioIO, which launched in 1999, became the world's first publicly traded internet radio company, and today listenership exceeds 1 million users per month, with 23 ad-supported channels, most of which are also available on iTunes Radio, WindowsMedia, Shoutcast, and through Real Networks.

Media players have extended the definition of radio as they can stream audio and video, import or copy content to and from disc, maintain a playback library, synchronize with other devices, and allow for purchasing and renting content. Microsoft's Windows OS comes pre-loaded with Windows Media Player, Mac OS with Quicktime and iTunes. Linux systems offer various players including VLC, MPlayer, Xine, or Totem. Rhapsody and Zune use Windows Media DRM for secure content delivery. Rhapsody was the first to offer unlimited on-demand streaming for all of their music including the catalogs for Sony/BMG, EMI, Universal, and Warner music.

'Pandora' is a different sort of media player. Developed by a group of musicians and technologists by assembling over 400 musical attributes into a very large 'Music Genome,' the goal was to create a comprehensive music analysis and recommendation system that would capture the fundamental essence of music. Attribute genes of course include: melody, harmony, and rhythm, but also parameters such as instrumentation, orchestration, arrangement, singing, range, syncopation, tonality, vocal harmonies, and instrumental proficiency, to name only a few. Users start by selecting an artist and Pandora programs a stream of different songs, with several from the chosen artist along with other songs based on similar attributes. Users can rate each track with a thumbs up or thumbs down feedback for the smart system, which then adjusts accordingly for future selections. MSN Radio is now powered by Pandora.

Social Networking

MySpace, one of the most popular interactive networks in the world, has helped new artists and bands get discovered utilizing their music player and social networking features. By customizing pages and posting blogs, photos, videos, and music as well as communicating with friends, the music player serves as an artist's or band's own radio station, and users can create networks of friends as well as sell up to four MP3's, as long as they have the rights to the music. YouTube is also an effective means of promoting music. After winning Time magazine's "Invention of the Year" for 2006, traffic levels went to an all time high and some have calculated that potential revenues from streaming and page view advertisements could be in the millions per month. The media player serves as an artist's or band's own TV station.

P2P

'Napster' paved the way for decentralized P2P file-sharing programs such as Kazaa, Limewire, imesh, and BearShare, and the popularity and repercussions of the first Napster have made it legendary. Today, online promotion allows musicians and composers to control their own distribution either from their website, or through pay services such as iTunes, Rhapsody and MP3.com. By providing free tracks for download and streaming through Napster and other file-sharing networks, many unsigned artists and bands without access to mainstream media, in effect have created their own 'radio' outlet helping them promote and improve their music sales.

Although underground musicians and independent labels originally expressed support for Napster and the P2P model, others criticized it. First released in 1999, Napster offered free MP3 tracks, and its enormous selection of music generated a huge following, making it massively popular. Early users viewed Napster as a simple search engine where they could download and trade music, oblivious to the rights of copyright holders who were getting hijacked on high-speed networks in college dormitories. In 1999 the RIAA (Recording Industry Association of America) claimed the practice illegal, following a long line of lawsuits from composers, record labels, musicians, and bands, including Metallica. Eventually Napster shut down. Complying with a court injunction and agreeing to pay copyright owners for past unauthorized use of their music as well as an advance against future licensing royalties, Napster was sold to media giant Bertelsmann who converted the network into a music subscription service, the antithesis of its original mission. The deal turned very bad for Bertelsmann as former users abandoned Napster, and its brand and logos were eventually acquired in a bankruptcy auction by Roxio, which has now rebranded the service as 'Napster 2.0.'

Podcasting & Blogging

MP3 blogs take the idea of radio, publicity and 'direct marketing' to another level by utilizing personal communication between the artist and the media, buyers, and fans. The first MP3 blogs were generally under the radar as online usage was relatively low and most blogs focused on unsigned and indie music. But today MP3 blogs deliver increased direct promotion and awareness for both known and unknown artists with music, video and information that are just a click away. The reaction is palpable, and major labels now routinely deliver artist content in this way.

Online Performance Rights

Prior to 1995, copyright owners in the United States did not have a digital performance right. Two laws, The Digital Performance in Sound Recordings Act, and the Digital Millennium Copyright Act amended that practice criminalizing the production and dissemination of technology, devices, and/or services used to circumvent DRM (Digital Rights Management) controls. Similar to ASCAP and BMI for terrestrial radio, 'Sound Exchange' is a non-profit organization authorized by the U.S. Copyright office to collect licensing fees from digital broadcasters on behalf of thousands of copyright owners (composers, record labels, artists). Started in 2000, Sound Exchange distributes performance revenues on a pay-per-play basis for transmissions on cable, satellite, and online. Utilizing parity in royalty distribution with everything split evenly between artists and copyright owners, annual payouts have been doubling every year, and accounting for tens of millions of dollars each cycle.

DRM (Digital Rights Management) allows the publisher and copyright holder to receive compensation for performances of their work by attempting to control copyright restrictions and digital piracy. By modifying media player software to include cryptographic controls, DRM can restrict how the player interfaces with specific content (e.g. burning a copyrighted song to disc).

DRM, vulnerable to hackers, has been openly criticized by Apple founder Steve Jobs and others in the industry who advocate selling music without DRM, citing that it encourages more people to steal music. In 2007, Apple announced DRM free music for EMI's complete catalogue for a $0.30 per track premium above the standard price. The decision has huge implications for the future of the music industry, and the remaining Big 3 labels still using DRM, Universal, Sony/BMG, and Warner Music.

In 2007, the Copyright Royalty Board set new webcasting licensing rates for the period 2006-2010, which could multiply broadcaster royalty fees by a stunning 300 to 1200 percent, threatening online radio. Still pending, Internet Radio has been singled out and burdened with fees not paid by AM or FM stations, and with rates at least 3-4 times paid by satellite and cable radio. Should this ruling stand, outlets such as Live365 may evaporate.

At the request of the Recording Industry Association of America, the CRB ignored the fact that Internet radio royalties were already double what satellite radio pays and multiplied the royalties even further. The 2005 royalty rate was 7/100 of a penny per song streamed; the 2010 rate will be 19/100 of a penny per song streamed. For small webcasters that were able to calculate royalties as a percentage of revenue in 2005, that option was put down by the CRB.

A new coalition of Internet radio stations is mobilizing in this wake of this increase. Tim Westergren, founder of Pandora, estimates that his company will end up paying out about 60 percent of its revenues in royalty fees once the new rates kick in. Terrestrial Broadcaster KCRW in Santa Monica, estimates that based on the station's traffic levels, with the new rates, they paid $140,000 in copyright royalties for 2006, and $190,000 for 2007. As a public radio station that is both a terrestrial and streams online, the new royalties will not kill the station, but will severely hurt it. Artists, listeners, and webcasters have joined coalitions to help save Internet Radio, lobbying members of Congress to create a structural solution for this problem and create an environment where Internet radio, and the millions of artists it features, can continue to grow for generations to come.

The term broadcasting was originally used in the field of agriculture and farming but today extends to various forms including: terrestrial, airborne, and online changing the definition of radio. This chapter has presented a brief overview and chronology of Radio in its changing landscape.

The Music Business in Action:

New Developments in Radio

Radio has a new tool for play list research; radio has found a replacement for the physical single as an indicator of song popularity. Digital tracks legally bought or illegally downloaded are increasingly playing a role in radio programming decisions. Radio program directors are using song information purchased from iTunes or downloaded from authorized or unauthorized peer-to-peer sites as an important read on developing hits.

Data company Big Champagne tracks the popularity of downloads on unauthorized sites and Neilson Soundscan on iTunes.

Those of you who are interested in any areas in the recorded music industry should check radio to find out how these resources are now being used for programming purposes.

The Music Business in Action 2:

Megastation Radio and Local Need

Radio in the 21st century is a business of multi-owned stations. In addition, the two largest satellite radio providers, XM and Sirius, have proposed a merger. What all this means is a more homogenized, less local sound.

Listeners have complained that their favorite local DJ's, talk show hosts, and reporters have disappeared, replaced by syndicated shows, automated programs, and song cycles. Local flavor and diversity are gone. In the past one could hear the sounds of Chicago, Philadelphia, Seattle, and New York, making hometown radio sound like home. Now this diversity is lost.

Today, broadcast stations are converting their signals to digital, which allows each station to function as multiple stations in the same space. Now you can go local and give the airways local and diverse life. The FCC needs to make this happen by creating policy that recognizes this possibility in the digital spectrum. After years of favoring big broadcasters and allowing them to own multiple stations in a listening area, it is time to give the listeners a break, and allow the public to sample as diverse a spectrum of music as possible.

Chapter 13

The Billboard Charts

Harmon Greenblatt

Note: *Much of the material for the first version of this chapter was gathered from an interview with Michael Ellis, former associate publisher of* Billboard. *This information has been supplemented in 2009 through an interview with Silvio Pietroluongo, Director of Charts for Billboard.*

INTRODUCTION

Of all of the trade publications in the music business, *Billboard* garners the highest circulation and the most respect within the industry. The *Billboard* charts function as the industry standard in determining the success of a song or album. This chapter will explore how *Billboard* gained its place of prominence in the music business and, more importantly, will examine its accuracy as a reflection of the tastes of the record-buying public.

HISTORY OF THE CHARTS

Billboard began more than 110 years ago as a total entertainment trade magazine. As it evolved, it began publishing charts for sheet music and, later, for the jukebox, which came into prominence during the 1930s. Beginning in the 1940s, *Billboard* published charts for music, and in the early 1960s the magazine began to concentrate on music and home entertainment. The methodology for formulating the charts was developed and improved throughout the '40s and '50s. The present formats for the *Billboard* 200 Album Sales Chart and the Hot 100 Singles Chart were created in the 1950s. In 1958, several small charts for sales, airplay, and others were combined into the Hot 100 Chart.

PURPOSE AND IMPORTANCE OF THE CHARTS

The purpose of the charts is to provide record labels and artists a way to measure their success against other labels and other artists. By measuring the relative popularity of a recording, it also helps talent buyers, producers and promoters of tours, booking agents, and anyone who needs to know which records are most popular in order to do their jobs better.

But why are *these* charts so significant? There are other publications with their own charts (see Chapter 12: Radio for a complete list), but *Billboard* has many advantages over its competitors in this area. First, it is the only one that circulates internationally. Second, it is the only one of its kind that has a name familiar to the average consumer of music. Although it is designed for music business professionals, *Billboard* has a strong readership among consumers as well. Its circulation, in the neighborhood of 30,000 with much sharing and online viewing that crosses many nations, is many times that of its nearest competitor. *Billboard*, therefore, has broad influence far beyond music industry insiders.

Many of the other music business publications, such as *Radio and Records,* cover only one part of the business or one kind of music. With *Billboard*'s dominance in the industry and by its multiplicity of charts among its print and online offerings (currently over 100 for U.S., more than 150 including world charts), it provides a vital service to many facets of the music industry.

HOW THE CHARTS ARE COMPILED

There are two basic types of information that go into the charts:
- sales information, which includes digital downloads and ringtones
- airplay information

Also included in the Hot 100 is streaming media data from AOL and Yahoo, with other online sites prepared to join the reporting panel in the near future.

These types of information are presented in three different kinds of charts:
- sales only charts
- airplay only charts
- charts that combine sales and airplay

Most of the charts in *Billboard* are sales charts. Specifically, of the 35 to 40 charts that appear weekly, roughly 10 are airplay only, and only two (Hot 100 singles and Hot R&B/Hip-Hop Songs) are a combination of sales and airplay. The remaining charts, which number 30 or so, are mostly sales. Exceptions include the Dance/Club Play Chart, which covers club play rather than radio play and a few third party-provided social network/streaming media charts.

The sales charts include:
- *Billboard* 200, covering all album sales
- Gospel and Contemporary Christian albums
- Country albums
- Latin albums
- Two charts for jazz albums, one for "Traditional" and one for "Contemporary"
- Two classical charts: one for traditional albums and one for classical crossover.

Other album sales charts include New Age, world music, reggae, R&B/Hip-Hop, and the Heatseekers chart for new artists. There is also a singles sales chart, Hot Digital Songs, based on digital download transactions. There are also a number of video sales charts.

Among the airplay only charts are:
- Hot 100 Airplay
- Adult Contemporary
- Adult Top 40
- Country
- Adult R&B
- Pop 100 Airplay
- Rhythmic Airplay
- Modern Rock
- Rap Songs
- Dance Airplay

In both sales and airplay categories, some charts appear weekly, others bi-weekly. New charts are added as taste and demand change.

But the dissemination of the sales and airplay information that make up the *Billboard* charts is only half the story. Just as important is how the information that makes up the charts is actually gathered and compiled.

COMPILING THE SALES CHARTS

The information is tracked and compiled by an organization called Nielsen SoundScan, which has participation with most of retail record locations, throughout the U.S. These locations include record chains, independent record stores, online retailers (iTunes, Amazon), and "racked" accounts (record departments in chain stores like Kmart, Target, and Wal-Mart). SoundScan tracks over 90% of all the records sold in the United States.

Whenever a customer purchases a recording, whether it is a CD, cassette, single LP, or through digital download, at a reporting retailer, SoundScan uses the company's inventory system to read the CD's bar code and communicates the information to Soundscan's main computer. The sales data from all retailers are tallied weekly. The resulting list of the best-selling records in the country provides accurate information based on more than 90% of the U.S. retail market that participate in SoundScan. SoundScan projects an estimate of the total units sold in the U.S. on any non-reporting stores.

Once *Billboard* gets its list of the top records from SoundScan, members of its staff, the charts managers, listen to all the records and decide which ones belong on each chart. The managers may consult with the record labels, radio people, or record retail stores. But *Billboard*'s chart mangers make the final decisions as to which songs qualify for which specialty chart: country, R&B, reggae, jazz, etc.

This system makes for some controversy and debate, which is probably unavoidable when there is so much at stake on each release. The labels, seeking the most visibility for every album, want each title on as many charts as possible.

Once the charts are compiled, the managers add "bullets," so named because in the old days they looked like bull's eyes, next to the chart position of each song. Today, *Billboard*'s bullet looks more like an ellipse, which it puts around the chart position number of the song. Whatever it looks like, the bullet means that the title has shown a significant sales increase over the previous week. The bullet represents *Billboard*'s chart managers' editorial judgment, based on weekly retail market conditions. If overall sales are up significantly in a given week, an album would need to show a greater improvement to earn a bullet than it would in a week where overall sales are down. SoundScan reports record sales in units sold this week and last week, but the chart managers decide which recordings should have a bullet.

COMPILING THE AIRPLAY CHARTS

Airplay charts don't utilize information from SoundScan. To compile airplay information, *Billboard* uses a different system called the Nielsen Broadcast Data System (BDS). BDS is a monitoring system that captures data on the music that is played on the radio. The BDS technology has been in existence since 1986. The corporation that owns *Billboard* also purchased the technology and began the company in 1989, and the first conversions to the system began in 1990. In the early 90's, all of Billboard's radio charts were converted to BDS technology.

How does BDS work? BDS's main computer in Kansas City contains each song's pattern, an audio fingerprint of each song using a technology based on sound wave patterns. The BDS monitors "listen" to the radio in 141 U.S. markets, and 32 in Canada and Puerto Rico. The stations in Puerto Rico are used in compiling some U.S. charts; the

Canadian stations are not used for U.S. chart information. The monitors listen and are able to recognize any music, and can identify a song as long as it is played in the same form as when it was encoded. This system can also differentiate between performances by different artists of the same song. The BDS system requires cooperation from the record labels, which must provide the company with all of their new releases so that they can be encoded. It is difficult, at times, for BDS to keep up with the hundreds of new releases that enter the market each week. The labels, of course, are careful to send every one of their new releases to BDS to be entered into the computer. They are well aware that for a song to get on to any of the airplay charts it first has to be in the system.

In each of its 141 markets the BDS computer "listens" to a number of major stations around the clock and records each selection played. All of these remote computers are connected to the main computer by phone lines. The main computer polls all the remote sites continuously and tabulates the results. Each week, BDS provides the totals to *Billboard,* which uses this information to compile the airplay charts. The chart managers select the stations to report to each chart based on the genre of music that each station plays. But programming decisions are made by radio stations' programming directors, so, for example, if a rap song is played frequently on several country stations, it is possible that the song may appear on the country chart.

The airplay charts and the three combined charts (Billboard Hot 100, Pop 100, and Hot R&B /Hip-Hop Songs) are also weighted to reflect the number of listeners at any time at each monitoring station. The two combined charts (Billboard Hot 100 and Hot R&B/Hip-Hop Songs) include airplay ranked by audience impressions. *Billboard* has an agreement with Arbitron, and Arbitron information on each radio station's listenership for varying times of the day is entered in to the BDS Computer. When a song is played, the computer counts not only that it was played but also estimates how many people were listening at that time. (See Chapter XII: Radio for an explanation of how Arbitron gathers information.) A song playing at noon in New York City on Z100, therefore, might have 200,000 listeners, while a record playing at 3 a.m. in Little Rock, Arkansas might have 200 listeners. A number one song might have four or five thousand detections in a week for a pop hit, but many less for a number one country song. Each detection is multiplied by the estimated number of listeners. A number one song typically gets 100-150 million gross impressions per week. Every person who listens is counted separately every time he/she hears the song. So, 10 gross impressions could mean 10 people hearing the song once, or the same person hearing it 10 times.

COMPILING THE "COMBINED" CHARTS

The Hot 100 and R&B/Hip-Hop Songs charts are the only two charts that combine airplay and sales. The Hot 100 is the most used of all the *Billboard* charts, and is quoted regularly around the world. The R&B/Hip-Hop Songs chart is also very important. There are two elements that go into each of these charts:
- SoundScan sales (both digital and physical singles)
- BDS airplay

The Hot 100 also includes streaming media play from various online sites.

The Hot 100 uses all the retailers; all sales of physical and digital singles are counted as well as all radio stations in the survey. R&B Singles uses selected retailers of physical singles and selected radio stations.

The number of units sold is converted into points, and then the weighted average of the number of times a record is played (see above) is also converted into points. Since February, the calculation has included digital sales.

Billboard weights its ratio 50% airplay, 50% sales to decrease the volatility of the charts.
An example of the point-system calculation: to get the number of points from sales of a song, take the number of units sold and divide by 10. If a record sells 75,000 units in a week, that would be 7,500 points. Next, for airplay, take the gross impressions and divide by 10,000. A hot record may get 80 million gross impressions in a week, which converts to 8,000 points.

CONCLUSION

So much is dependent on these charts that the utmost care is needed to keep them beyond reproach. Before the advent of SoundScan and BDS, *Billboard* compiled its charts by phoning radio stations and record stores and getting the information verbally. The potential for abuse and misinformation was certainly present, and this called into question the accuracy and reliability of the charts. Using the state-of-the-art technology of SoundScan and BDS, *Billboard* has created a fair and arbitrary system that, while not perfect, is much more accurate and reliable than in the past.

Who have been the major beneficiaries of the computerization of the charts? Most people feel that the traditionally under-counted parts of the industry, country music and independent labels, have seen the greatest benefit. But all artists, composers, and anyone who is working in the field stand to benefit. There is now an accurate count of impressions to determine royalties for payment purposes, record companies can now more closely monitor how songs are performing and adjust their marketing plans accordingly, and artists and their managers can negotiate with record companies and promoters with more authority based on these figures. The *Billboard* charts were always important. Now, more than ever, they are the most important source of information for the entire music industry.

Chapter 14

Music Publishing

Harmon Greenblatt

Note: Much of the material for this chapter was taken from interviews with Les Bider, former chairman and CEO of Warner/Chappell Music, Inc.

Music publishing begins with the songs. Without the songs, of course, there is nothing. With the songs, it's important to have an organization that can maximize the profit from those songs. That is the publisher's job: to exploit those songs in the territories that have been assigned to him or her, to have them earn money for the songwriter and for the company. Exploit means taking those compositions and getting them recorded on records or CDs, getting them used in film and television, having them used in commercials, printed on sheet music, anything that is consistent with each particular piece of art. "Territories" refers to the fact that frequently an artist will use different subpublishers in different countries. Some publishers are international; others operate within a single country, so a songwriter or composer may assign rights to a different publisher in each country. A writer may sign an exclusive agreement with a publisher either for a certain number of compositions for a certain length of time, or, in the case of writer-performers, for a certain number of compositions as they relate to certain albums.

Most songwriters don't realize that there has to be demand for the songs before a publisher will be interested in publishing them. If there is demand, the composer may have his/her choice of publishers. If not, the writers only choice may be self-publishing, that is, to be his/her own publisher.

The composer whose music is in demand has a number of options as to how he or she handles the publishing. He or she may sign with a large publisher, an independent publisher, or a publisher affiliated with his or her record company (if he or she has signed with one). Some artists, composers and performers choose to become their own publishers. The main advantage of a large publisher is that a large publisher has staff who work solely for the exploitation of music copyright in each area: recordings, film and TV shows, and commercials. Also, a large publisher is thinking globally, viewing each of the individual elements of music publishing from an international perspective.

A small, independent publishing firm also has advantages. First, a large publisher may not be interested in an individual's music, may not see a big enough return on the music, while a smaller publisher might see potential and become interested. The smaller company can deal with music that finds a smaller niche, and does not necessarily require worldwide success. Further, a smaller publisher may say that it can offer better service; that a new artist will get lost in a mammoth company which would never deal with his or her small number of songs. Also, an artist may want to make a deal with a local publisher in the U.S. and want to make other deals with publishers in foreign countries. He or she could sub publish songs with a publisher in France, another in Germany, another in Italy, and get the kind of attention he or she wants, rather than being one more U.S. artist signing to a big multinational.

Signing with a label-affiliated publishing company also presents advantages and disadvantages. Often, record companies demand the artists sign a publishing contract as part of the recording contract. Those that balk may find it imperils their ability to get signed. But other artists find that one result of this arrangement is to make it easier for an artist/writer to get the record company publisher to accept more of the writer's songs for recording. For most songwriters, a recording contract is an excellent way to promote their songs. Others say that being affiliated with the same record company and publisher helps to get their songs exposure in other media. Should a writer sign with a record company affiliated publisher? It's up to composers to make what they think is the best long-term deal.

Many artists and writers have set up their own publishing companies. There are several reasons for this. First, they do not want to split their income with a publisher. Second, writers may not be able to get their material accepted by a publisher, so they set up their own companies. Others have had bad experiences with publishers or feel that their music has not been given sufficient attention by the publisher, so some writers make a decision to publish on their own.

PUBLISHERS TODAY VS. THE PAST

The role of publishing has changed radically from its beginnings a century ago. In the early days, publishers were most concerned with sales of sheet music. As sheet music sales increased and recordings came on the scene, publishers became the most powerful people in the music business. The most effective song promoters were the performers in the theaters and vaudeville houses, particularly in New York City. Star performers would make the rounds of the publishing houses looking for appropriate material. The publisher would match up certain songs with certain artists. So it frequently was the decision of the publisher which artist would get to perform and record which song. This also gave the publishers power over the songwriters, because the publishers were the vital link between the songwriters, their songs, and the performers.

Publishing today is far different. Many performers write their own material, so the publisher does not play the same part in matching writer and performer. Also, as mentioned previously, many performers are their own publishers, retaining their own copyrights and avoiding the publishing companies completely. Some publishers still do match up artists with writers, or writers with other writers, or critique the writer's work. But the publisher has a different role to play in the modern era: to take advantage of the explosion of different sources of income now open to any song.

One of the reasons that publishing is so lucrative is that there are so many sources of income possible. Broadcast performances, live performances, mechanical royalties, including samples used within other songs, cover records, sheet music sales, synchronization rights, jukeboxes, and foreign rights are just some of the traditional income sources that publishers have used to generate income. With the explosion of new media, the publisher sees many new income possibilities that did not even exist a few years ago. Technologies such as computer software, CD-ROM's, digital, downloadable possibilities, and cable radio are just beginning to penetrate the mass market. As they become more popular, income from these and other similar sources will continue to grow into the 21st century.

COLLECTION OF ROYALTIES

The publisher's ability to collect the royalties earned by the songs is another important consideration in choosing a publisher. Exploiting the songs is one matter, collecting the money earned by these songs is another matter. Here, again, the organizational structure of large publishers seems to place them at an advantage. A large organization has separate information technology, as well as copyright, royalty, licensing, legal and business affairs departments. All of this technology and manpower is at the service of the songs, to get them used and to collect the income generated from their use. A small publisher may have one person who fills out the copyright license, collects the royalties, and issues the royalty statement. It's difficult for one person to be an expert in all the different areas. Further, if someone goes unpaid, it won't be the big company that controls hundreds of titles. The one who will go unpaid is the small publisher that controls only a few titles and can be made to wait get his or her money.

Before even approaching a publisher, a writer must affiliate with one of the performing rights societies, ASCAP, BMI, or SESAC, to collect royalties on performances of the music. ASCAP, BMI, and SESAC are collection agents for publishers for performance royalties. For mechanical royalties, many publishers use the Harry Fox Agency. Warner/Chappell, EMI, Universal, BMG and many others all use the Fox agency. They have a non-exclusive agreement, meaning that they can use the Fox agency, but are not required to do so. At times, they do a lot of direct licensing themselves. For example, if Warner/ Chappell is licensing within the Warner Music circle, it will license directly to the record company. It's faster, more efficient, and Warner/ Chappell doesn't have to pay the Harry Fox fee, which is 7.75% of the mechanical royalties received.

It is important for the publisher to have good relationships with the record companies. Once a song is recorded, a record company does not have to contact the publisher about making another recording of the song. All the company needs to do is pay the mechanical royalty on each copy sold. But the record company may not know exactly who gets the royalty, and so may not be able to pay anyone. The publisher does not want to make trouble, because he wants this song and other songs to be used by the record company, so it can be a delicate situation for the publisher. By nature, the relationship between the publisher and the label is adversarial, because the record company has to pay the publisher. Maintaining good relationships not only helps get the songwriters paid for the songs used, but increases usage and payments for other songs as well.

FOREIGN ROYALTIES

The international scope of the music business makes income from foreign royalties an important element in music publishing. The large international music publisher is able to consider the international potential of each U.S. song. A commercial advertiser will only license a song for the least number of territories that it will cover in its advertising. Also, many songs that are recorded and released in the U.S. are not automatically released worldwide, but when a song is released in a foreign country, the publisher needs to be aware of it.

Each of the mega-publishers has affiliates in the large countries where it does substantial business. The smaller companies may affiliate with publishers in the foreign countries to collect royalties, or they may use Harry Fox's foreign service branch, but keep in mind that Harry Fox handles only mechanical royalties, so other sources must be used to collect other royalties. Fox has reciprocal arrangements with most foreign collection agencies, which charge about 15% for their service. Fox deducts its fee, then sends the balance to the U.S. publisher. But this 15% fee varies substantially depending on the country. The good news about foreign payments is that as use of songs in foreign markets increases and foreign territories become an increasingly large share of the world record market, payments are increasing to publishing firms in the U.S.

The foreign collection agencies differ from their U.S. counterparts in that they are governmental bureaucracies set up under a monopoly that is granted by each individual country. There are performing rights societies in every country of the world that recognizes copyright law, but in every country except the U.S. there is only one society and it is government controlled. The major agencies include the following:

Country	Agency
Israel	ACUM
Greece	AEPI
Australia, New Zealand, Fiji, Pacific Island Territories, Papua New Guinea	AMCOS
Hungary	ARTISJUS
Hong Kong	CASH
Germany, Austria, Bulgaria, Romania, Turkey, Czech Republic	GEMA (based in Munich and Berlin, Germany)
Croatia	HDS
Japan	JASRAC
Republic of Korea	KOMCA
England, Scotland, Wales, Ireland,	MCPS (based in London) (mechanicals)

Northern Ireland, Bahamas, Bermuda, British Virgin Islands, India, Jamaica, Kenya, Nigeria, Uganda, Zimbabwe, Denmark, Sweden, Norway, Finland, Iceland	PRS (based in London) (performances) NCB
Belgium	SABAM
Argentina	SADAIC
South Africa, Botswana, Lesotho, Swaziland	SARRAL
France, Andorra, Luxembourg, Monaco, Egypt, Lebanon, Morocco, and many African countries	SDRM/SACEM
Spain	SGAE
Italy, San Marino, Vatican City	SIAE
Portugal, Azores, Madeira	SPA
Netherlands, Aruba, Dutch Antilles, Irian Barat, Surinam	STEMRA
Switzerland, Liechtenstein	SUISA
Russia	VAAP

Just as the international branch of a U.S. record company is responsible for signing and exploiting music from its own country in addition to exploiting U.S. music in that country, so the multinational publishers sign local Italian, French, or Dutch repertoire in different countries. Some of it is popular only in its own territory, but sometimes some of it sells well outside as well. For example, Spanish repertoire may sell well in Latin American countries, and Brazilian repertoire may do well in Portugal. Once again, the large companies with their world-wide rights and enormous clout are in the strongest position to take the songs and exploit them outside the territory of origin.

HOW AN ARTIST IS SIGNED BY A PUBLISHER

If the most important thing to any artist is to be signed to a record deal, the second most important is to be signed to a publishing contract. As previously mentioned, sometimes the recording and publishing contracts are signed simultaneously or are connected, but how does a non-performer get his or her music exploited?

The first thing to remember is that today no publisher accepts unsolicited material. Publishers are afraid of being sued, and the only way to protect themselves is to not accept unsolicited material. To get through this blockade, an artist has to be represented by a lawyer with whom the publisher has done business, a manager with whom it has done business, or have some other reputable inroad into the company.

If one of those options exists, then the artist's representative can call his contact at the publisher and say that he or she has a client whose music the publisher might like to hear, and offer to send material.

When solicited material comes in, somebody does listen to it. Then it's either sent back to the lawyer as rejected, or it's held on to. If the publisher holds on to the material, this means he or she is interested in what has been heard, and a meeting is scheduled. At the meeting the discussion with the writer usually consists of topics such as what the writer's goals are, whether the writer is also a performer and whether that person wants to be a singer/songwriter or just a staff songwriter who is writing for other artists. There are few staff writing positions available in a music publishing company, because of the greater number of performers who write their own material. When these performers aren't doing their own material, they're frequently performing standards, not new material written by others.

If the initial meeting is successful, the next step is to bring the writer's material to be reviewed at a weekly creative staff meeting. The person who wants to sign the act gives a brief introduction and then plays three or four songs. The rest of the department then may comment that they see no profit in it, or that it sounds too much like another artist, or, in the best case, the songs are great and they recommend signing the artist.

Once the publisher and writer have reached the signing phase, the terms of the agreement are subject to the entire realm of possible negotiations as to how much the writer will receive and under what circumstances. As usual, the better known the artist and the greater the demand there is for his or her songs, the better deal he or she will be able to negotiate. Usually, the writer is signed for his or her entire output, not on a per song basis. More commonly, the publisher will give the artist a flat fee, $40,000 for the year, for example, and the writer will have to deliver something like 12 finished songs to the publisher. Again, depending on the negotiations, this money may be recoupable against royalties, or may not be, and the agreement may go on for several years.

RELATION TO RECORD COMPANIES

If the writer is also a performer and already has a record deal before coming to a publisher, it becomes much easier to get a publishing agreement. The publisher knows that there will be money generated by the songs from the release of the record, so that is a big step forward in getting acceptance. The publisher will want to know which label signed the artist, who signed him or her, and what the job security of that individual is at the label. One of the harsh realities of the music business is that if an artist has been signed by someone who has just departed a record company, the publisher will probably not want to sign that artist. Once a person has departed a record company, the artists that person signed tend to be dismissed, or get minimal attention.

When an act is unsigned by a record label, sometimes it can negotiate a publishing deal and use the publishing money to record a studio-quality demo that can gain a record deal. The publisher can sometimes help get the act signed by calling a friend at one of the labels and having someone listen to the music. But signing with a publisher is no guarantee of getting signed by a label, even if it is owned by the same parent company. Nor is a label signing a guarantee of getting a publisher. Ideally, a band will sign with the publishing company it feels can do the most for its career. One may think that because Warner/Chappell is affiliated with Warner Brothers Pictures, it would be good to sign with Warner/Chappell. Signings may also occur for any number of capricious reasons. Someone may sign with Sony Music Publishing because he or she wants a Walkman or may sign because he or she wants to be on MTV, and thinks that a certain publisher can accomplish that.

Lawyers frequently are determining factors in which groups sign with which publishers, as is the publisher's location. Lawyers will certainly steer their clients to publishers with whom they have good relations, and the publisher is more willing to work with a lawyer that he or she knows and trusts. Sometimes, location makes a difference. Certain lawyers do more business with EMI, because they are centered in New York. Others do more business with Warner/Chappell, because they are headquartered in Los Angeles.

AFTER SIGNING

Once the writer is signed to a publishing agreement, the publisher begins to exploit the music. The first matter is a demo tape. If there is no demo, or if it is not of sufficient quality, making the demo is the first thing that needs to be done. Once the demo is made, the publisher sends it to record companies. If the writer is a performer, the object is a record deal. If the writer is not a performer, the object is to interest record companies, performers, and managers in using the songs on recordings.

The publisher will work with the act and the record company to help close the record deal. If the company wants to see the act live, the publisher will suggest some kind of artist's showcase to give the record company a chance to judge the group's appeal and marketability.

If the artist has a record deal, or is even fairly close to having one, the publisher will not shop his songs to other artists. If the song has potential as a single, the publisher wouldn't want it to be used by another artist. However, if the song is going to be on a CD, the publisher might try to get the song used in another medium, such as a movie, a film or TV show.

OTHER PUBLISHING OPTIONS

Until now, we have discussed only the standard publishing agreement, in which the publisher buys the copyright and the income is split 50–50 between the writer and publisher. But there are many other deals possible between artist and writer. Following are the most common ones:

- Co-publishing. In the pre-rock era, the writer created the song and the publisher exploited the song, so it was considered fair to split the profits from the song in half. With the advent of rock music and, more importantly, the songwriter and singer becoming the same person, the writer/performer has automatically become involved with exploiting the song. The publisher's role was diminished and lawyers negotiated a concept called co-publishing, in which the writer keeps all of his or her share and half of what was traditionally the publisher's share, or 75% of the royalties to the artist, 25% to the publisher. This concept was successful for popular artists, because the publisher was forced to accept the reduced fee or get nothing at all. If other companies are offering co-publishing deals to the artist, the publisher is forced to meet the competition or lose the business altogether.

- Administration. There are times when an artist does not want his or her songs exploited by the publisher, believing that he or she is getting enough exploitation and not wanting his or her songs pushed into other media. The artist may feel that he or she doesn't want to share the publishing income, but still needs someone to collect the money and handle the paperwork, which is the administration of the songs. The most important differences between administration and publishing are that the artist maintains the copyright of the songs, and that the administration is usually for a set number of years, not for the entire duration of the copyright. The other difference, of course, is that the payment to the publisher is less, usually in the area of 20% of the gross. Note that this is not 20% of what the publisher received before. Because the pie was split down the middle, i.e., each party getting 50%, the publisher is now getting 20% of the whole, or 40% of his previous income. He or she receives substantially less than if publishing the songs, but the responsibilities decrease tremendously as well.

- The terms administration and subpublishing are often used interchangeably. Subpublishing is the publishing of some other publisher's rights, and administration is one form of subpublishing. But when subpublishing is used today it usually refers to a foreign publisher affiliated with a U.S. company providing publishing services for U.S.-copyrighted songs. This is particularly important to U.S. publishers who do not have world-wide presence. In order to exploit their songs in foreign countries, and to collect royalties on those songs that are being played, there needs to be an agreement with a publisher in each country to publish the songs and collect the money in that country. There is a wide range in the percentage of money that the subpublisher can keep, but it is usually between 15% and 25%.

CONCLUSION

What is the future of music publishing? Almost everyone is in agreement that the booming new technologies will have a great impact on publishing and result in many new uses for music. The exploitation of music on the Internet, especially in regard to technology which will enable users to download and upload high quality, full length recordings is of great interest to publishers who are looking to the future. Publishers are most concerned with tracking issues, and agree that a negotiated, flat-fee basis would be the method by which these works should be licensed. The types of online usages that most publishers would expect to be compensated for include music used to advertise or sell a product, and music associated with individual Web sites. Promotional Web sites set up by record companies are of lesser concern as these promote rather than interfere with or displace record sales.

Many feel that new technologies will mean much additional income for publishers and that publishing will be THE place to be in the music industry in the immediate future. Others fear that the new technologies will mean extra income, but at a greater cost of income from traditional sources. They reason that TV and radio, the greatest sources of income at present, are most in jeopardy from these alternative sources of entertainment. If the TV and radio numbers decline, and publishers' income declines with them, can this income ever be made up in what publishers will receive from CD-ROMs, cable radio, and the other new media?

The practice of sampling is the other issue on the minds of many publishers. It remains a difficult-to-license, yet profitable means by which songs can be further exploited. At this point, most publishers have established policies by which they license samples. For instance, many who are represented by the Harry Fox Agency will license all samples directly with the record company so as not to introduce a third database into an agreement involving complex issues (negotiated rates, colloquial spellings, etc.)

As new technologies continue to develop, music publishers want to be able to track and enforce the licensing and payment of royalties without discouraging music users from using their songs and/or complying with the Copyright Law.

Chapter 15

The Record Business and the Law

Lewis S. Kurlantzick

Lewis S. Kurlantzick is the Zephaniah Swift Professor of Law at the University of Connecticut School of Law.

INTRODUCTION

The legal system affects the production and distribution of recorded music at a variety of points. For example, Chapter 5 examines the details of the contract between the record company and the recording artist. That arrangement spells out the obligations that these two parties owe to each other. The interpretation and enforcement of that commercial agreement is governed by the law of contracts. Similarly, distribution agreements between record companies and their distributors and retailers, including online arrangements, are shaped by contract law.

Another example of the background pervasiveness of legal involvement is the law of business organizations. The duties that record company executives owe to each other and to the shareholders of the company are largely determined by the law of corporations. Finally, the organization and operation of the music public performing right societies are extensively regulated by federal antitrust law.

However, the body of law of prime importance to the record executive is intellectual property, which is dedicated to the fostering and dissemination of musical creation. Accordingly, the first part of this chapter is devoted to the fundamentals of intellectual property law. Later, other topics of interest to the record company professional will be discussed. Some of these topics have received considerable publicity; others are likely to be relatively unknown to the reader.

INTELLECTUAL PROPERTY LAW:
COPYRIGHT, TRADEMARK, TRADE SECRET, PATENT

The term "legal protection of intellectual property" is usually thought to comprise patent, copyright, trademark, and trade secret law.

Patent

Patent law is aimed at the protection of novel and useful inventions and discoveries, and it grants the inventor the exclusive right to exploit his machine or process for a limited period of time, usually twenty years. The complexity of patent law and procedure far surpasses any other method of intellectual property protection, and is of little relevance to the everyday operation of a record company. Patent law could prove important, however, when new methods of creating, storing and distributing music are developed. Historically, the development of the long-playing record (LP) is an example of the kind of technical advance which would involve patent law and for which it would make sense for a company to secure patent protection.

Copyright

Copyright law is designed to encourage the production and dissemination of intellectual, artistic, and musical works. Copyright is most familiar in the context of books, but it also governs paintings and sculpture, records, computer programs, and many other artifacts.

A key point to keep in mind is that a typical compact disc (CD) incorporates two distinct, yet related, copyrighted works. The first copyright covers the composition, the music and lyrics, being performed. The second copyright protects the sound recording, the performance of the composition captured on the disc. Different people and different institutions are often involved in the commercial exploitation of these two works. The composition is the domain of the composer and music publisher; while the sound recording is the domain of the recording artist and record company.

The Set of Exclusive Rights

Copyright seeks to affect the objective of production and circulation of creative works by guaranteeing to authors and publishers a qualified set of exclusive rights. For most works these rights consist of the right: 1) to reproduce the copyrighted work in copies or phonorecords; 2) to prepare derivative works based upon the copyrighted work; 3) to distribute copies or phonorecords of the copyrighted work to the public by sale or lease; 4) to publicly perform the copyrighted works; and 5) to publicly display the copyrighted work. The result of this protective scheme is that no one can make any of the listed uses of the work without permission from the owner of the copyright on the work.

In the case, therefore, of a composer who authors a musical composition, his interest in the marketing of sheet music and recordings of his work is protected by exclusive rights to reproduce and publicly distribute copies or license someone else to reproduce and distribute copies of the work. His interest in arranging the music or adapting it for a stage production is protected by his right to control the preparation of derivative works, that is, works based on a preexisting work. The composer's interest in being compensated when his song is played in concert or on a television or radio broadcast is secured by the right to control public performance of the music. (For purposes of this public performance right it is irrelevant whether the performance is by live musicians or by a disc jockey playing records.)

In the case of a recorded performance of music with the record company holding the copyright on the sound recording, the company's interest in preventing unauthorized duplication of the recorded performance by CD "pirates", for example, is protected by the exclusive right to reproduce phonorecords of the recording. Similarly, the company's control of distribution of the record is assured by the exclusive right to publicly distribute the work. That right also prevents anyone from renting out a record without the company's permission. (Control over rental is important because often unauthorized duplication of the recording accompanies the rental of the record.)

However, unlike the musical composition, copyright protection for the sound recording does not include a broad public performance right. Accordingly, when a copyrighted musical composition is embodied in a copyrighted sound recording and the recording is played on an over-the-air broadcast, the broadcaster is not obligated to make any payment to the recording artist or record company, although it is obligated to compensate the owner of the copyright on the recorded music, which in practice is the composer and/or music publisher. Thus, neither Capitol Records nor Frank Sinatra receives performance royalties when Sinatra's recording of a Cole Porter song is played on the air. Only Porter's music publishing company is due royalties.

Record companies and artists have long been unhappy with this disparate treatment with respect to a performance right. As a result, for several decades they have petitioned Congress to grant a public performance right in recordings comparable to that for musical works. However, these efforts have been largely unsuccessful. In 1995, record companies did secure a measure of performance right protection with the passage of the Digital Performance Right in Sound Recordings Act of 1995, but that protection is limited in its coverage. The Act was a response to new interactive services that permit consumers to use their television sets and computers to hear any record at any time. Home subscription services for the digital transmission of music allow the home subscriber to select music that can be enjoyed without the need for a CD purchase by the consumer. The new Act granted record companies and recording artists a digital performance right so that interactive music services are required to obtain licenses from both the company and the artists. Artists are entitled to royalties when recordings of their performances are distributed digitally.

The sound recording copyright is qualified in one other significant respect. The exclusive rights are limited to the right to prevent duplication or use of the actual sounds embodied in the recording and do not reach prohibition of an independent fixation of other sounds even though those sounds simulate those in the copyrighted sound recording. An independent recording by another performer is not proscribed no matter how closely that second performer imitates the style and sound of the performance on the copyrighted recording. In other words, nothing in the sound recording copyright stops an entrepreneur from employing a singer to mimic the original artist or hiring a band that sounds just like the original recording. Such "sound-alikes" do not constitute copyright infringement.

Although an imitative recording does not violate the Copyright Act, the marketing of that recording, if misleading, will run afoul of federal and state laws against misrepresentation and false advertising. Thus, while an entrepreneur may enlist a singer to imitate Diana Ross, he can not truthfully promote the resulting sound-alike recording as Diana Ross's Greatest Hits.

The Mechanical Reproduction Right and Compulsory Licensing

Composers and music publishers earn most of their income from licensing broadcasters to perform publicly records using their copyrighted music. These licenses are accomplished through the performing rights organizations, ASCAP, BMI, and SESAC. They also earn substantial revenues through licensing record companies to record their music pursuant to their mechanical reproduction right.

 The mechanical reproduction right permits composers to control the initial recording of their music and to profit from all subsequent recordings. This right, however, is subject to compulsory licensing which limits the degree of the composer's control in this regard. (The term "compulsory license" means that one must issue a license to someone who wants to use the work, whether or not one would voluntarily license the use.) Under the compulsory licensing provisions, whenever a recording of the composition authorized by the composer is distributed, anyone else may record the song and distribute phonorecords of it upon following the statutory formalities and paying the statutory rate of 9.1 cents per record to the copyright holder. This prescribed royalty amount is adjusted periodically in a public proceeding.

In other words, when a record company issues a recording of a song, any other company can then have that song recorded by one of its artists even though the company does not control the copyright on the song and has not negotiated a license from the owner of the copyright on the song. In fact, record companies usually obtain voluntary licenses that permit them to avoid many of the burdensome statutory formalities accompanying the compulsory license, such as monthly accountings. These licenses are obtained from the Harry Fox Agency, which represents most of the popular music publishers in handling the mechanical reproduction right.

Technological change often poses questions for copyright law and practice. An example is the recent advent of digital transmission of music. Subscription services may enable their subscribers to tape or download copies of recorded musical works, thereby making a distribution of those works to the public. The relationship of such transmissions to the scope of the mechanical license was initially unclear. In response, Congress in 1995 confirmed and clarified that the compulsory license to make and distribute phonorecords of musical works includes digital transmissions which constitute digital phonorecord deliveries, and that the same royalty rate applies to these transmissions. A "digital phonorecord delivery" refers to those digital transmissions of sound recordings that result in a specifically identifiable phonorecord reproduction for the recipient of the transmission. In such instances, a mechanical distribution royalty will be due the owner of the copyright on the music just as if the work had been distributed through a compact disc sale at retail.

Fixation: The Point at Which Protection Attaches

Through most of the history of American copyright law the behavior that triggered federal copyright protection was publication of the work with the appropriate notice affixed. The present law, however, radically alters that scheme. Exclusive rights arise not from registration or publication of a work, but from creation of the work. Copyright protection now attaches to original works of authorship "fixed in any tangible medium of expression". As a result of this change, publication recedes as an important legal concept and event, and fixation becomes the central idea. Copyright is secured automatically when the work is created, and a work is created when it is fixed in the tangible form of a copy or phonorecord for the first time. A work is "fixed" when "its embodiment in a copy or phonorecord...is sufficiently permanent or stable to permit it to be perceived, reproduced, or otherwise communicated for a period of more than transitory duration."

What impact does this definition have on the music industry? Two typical examples should clarify its meaning and import. First, when a composer writes down the notes of his composition or inputs them into a computer or sings and plays them into a tape recorder, a fixation of the musical work has occurred, and copyright protection of that work exists. Thus, a song can be fixed in sheet music ("copies") or in phonograph discs ("phonorecords") or both. Similarly, when a recording artist performs a musical work and that performance is captured on tape, a fixation of the performance has occurred and copyright protection of the sound recording exists.

In addition to fixation, to be copyrightable a work must be "original". In this context, originality does not mean novelty or some advance over the prior art, nor does it imply a requirement of artistic or intellectual merit. Instead, it means simply that the work was independently created by the author and that he has not copied the work from something else. Copyright protection does not depend on the quality or purpose of the work.

Ownership of Copyright

Who is the owner of the copyright in a protected work? To what extent can the owner transfer all or part of his interest?

Generally the author of a work is the initial owner of the copyright on his creation. Accordingly, the composer of a musical piece is the owner of the copyright in the piece. If different people create the music and the lyrics, the resulting creation is regarded as a joint work, and the people are treated as co-owners of the copyright. However, in the case of a "work for hire", which includes a work prepared by an employee within the scope of his employment, the person for whom the work was prepared is deemed the author for purposes of copyright law. As a result, the record company is usually regarded as the owner of the copyright of a sound recording.

The bundle of rights that comprise a copyright is divisible. Divisibility means that each of these interests can be licensed or transferred separately from the others. For example, the holder of a copyright on a piece of music might license one person to record his song, another person to market sheet music, another to use the music in a film, and yet another to monitor the public performance of the song. The performing rights societies, ASCAP, BMI, and SESAC, are organizations to which composers and music publishers have assigned their interests so as to best exploit their public performance rights.

No matter who is designated as the initial owner of the copyright, that ownership status can be changed by agreement. For example, the copyright on a musical composition is usually held in the name of the music publisher rather than the composer, with the division of mechanical reproduction royalties between composer and publisher specified by the contract establishing their mutual rights and duties. The transfer of a copyright or of any of the constituent elements of the bundle of rights must be in writing to be valid.

Duration of Protection

How long does copyright last? The constitutional provision that authorizes Congress to enact patent and copyright laws empowers it to "promote the progress of science and useful arts, by securing for limited times to authors and inventors the exclusive right to their respective writings and discoveries." While protection is limited in time rather than perpetual, the period is lengthy. Indeed, the history of copyright duration in the United States has been one of an ever-lengthening term of protection. The most recent extension of the term of protection occurred in 1998.

Under present law copyright in a work endures for a term consisting of the life of the author and seventy years after his death. What does this protective period amount to in practice? Imagine a musical composition created by composer C in 1980. The copyright in that composition will last for C's life plus seventy years after his death. Thus, if C dies in 1995, copyright will expire in 2065. If C dies in 2006, copyright protection will last until 2076. Note that C's death will determine the period of protection even if C has transferred his interest. Assume that C sells the full copyright interest to B in 1990. B's protection will still expire in 2065 if C dies in 1995 and in 2076 if C dies in 2006.

In the case of works made for hire, copyright endures for a term of ninety-five years from initial publication, or 120 years from creation, whichever expires first. Thus copyright protection in a sound recording, if deemed a work for hire, lasts ninety-five years from its public distribution. Imagine record company X tapes a studio performance in 1997 and releases it on compact disc in 1999. The copyright on that recorded performance would expire in 2094, ninety-five years after its first distribution.

Remedies

Copyright infringement is the unauthorized exercise of one of the rights that the law reserves exclusively to the copyright owner. Anyone who duplicates a disc without authorization, for example, infringes the reproduction right held by the owner of the sound recording copyright. Similarly, a concert promoter who performs songs without permission violates the public performance rights held by the owners of the copyrights on the musical compositions. A copyright owner whose work has been infringed has a variety of judicial remedies available to him. He may obtain an injunction, a court decree ordering the infringer to cease his infringing behavior. Serious sanctions lie behind this order, as an infringer who violates an injunction is in contempt of court and may be fined or imprisoned. In addition, the owner may be able to secure impoundment and destruction of the infringing copies of his work.

The owner is also able to recover a monetary award. He may choose to sue for the profits that the infringer made due to the infringement and for any additional damage he suffered that is not taken into account in figuring the infringer's profits. Alternatively, the copyright owner may elect to sue instead for "statutory damages"; under this option, he is entitled to a minimum recovery of $750 and a maximum of $30,000, according to what the court finds just. If the infringement is willful, the statutory damage award may go as high as $150,000. One advantage of statutory damages is that the owner need not provide as detailed evidence of damage in order to obtain a monetary recovery. Finally, the court has discretion to award a reasonable attorney's fee to the winning party in a case.

The willful commercial infringer is also subject to criminal remedies. Such an infringement qualifies as a federal misdemeanor or felony–depending on its scope–and is punishable, for the serious first offender, by up to five years in jail and/or up to a $250,000 fine. Criminal prosecutions under the Copyright Act were quite rare until three decades ago. In the past three decades, however, the practice of large-scale record, video, and computer software piracy has elicited much more frequent criminal investigation and prosecution. And Congress has both increased the criminal penalties substantially in recent years and broadened the scope of behaviors to which they can apply.

Formalities: Notice and Registration

Notice. Most of us are familiar with copyright notice from our reading of books. That notice generally consists of the letter C in a circle, the word "Copyright", or the abbreviation "Copr." followed by the year of first publication of the work and the name of the owner of the copyright. Prior to 1978 the affixing of notice played a major role in securing copyright protection for a work. Indeed, a failure to properly comply with the notice requirement on the first publication of a work could result in a complete loss of protection.

The 1976 Act began a process of progressive de-emphasis of formal requirements. In particular, while affixation of notice remained mandatory, the stringency of the notice requirement was dramatically lessened. No longer were disastrous consequences for noncompliance likely. The Act granted protection for some works despite the lack of any notice at all, provided for the correction of errors in otherwise defective notices, and significantly reduced the negative legal effect of a failure to attach notice to a work.

This decline in the significance of formalities was accelerated in 1988 by the United States' accession to the Berne Convention, the foremost international copyright treaty. Under that convention, the enjoyment and exercise of rights may not be subject to any formality. Accordingly, the amendments to American law that were passed in 1989 to bring that law in accord with our Berne obligations eliminated the mandatory character of notice. For works presently distributed, copyright notice is not required to assure protection; it is completely elective. Its only legal significance now is that it prevents an infringer from pleading innocent infringement--that is, infringing without the knowledge that he was doing so.

While notice is no longer legally required, as a practical matter it is still advisable to attach it to the work. The notice informs the public that the work is protected, and it identifies the copyright owner. This information and identification will facilitate licensing transactions between the owner and those who want to make use of the work. In the case of works for hire, such as sound recordings, the notice will also provide a basis for determination of the copyright's expiration (ninety-five years after the notice date).

One aspect of notice distinctive to the music business should be noted. The common notice form of C in a circle applies to works, such as books or sheet music, which appear in visually perceptible copies. The notice form for phonorecords of sound recordings is slightly different. Rather than the C in a circle ©, the letter P in a circle is to be used along with the year of first publication of the recording and the name of the owner of the copyright. This notice is placed either on the surface of the disc or on the disc's label or container.

Registration. Copyright protection, unlike patent and trademark, is essentially self executing. As has been noted, protection attaches as soon as an author fixes his work in a tangible medium of expression. No approval of or registration with a government agency is needed, although registration does significantly affect the legal relief available to the author.

There are copyright registration procedures and deposit requirements. These procedures, however, are not a condition to protection. That is, copyright protection will exist despite lack of registration or failure to deposit the called-for copies of the work. Registration and deposit, however, do have significant legal consequences. Most importantly, an owner of copyright in the work of an American author cannot sue for copyright infringement until he has registered the copyright. Thus, while registration is not a precondition to protection, it usually is a precondition to suit; in other words, no registration means no ability to initiate litigation to take full advantage of the anti-infringement remedies provided by the law.

Registration, moreover, is a prerequisite to certain remedies, and these remedies can be lost by failure to register soon enough. First, attorneys' fees cannot be recovered for infringements that occur prior to registration unless registration is made within three months after first publication of the work. Second, statutory damages are also not recoverable under the same circumstances.

The practical implication of this system is that while registration is largely optional, it is advisable to register a work promptly after its initial distribution in order to safeguard litigation and remedial advantages. Registration is a simple, inexpensive process that requires submission to the Copyright Office of an application form, the specified fee, and deposit of two complete copies or phonorecords of the work.

Home Recording

Periodically technological change significantly alters the manner, form, cost, and ease with which intellectual or artistic works are disseminated. The photocopying machine, for example, has had such a dramatic impact in the case of printed materials. The audio tape recorder and player similarly affected the distribution of recorded music. Its effects were multiple. On the one hand it created a new market for recorded music in the form of prerecorded tapes and cassettes. On the other hand, it facilitated the practice of home recording, the practice of individuals making tapes at home of their own or friends' records or taping broadcasts of recorded music off the air. Home recording and the inexpensive taping technology supporting it undoubtedly expanded access to music and increased public exposure to various works. At the same time, however, the practice had a displacement effect on record sales; to some extent, home taping replaces purchases.

The question of the appropriate public response to this practice presented the legal system with a serious dilemma. The standard copyright law paradigm of a voluntary transaction between the copyright owner and the prospective user of his work is unworkable in this context. It is not feasible for an individual contemplating home taping to seek and arrange permission with the copyright owners. From the music and record producers' perspective, the new technology not only made it possible for individuals to make quality copies of copyrighted works easily and cheaply but also to do so in a setting where detection of the copying is either impossible or practicable only by intolerable invasions of people's privacy.

Congress responded to this dilemma by enacting the Audio Home Recording Act of 1992, which creates a levy scheme similar to those in place in other industrialized countries. First, the Act legitimizes the practice of digital audio (DAT) home recording. It declares that such home taping is not to be deemed a copyright infringement. Second, it imposes a royalty charge on the importation and distribution or the manufacture and distribution of digital audio recording equipment and digital audio tapes. Normally the royalty due on recording devices is 2% of the transfer price and on blank tapes 3% of the price. The initial importer or manufacturer is responsible for payment of the royalty.

The money collected by the Copyright Office via these levies is pooled, with the pooled funds to be distributed among music publishers, composers, record companies and recording artists whose works have been subject to home taping. Two separate royalty funds exist. Two/thirds of the royalty payments are allocated to the Sound Recordings Fund; in turn approximately 60% of that fund goes to record companies and approximately 40% to featured performers. (A small percentage of this fund is reserved for backup musicians and vocalists who have performed on sound recordings.) One/third of the royalty payments are allocated to the Musical Works Fund, which is divided equally between music publishers and songwriters.

In addition to establishment of this royalty arrangement, the Act requires that all digital audio tape recorders be equipped with the Serial Copy Management System (SCMS) or an equivalent technical control that prevents copying from copies of digital audio recordings. The SCMS is a device that can distinguish between a prerecorded tape and one that is a copy of a prerecorded tape. The device prevents a digital audio recorder from making a copy of the latter. The objective is to permit one copy by the home taper but to discourage the making of multiple high quality duplicates, as that practice may well displace sales of prerecorded works.

Due to its narrow scope the amounts generated from the Act have been quite small. More fundamentally, because its focus is on DAT technology, which never became widely used by individuals, and because judicial interpretation has held that personal computers, the devices most commonly used by consumers to make digital copies of music, are not covered by the Act, this statutory arrangement does not reach the most recent and extensive form of home recording.

Anti-Bootlegging Legislation

Federal law has for several decades protected recorded performances against unauthorized reproduction. That protection is accorded by the grant of copyright to the sound recording. However, no federal protection of live musical performances existed. In 1994 passage of the Federal Anti-Bootleg Statute changed that situation. That law prohibits unauthorized recording, manufacture, distribution, or trafficking in recordings of artists' live musical performances. Violators can be sued civilly by the affected performer and can be punished criminally with up to five years in prison and $250,000 in fines.

Trademark

 The prime purpose of trademark law is to insure accurate identification of the source of a product, and the prevention of consumer confusion is the principal aim of conventional trademark doctrine. Accuracy of identification is important to any company because its reputation is at stake when it is marked as the producer of an item, and its good will will be damaged and future sales suffer if the product is defective and the company is misidentified as the manufacturer. Accuracy of identification of source is also important to the consumer because misidentification is a deceptive act, and the result of the deception is often consumer dissatisfaction, as he is not, in fact, purchasing the product that he thinks is being purchased. Trademark law protects a company's investment in the development of positive relationships with customers.

A good example of violation of trademark law is the case of the record "pirate" who not only reproduces the recording without permission, but also duplicates the name and corporate logo or symbol of the original producer that appears on the packaging of the compact disc. The purpose of this behavior is to induce the buyer into thinking that this item was made by the original record company. Accordingly, to the extent that the identity of the source affects the purchaser's decision to buy, revenues that should go to the original manufacturer will be diverted to the duplicator. The duplicator, often referred to as a "counterfeiter," has violated both copyright law by reproducing the music and sound recording without permission of the copyright owners, and trademark law by identifying the source of the product in a way which would confuse purchasers of the item.

Trademarks and trade names refer to words and symbols used on goods to identify the source of the good. (Service marks are words and symbols used on services to identify the source of the service.) Examples in the music industry are the picture of a palm tree enclosed in a circle, which identifies Island Records, and the stylized capital letter "A" boxed in a rectangle, which indicates the products of Atlantic Records. Trademarks differ in distinctiveness. An example of a strong mark is "Kodak", as it is arbitrary, non-descriptive, prestigious, and without generic overtones. Weak marks are typically descriptive or common, such as "Gold Medal". The stronger the mark the greater the scope of protection provided by the law. When a designation is said to be generic, it signifies that it is used as the name of the article itself, regardless of source, and as a result cannot be monopolized by a single producer. Even a coined word that initially qualifies as a trademark because of its capacity to indicate source can become generic and therefore non-protectable. "Cellophane" is a famous example.

Historically the laws of various states offered, and still offer, protection for trademarks by providing civil remedies against the fraudulent marketing of goods through the imitation of another's mark. Today, however, for those who wish to market goods in more than one state, the prime source of protection, through a system of trademark registration, is the Lanham Act, the federal trademark statute. This system is administered by the Patent and Trademark Office of the U.S. Department of Commerce. The "R" in a circle ® is a symbol that the holder of a federally registered trademark uses to give notice that its mark is registered. This designation calls attention to the mark and alerts other companies that the mark is protected and should not be used without authorization. Before the 1988 amendment of the Lanham Act, actual use of the trademark or service mark in interstate commerce was a prerequisite to registration. In other words, a company could not apply for registration until the identifying mark had been in commercial use. However, since the 1988 revision, application for registration can be made based on an intention to use the mark. This change provides a greater measure of security to a company for pre-marketing expenditures.

A registration system needs to generate a list that companies can consult in order to avoid adopting marks that are already taken. Under the Lanham Act that list is known as the principal register. A system also requires a priority rule to solve the problem of multiple use, i.e., a way to determine who among multiple users of a mark has the right to keep the mark and who must pay to switch to a new mark. Historically, the general rule has been that conflicting claims to trademark ownership are resolved according to priority of appropriation; in other words, the rule favors the first user in a geographical area. Under federal registration, however, the rule of priority is altered due to the doctrine of constructive notice. Upon federal registration the owner of the registered trademark can claim nationwide constructive notice. Another user cannot claim lack of notice because everyone is presumed to have the notice that the federal registration legally provides. Accordingly, there can be no good faith use after federal registration, despite the fact that factually a second user may proceed innocently and in good faith.

What is the test for trademark infringement? What behavior is proscribed? The standard of infringement is the likelihood of consumer confusion about the source of the product. Under the Lanham Act, anyone who uses a reproduction or imitation of a registered mark in a way that "is likely to cause confusion, or to cause mistake, or to deceive" is liable to the owner of the registered mark. Whether the user intended to deceive or acted in innocence is irrelevant. This test is rooted in the informational function of marks; accurate identification of source is the norm. Thus, the exclusive right given to a registrant and user amounts to the authority to prevent others from using the same mark, or a confusingly similar mark, on the same or related goods. This trademark right continues so long as the company uses the mark.

Registration under the Lanham Act provides a variety of procedural and remedial advantages. One of these advantages is incontestability, which attaches after five years of registration and which radically limits the challenges and defenses available to an alleged infringer. The remedies for infringement are several, and they are cumulative. First, the trademark owner can seek injunctive relief, i.e., a court decree ordering the infringer to stop using the confusing mark. The owner is also entitled to recover the profits the defendant earned while using the infringing mark, as well as a damage recovery of any other loss he suffered due to the infringement. In addition, if the defendant has an inventory of infringing goods, a court may order their destruction. Finally, in exceptional cases, the defendant may be entitled to an award of attorneys' fees.

Dilution. While prevention of confusion and deception in the marketplace is the focus of traditional trademark law, there is an additional concept in this area that emphasizes not the identification function of marks but rather the advertising and commercial values inherent in successful, highly distinctive symbols. That concept is "dilution", and it protects good will by acting against uses that may drain off the potency of a mark, regardless of the likelihood of source confusion. Dilution has been recognized by statute in more than twenty states, and in 1996 Congress enacted the Federal Trademark Dilution Act to provide relief against dilution of the distinctive quality of registered marks that have become famous.

Generally, two forms of dilution have been recognized: blurring and tarnishment. Blurring takes place when use of a mark on other goods and services reduces the mark's ability to serve as a unique indicator of source. For example, the LEXIS legal research service relied on this blurring theory, unsuccessfully, in its attempt to prevent the use by Toyota of LEXUS on luxury cars. Tarnishment takes place when a mark is associated with goods of inferior quality or is portrayed in an unsavory context, causing it to lose its wholesome identity. Therefore, under a good will theory of trademark, an owner may succeed in halting the use of its mark on an unrelated product, even though consumers are not confused about the owner's actual products, because of a concern that consumers will think less of the owner if the other goods are inferior,

The major practical implication of this summary of trademark law for the record executive is the need to be aware of potential liability when a name or symbol is being considered for use to identify a company, product, line of product or service, recording group, or other similar entity. If the name or symbol turns out to be confusingly similar to a mark already in use, the company would be subject to suit with the possibility of being ordered not to use the name. Accordingly, it makes sense to try to assure oneself that no trademark infringement will occur before starting to make use of the name or symbol. The larger the present and potential investment in the name, the more prudent is an advance investigation to avoid adopting marks that are already taken. A trademark search can be conducted by the company's legal department. However, it generally makes more sense in terms of efficiency and coverage to employ one of the trademark search services that specialize in conducting these investigations. The cost of a professionally conducted search is modest, and the search can be completed quickly, often within a few days.

Musical Performers' Names

The protection of musical performers' names, including the names of musical groups, when the public associates that name with the particular service being given, is related to a discussion of trademark law. When, for example, the law of unfair competition acts against the use of a name by a second performing group which is likely to cause confusion, it is vindicating the common policy concern to protect the consumer from being misled as to the source of services and to protect these sources from having their efforts exploited.

Questions about the ownership of a group name, how it is to be shared among the group's members, and the effect of departures and additions of individual performers are usually the province not of the record company but of the performers and their manager, with partnership law acting as a backstop. Ideally, an agreement at the outset will deal explicitly with these contingencies, although such formal advance agreements are hardly common.

On occasion the record company may have a role to play in this name game. Thus, if a group with whom the company is dealing is considering adoption of a name (or changing its existing name), the company, out of prudence, should insure that great care is exercised to prevent selection of a name that is confusingly similar to an already existing name in the field. Not only should "The Rolling Stones" be shunned, but it is advisable to avoid "The Rolling Rocks" as well! Professional help can be engaged in the effort to avoid duplicative and confusing names. Firms specializing in this kind of search are available, and valuable data is available through AFTRA (The American Federation of Television & Radio Artists), the union for performers on radio and television, which maintains a list of the names of performers on its roster. Caution is advisable not simply because names are valuable and can sell records, but also because the record company is out to forestall both its possible financial liability to a prior user of the name and the loss of resources expended in the creation of promotional material using the group's name, such as album covers and advertising copy.

Trade Secret

Trade secret law may be used to protect items, such as commercially valuable ideas, which are not accorded protection by copyright, patent or trademark law. A trade secret encompasses any commercially valuable information that a company has taken reasonable steps to keep confidential In other words, a trade secret is any confidential information that is valuable to a company because it provides the company with a competitive advantage. Some pertinent examples of trade secrets are a closely guarded advertising scheme or marketing strategy or customer list. Frequently secrecy is sought not just by means of physical security but by non-disclosure agreements between a company and its employees.

Let's assume a case of a guarded marketing strategy known to only a few executives and that these executives acquired that knowledge solely in the course of this confidential relationship. In this case, the employees are obliged not to make use of the secret for their own commercial purposes or to disclose it to other people. Furthermore, that obligation not to use or disclose the idea may well continue even after the employee's term of employment with the company ends; the employee who later goes to work for a competitor may still be bound to secrecy.

In addition to protection against unauthorized disclosure, a trade secret is also protected against improper acquisition by a competitor. Examples of clearly improper methods of obtaining another's trade secret are industrial espionage via electronic surveillance, bribery of employees, and placement of spies within the other's organization. All of these behaviors would give rise to civil liability for trade secret misappropriation. Finally, liability is not confined to those who breach a confidential relationship or improperly obtain another's secret but includes as well those who make use of a trade secret knowing it to have been improperly disclosed by another.

Trade secret law imposes no time limit on protection. Protection is available for as long as the information remains secret. The remedies that law supplies are both injunctive and monetary; that is, in a case of trade secret misappropriation a court may prohibit future use of the secret and may also award a compensatory financial recovery for the economic loss caused by the misappropriation.

As a practical matter, trade secrets are most frequently misappropriated by people who properly receive the information and then improperly disclose or use it. That pattern suggests the need for efforts to educate employees as to the sensitive nature of certain information and the company's intention that such information remain secret. That message should also be manifest not only in physical security measures but also in a uniform document handling policy within the company, including the marking of appropriate documents as "confidential". In addition, employees with access to trade secrets should sign a non-disclosure agreement. A serious policy of safeguarding the company's secrets requires that employees be made aware through education of what information is considered to be trade secret information, what their role is in the protection of that information, and what the consequences of misappropriation are. Employees should also be cautioned against letting secrets slip through lack of care or by disclosure in social settings.

The business executive intent on taking practical preventive measures to protect his company's trade secrets faces two tasks. First, he must clearly define the information that the company wants to keep secret. And second, he needs to implement policies and security procedures reasonable under the circumstances to maintain the secrecy of that information.

While historically the protection of trade secrets has been the province of state law, the enactment of the Economic Espionage Act of 1996 made the theft of trade secrets a federal criminal offense. This legislation represents a major development in the law of trade secrets in the United States and internationally. It is designed to create a national scheme to protect U.S. proprietary economic information, particularly against high-tech theft via the Internet. Persons engaged in trade secret misappropriation can now no longer be assured that liability will be limited to civil remedies and monetary damages imposed for such misconduct. Violation of the Act can result in stiff criminal penalties.

The Content of Recordings: The Record Industry and Censorship

The content of a recording--that is, the lyrics of the song being performed-- may expose a record label to the risk of legal liability. It is conceivable, for example, that the words of a song might disparage an identifiable individual in a way that damages his reputation. In such a case, the law of defamation (libel and slander) might come into play and afford that individual a monetary claim against the company.[i]

A more likely encounter between a recording and the legal system, however, is with the state and federal laws proscribing the distribution and sale of obscene materials. These laws subject producers, distributors, and retailers of obscene material to possible fine and imprisonment as well as confiscation of the obscene matter. While obscenity prosecutions are uncommon, the threat of the laws' invocation remains a real one. A prime example centered on the album "As Nasty As They Wanna Be" by the rap group 2 Live Crew. In 1990, the recording's graphic lyrics prompted the arrest on obscenity-related charges of the performers as well as record retailers in several states.

It is a firm constitutional principle that freedom of expression requires that governments refrain from regulation of speech based on the content of that speech. That principle would seem to rule out the possibility of legal action against the makers or distributors of a recording based on its lyrical content. However, the Supreme Court has consistently ruled that "obscenity" is outside of the protection of the first amendment. Thus, obscene materials, whether printed or aural, can be regulated. And both the federal and state governments have some proscriptions in place. The federal law prohibits the distribution of obscene matter through various methods such as importation, mailing, interstate transport and sale. Violators are subject to criminal prosecution and face the possibility of significant fine and imprisonment. Similarly, the state of California, for example, condemns the sale, distribution, promotion, or exhibition of obscene materials.

The ongoing difficulty, however, is with the definition of "obscenity"; exactly which materials may be suppressed? According to the Supreme Court, obscene expression describes sexual conduct in a patently offensive way, appeals to the prurient interest, and lacks serious literary, artistic, scientific or political value. Unfortunately, for those who must try to guide their behavior by reference to this definition, its vagueness often makes confident application problematic, particularly as community standards may vary among geographical areas. The defects in this attempt to draw an intelligible line between protected and unprotected material so as to give fair advance warning as to what is forbidden suggest that it is unlikely that the development of the law in this area has reached a state of rest. Rather, it is likely that we have not seen the end of marked movement in the constitutional law of obscenity and in the Supreme Court's response to the contention that legal restraints on the publication of obscenity are an unconstitutional violation of the first amendment's guarantees of freedom of speech and press.

The character of a recording's lyrics is of legal and practical import not only to the record company and those who distribute its product but also to radio broadcasters who play recorded music as part of their daily programming. And in the broadcast context the constraints on content go beyond prohibition of obscenity. Federal law prohibits the uttering of "any obscene, indecent, or profane language by means of radio communication." The acceptability of what is broadcast is regulated by the Federal Communications Commission (FCC). Under the FCC's regulations, "indecency" encompasses more than the obscene, and the term is defined as language or material that depicts or describes sexual or excretory activities and organs in terms patently offensive as measured by contemporary community standards for the broadcast medium. Language, then, can be "indecent" even though it has artistic value and lacks prurient appeal. As with "obscenity" the definition is vague and in many cases will not supply reliable precision as a guide to decision.

Radio airplay, of course, is a prime promotional vehicle for records. Sales are assisted by the advertising provided by these broadcasts. Accordingly, in order to secure airplay and to minimize broadcasters' legal risk, record companies often release two different versions of the same song, the "clean" or radio form and the original or "street" form with explicit lyrics intact. The object is to remove raunchy words deemed unfit to be heard by broadcast audiences, especially children. This technique responds to the indecency limit on programming and at the same time assures the record company's promotional interests in its product by issuing to broadcasters a different version than that distributed to retailers, and is especially common with rap music and artists.

Labeling

The record company's interest in lyrical content is prompted not only by anti-obscenity and anti-decency laws but also by potential negative reaction by consumers and private watchdog groups. In 1985 the Recording Industry Association of America (RIAA), the industry trade association, reached an agreement with the National Parent Teacher Association and the Parents Music Resource Center, under which record companies would voluntarily identify and label newly released recordings that may contain strong language or expressions of violence, sex or substance abuse. Then, in 1990 the RIAA implemented a uniform parental advisory logo that continues in wide use today. The purpose of this program is to provide information on the basis of which parents can guide their children's music consumption while at the same time not inhibiting the expression of record companies and their artists. That information may also be helpful to radio stations and retailers when deciding whether specific explicit recordings should be broadcast or made available for sale to minors. The decision to label a particular recording (or music video) is left to each company. The visible black-and-white logo, measuring 1" x 1 5/8", is placed on the front of the permanent packaging, and appears as follows:

PARENTAL
ADVISORY

EXPLICIT CONTENT

ANTITRUST LAWS

The Sherman Act

Federal and state antitrust laws are aimed at the prohibition of anti-competitive practices. These proscriptions reflect a commitment to competitive market processes as the preferred social means to achieve efficiency in resource use and enhancement of the welfare of consumers. Arrangements that interfere with the operation of reasonably competitive markets are condemned.

The Sherman Act is the federal antitrust statute that is of principal interest to business executives. State laws are typically modeled on the federal statute. The Sherman Act addresses improperly restrictive agreements. More precisely, section 1 of the Act does not specify prohibited conduct in detail but rather declares illegal "every contract, combination... or conspiracy in restraint of trade or commerce among the several States. . . ."[ii] This broad proscription has been flexibly interpreted as a condemnation of unreasonable conduct; that is, the Act condemns not every contract but rather only unreasonable agreements in restraint of trade.

The assumption underlying section 1 is that the social benefits of competition may be lost if rivals are permitted to join together and to consolidate their market power. Agreements to limit output and raise prices above competitive levels directly impair competition. Accordingly, in looking to control the misuse of private economic power the prime concern of the Act and its enforcers is with such concerted arrangements. The most egregious example of this kind of illegal interference with the market mechanism is an agreement by competing firms to fix the price for their product; for instance, an arrangement among record producers to set the prices they will charge wholesalers and retailers for recordings. It is not difficult to appreciate why competitors would find price-fixing attractive. If successful, such an arrangement yields a higher price and more profit for participants than would occur in a competitive market free of such restraints.

While price-fixing is financially attractive to businessmen, its social effects are undesirable. One major effect is a decline in the welfare of consumers, for this plan deprives consumers of two major benefits of a competitive market: lower prices and increased output. Direct price-fixing agreements are not the only way prices can be controlled and price competition reduced or eliminated. This consequence can be affected indirectly by various forms of agreements not to compete with one another. An agreement to divide markets, for instance, a geographical allocation under which one firm serves one area and the other firm a different location, is an example of an arrangement that suppresses rivalry. Since this concerted action has the same negative consequences for consumers as does direct price-fixing, it is similarly condemned outright by federal and state antitrust law.

The antitrust laws' concern is not only with "horizontal" arrangements, agreements between rivals at the same level of the production and distribution process, but also with "vertical" relations between firms and distributors, such as the relations between record companies and wholesalers or retailers. An example of such an arrangement designed to confer distributional advantages is an agreement under which a producer promises to sell to only one distributor in a certain geographical area. While the law governing vertical relationships is complex, and an explicit resale price maintenance understanding should be avoided, one can say that producers and distributors generally have considerably more latitude in defining their relationship than do producers or distributors and their rivals.

The legal ramifications of illegal restraints are significant. The Act supplies powerful remedies, and enforcement of the statute takes place both publicly and privately; that is, civil actions may be brought both by a public agency and by a private business which has been damaged by the violation of the law. The Antitrust Division of the U.S. Department of Justice and the Federal Trade Commission are the public agencies charged with enforcement of the antitrust laws, and one of their remedial options is to seek a judicial order enjoining specific restrictive behavior. (State attorneys general may also sue in some circumstances.) A private suit can be particularly expensive for a defendant because a successful plaintiff is entitled to an award of treble damages, i.e., in fixing the amount of money owed by the defendant the financial injury sustained by the business is assessed and that sum is then multiplied by three. In addition, the prevailing claimant is entitled to recover its attorneys' fees from the defendant.

The criminal provisions of the federal antitrust laws are enforced by the Department of Justice and authorize substantial penalties. These sanctions have increased significantly in the recent decades. The Sherman Act now fixes a maximum fine of $10 million for corporate defendants. Individuals may be punished by fines of up to $350,000 and jail sentences of up to three years. Generally, criminal felony prosecutions of trade restraints are limited to core violations of Sherman Act section 1, such as price-fixing and market division schemes and collective acts to exclude rivals from a market, which can produce similarly deleterious effects. Also, criminal (and government civil) cases usually lead to major private treble damage suits.

What are the practical implications of this legal structure for the record industry executive? Most obvious is the need to refrain from any kind of price-fixing or market division. Such behavior carries unmistakable dangers, including possible criminal prosecution.[iii] Care needs to be taken not only in the agreements reached with other companies but also in what topics are discussed with rival firms.[iv] Businesses often share information with competitors to identify best practices, cut costs, and improve distribution. While courts and government agencies have applauded many forms of cooperative activity, relations among rivals continue to attract close scrutiny.

The use of trade associations provides a good example of the caution needed. Not all joint activity or inter-firm communication restricts output and raises prices. Trade associations, for example, may legitimately promote an industry to potential customers and do so in a manner that is cheaper than it is for individual firms to advertise. Trade groups also often disseminate trade information among group members. The Record Industry Association of America (RIAA), for instance, compiles and publishes statistics on record sales, and is responsible for awarding gold and platinum records based on those sales.

The exchange of information between competing businesses often raises antitrust problems, however, because these exchanges may be a vehicle for group members to fix prices or allocate sales opportunities. Accordingly, such exchanges of information should be limited to past prices and should not bind members to abide by any announced prices. For the industry executive, antitrust risks can be minimized by limiting his communications to data other than current or future prices. To reinforce this caution, a lawyer should be present at trade association meetings to monitor the direction of formal and informal discussions. Finally, before entering any arrangement with rival firms, one must ask whether there are ways to achieve the firm's objective by unilateral action, as record companies acting alone face relatively few antitrust risks.[v]

Price Discrimination and the Robinson-Patman Act

Price discrimination refers to the behavior of a seller charging different prices to different buyers for essentially the same product. In one sense, of course, such differential pricing behavior is commonplace. That a gallon of gasoline costs the consumer a different price in New Jersey than in Connecticut hardly causes a raised eyebrow.

Certain versions of price discrimination, though, do implicate the antitrust laws, most specifically the Robinson-Patman Act. That act applies to sales of commodities of like grade and quality in interstate commerce when the discriminating sale, involving a price below cost, has the effect of lessening competition. Essentially the act bars price discrimination unless it is supported by cost savings to the seller or by a good faith belief that it is necessary to meet a competitor's price offer. Originally designed to protect small businesses from the more efficient buying and selling practices of larger, more integrated chain store operations, the language of the Robinson-Patman Act is a troublesome tangle of complicated and highly indeterminate terms. Also, the Act has been heavily criticized as a policy failure that is at odds with the pro-competitive aims of other antitrust statutes. Accordingly, suits initiated by the government are extremely rare. (In the period from 1981 through 1990, the FTC filed only one Robinson-Patman Act complaint and have initiated none since.)

Although the act is flawed, it still influences pricing decisions as the risk of private suits remains. However, in an industry such as the record business where no single producer enjoys monopoly power, it is unlikely that an executive and company that price its products in pursuit of maximum profitability (and whose selective price cuts do not reflect an effort to drive rivals out of business) will run afoul of this Act.

Record Clubs and the Federal Trade Commission (FTC)

In addition to sales through retailers and on-line distribution, records are marketed through other channels of dissemination. One of these channels is direct-mail sales through record clubs. Record clubs are mail-order arrangements that members usually join by agreeing to purchase a certain number of CDs. Typically clubs solicit and sustain membership by bonus and free CD offers. BMG Music Service is the principal contemporary music club. While Columbia House, the first record club, originally offered sales of only its own label, record clubs now commonly distribute the product of diverse record companies.

Record club arrangements early attracted the attention of the Federal Trade Commission (FTC). Acting under Section 5 of the FTC Act, which prohibits "unfair methods of competition" and "unfair or deceptive acts or practices" in commerce, the Commission in 1962 charged the Columbia Record Club with monopoly practices and the illegal suppression of competition. Two club practices, in particular, were challenged. The first was Columbia's agreements with other labels under which Columbia was the exclusive record club distributor of these labels. In response to the FTC challenge Columbia agreed to terminate the arrangements under which it acted as the exclusive record club for the labels of other record manufacturers. And it is now the common practice of all major record clubs to obtain their product from labels on a nonexclusive basis. Indeed, clubs now offer for sale virtually any CD that proves sufficiently popular to earn a listing in their advertisements. The other practice on which the FTC focused was the so-called "negative option" procedure. Under this method of operation, record club members are sent and billed for records periodically unless they explicitly reject the offerings. As a result of the FTC proceeding, the negative option procedure may still be employed by record clubs but the practice is subject to detailed federal regulations which are designed to insure that club members are aware of the practice and are given a clear opportunity to reject the records offered.

Payola

Payola refers to the secret payment to and acceptance by broadcasting personnel of money, services or other value in exchange for their on-air use of a particular record or song. The payments are typically made by record company or independent promoters, and the broadcasting personnel involved are usually disc jockeys, music directors, and program directors. Payola is indefensible in that the recipients are employees of radio stations who, presumably, are pocketing the proceeds from the sale of an asset belonging to their employer, the use of air time to promote records. In addition, the practice contradicts the representation to the public that the radio station selects records on the basis of popularity or the music or program director's judgments of each song's intrinsic artistic merits.

Congress responded to the practice in 1960 by amending the Communications Act to make payola, in effect, a federal criminal offense. Under this law a broadcast employee accepting a payment to promote the play of particular records is obliged to inform the station, which must, in turn, inform the public through an announcement on the program involved. Any violation of these provisions of the Act subjects the offender to a fine of up to $10,000 or imprisonment for up to one year or both. In addition, payola may run afoul of state commercial bribery statutes; and the Federal Trade Commission has declared the behavior an "unfair or deceptive" practice under section 5 of the FTC Act. While the sanctions provided in the 1960 anti-payola statute are minimal and that law has not been vigorously enforced, payola today may trigger liability under the RICO (Racketeer Influenced and Corrupt Organizations) statute, which can impose heavy penalties on a company that engages in bribery.

Reports of continued payola and public investigations of the practice appear periodically. The persistence of the temptation of those interested in record sales to bribe those selecting records to be broadcast is unsurprising. It stems from the accepted fact that radio play stimulates record sales by exposing new releases to potential buyers; in other words, radio play advertises records. Moreover, unlike most advertising, which only describes the product and its effectiveness, a record broadcast precisely apprises potential record buyers of the nature of the product involved; and by playing the record also gives the song the endorsement of a supposedly neutral source, the station's music programmer or the disc jockey who plays it. The effectiveness of radio play as a means of advertising new records and the inability of broadcasters to charge directly for this advertising create fertile ground for payola.

LEGAL CHALLENGES, PRESENT AND PROSPECTIVE

Digital Sampling

The spread of digital technology raises new problems for the owners of copyrights in a variety of intellectual and artistic works including musical compositions, sound recordings, and works of visual art. For example, as a result of the combination of computer and laser technologies, photographs now can be scanned by lasers and converted into digital data capable of being manipulated by a computer. The digitized image can then be altered to create a new scene that never existed; and portions of different works can be combined into a single image. The dilemmas posed for the law of copyright are manifest. Is it an infringement to take a tree from a copyrighted photograph and use it as background in a new picture? And how can the owner even know that a part of his work has been copied?

Similarly, the limits of the reproduction right in sound recordings and musical compositions are being tested by the practice of digital sampling. A digital sampler is a machine capable of taking an instrumental sound (e.g., a drum riff or horn blast) or voice and making a perfect digital duplication. That sound can then be edited and reworked as part of a new composition or recording. In other words, digital recording of music makes possible by computer analysis the extraction of bits of sound and the manipulation of samples in innumerable ways. Sampled sounds can be combined electronically to produce music without musicians. Similarly, samplers enable a producer to excerpt sounds from one recorded performance and insert them into another recording. Rap music performers, in particular, are known to sample freely from others' works.

Although few sampling cases have been litigated, perhaps because record companies sample as much as they are sampled, placing a sample in a record is a matter of consequence. In the most recent dispute, Bridgeport Music, Inc. v. Dimensions Films, a federal appellate court condemned the use of three notes and held that any taking of sounds, no matter how quantitatively small is an infringement. The result is a bright-line rule that sends the message, "Get a license or do not sample a sound recording." One might legitimately argue that a more flexible and expansive legal response to sampling would represent a better accommodation of the interests in protection of artists' rights and facilitation of the creation of new musical works. Though the propriety of the court's restrictive approach may be questioned, particularly as most instances of creative sampling involve taking only a small portion of sound from a prior recording, it is clear that the practice of sampling may constitute infringement and that samplers must be careful and should normally clear samples. Since two copyright interests are involved in a recording, the record company and artist looking to sample must deal with both the record company that owns the copyright on the recording to be sampled (master use license) and the publisher of the sampled musical composition (mechanical license).

The price for a license typically varies with the notoriety of the recording and song being sampled, the importance of the sample in relation to its intended use, and the extent of the use. In securing or granting a license, one needs to be thoughtful and clear about the scope of permission being sought and granted. Thus, often the sampling rights initially granted are only for records and promotional videos; and if more rights are required, a new round of negotiations is necessary in which an additional fee is charged or permission denied.

Unlike the situation with the Internet, record companies are regularly on both sides of the sampling transaction. That is, they both sample and are being sampled; they both request and grant permission to sample. Their familiarity with both sides of this transaction suggests that the problems posed by digital sampling will elicit reasonable rather than ornery responses as a matter of self-interest and those consensus standards and licensing practices will emerge within the industry.

Indeed, the fact that record companies are regularly on both sides of the sampling transaction suggests that a desirable legal framework would be a permissive one that tolerated generous sampling with the result that much of the considerable costs of license negotiation would be eliminated.

The Record Industry and the Internet

A number of phenomena already present or on the horizon pose significant challenges to the existing business and legal regimes. Historically, technological advances have affected both the industries responsible for the production and dissemination of intellectual and artistic works, and the intellectual property law governing these pursuits, in at least three ways: first, technical advances may affect the manner in which works are created; an example is computer-generated works. These effects may pose problems for traditional categories of copyright law, such as the definition and understanding of who is the author of such a work. Second, an improvement may produce social benefits by providing easier and cheaper access to works. The photocopying machine and the tape recorder are examples of such improvements. Third, an advance may create practical problems in the enforcement of existing copyrights by making detection of infringements difficult. Again, the photocopying machine and the tape recorder are examples of such advances.

For the creators, distributors, and users of musical compositions and recorded performances, the most important and most challenging contemporary technological development is the interconnected set of computer networks known as the Internet. Through this large network, home computer users can communicate, via telephone lines, with one another and with large computer databases containing an abundance of information. The Internet enables a single keystroke to broadcast information around the world without regard to its copyright status; and individuals can easily make high quality duplicates of works. In fact, a computer can copy audio content with speed and digital accuracy not previously available in any other appliance. In addition, computers create significant redistribution opportunities as demonstrated by the proliferation of websites and bulletin boards maintained by organizations and individuals.

On one hand, the Internet can be viewed benignly as akin to the photocopying machine. That is, the Internet facilitates the speedier dissemination of informational and imaginative works to more consumers and users. Under this view, just as predictions of the death of the publishing industry due to photocopying were overdone, so the alleged threat of the Internet to copyright law and practice should be discounted. Licensing systems to permit digital use and technical metering devices to monitor and charge the computer user for the content he downloads and the programs he uses can be devised in response.

On the other hand, the Internet (and satellite communications) can be seen as posing a radical challenge to the manner in which recorded music is created, disseminated, and paid for. In particular, it raises serious questions about the definition and enforcement of intellectual property rights in musical compositions and recorded performances. Such questions arise, in part, from the changed character of objects in cyberspace. From the beginnings of modern copyright law in the early eighteenth century, that law has assumed and focused on the tangible fixation of intellectual and artistic works. The original fixed physical medium was, of course, the book. Sheet music, cassette tapes, and compact discs are contemporary examples of "hard" copies which embody musical compositions and performances. Commercially, revenues from copyrighted works have largely, although not exclusively, issued from sales of these copies. The Internet, however, effects a fundamental alteration in copyright markets. With digital network technologies we face a move from a system based on the distribution of hard copies to one of online access to virtual libraries, book and record stores. In place of pre-recorded tapes and compact discs we confront fleeting electrical impulses. Technological change, in the form, for example, of file-sharing, permits an ease and rapidity of dissemination far greater than under traditional methods of distribution. With the spread of computer technology, and the evolution of online music services, it is likely that transmission of sound recordings will supplement and may eventually replace the current forms of distribution of phonorecords. Moreover, music consumers are able to receive digital transmissions of sound recordings on demand for performance in the home or for downloading. Webcasters can stream audio on the Internet, such as with Internet radio. And as available user bandwidth increases, more and more entertainment websites are streaming audio and creating genre-based, commercial-free programming. Indeed, people using computer networks could begin creating and distributing recorded music in competition with record companies and stores.

These developments pose a challenge to longstanding licensing and legal arrangements for the support of the creation and distribution of recorded music. The practical challenge to the industry is to create new distributional methods that again link producer and consumer so as to maintain both financial support for sustained music and record production and widespread dissemination of these recorded performances. These business models are presently in flux: it is unclear what the lasting structures responsive to technological change will be and to what extent they will find their source in private or public initiative.

Accordingly, it is in the best interest of both the record industry and the legal profession to sort out what protection is available to copyright owners and how to enforce it. (And the geographical reach of the Internet underlines the need for international responses as well.) Immediate issues under existing copyright law concern the liability of both service providers and ultimate users. At the core is the issue of which typical computer usages should be deemed making of a copy and a violation of the copyright owner's reproduction, distribution or performance right. To what extent do the uploading, downloading, or storage of material in digital form constitute reproduction or performance? Similarly, does the practice of "browsing" the Internet, the calling up of digitized images and sounds on a computer screen, constitute the creation of a copy within the meaning of the present law. If any of these practices are deemed infringements, the next question is who should be held legally responsible. In particular, should bulletin board operators and network service providers be held liable for every electronic communication that passes through their systems, or must the provider have some awareness of the transmission's content before copyright law would hold him liable?

There has been sparse judicial guidance on these issues, as the courts have only recently begun to address the question of copyright infringement over the Internet. While there is no doubt that copyright law applies in the online world, the law has yet to apportion the protection and enforcement burdens clearly among copyright owners, access providers, website operators, and consumers. Although there have been some cases in which copyright owners have sued individuals, the prime focus has been on suing bulletin board operators and online communications service providers that provide or operate facilities through which users violate copyright law. The economics of copyright enforcement support the targeting of distributors of information rather than the individual downloader.

A key, and increasingly important, contemporary issue is the definition of secondary liability or indirect infringement, i.e., the legal status of those who do not directly infringe by making unauthorized copies but who supply the technology, e.g., file-sharing software, that facilitates infringement. A significant problem for copyright law is that many such technologies can be utilized for both socially useful and socially harmful purposes. And it is difficult to regulate these facilities in a way that prevents social harms while at the same time expediting social benefits.

The test for secondary liability of providers of technology that has both infringing and non-infringing uses is not clearly defined at this point. The issue is of moment as the answer to the question of third party copyright liability may affect the viability of entire industries. However, in 2005, in the case of *Metro-Goldwyn-Mayer Studios Inc. v. Grokster, Ltd.*, the Supreme Court provided an answer to one aspect of the issue of third party copyright liability or contributory infringement.

Grokster involved a claim of third party liability against defendants whose technology supported the sharing of music over the Internet. In that case the defendants, Grokster and StreamCast Networks, produced and distributed software that enables users to exchange music, movies, and other digital media through a peer-to-peer network. This software allows users to share digital files by searching libraries on computers belonging to other users. However, unlike previous systems, the programs do not involve a website or a centralized communication center to identify MP3 files and make them available for download. With these programs, an Internet user is able to search directly the MP3 file libraries of another user's computer and then download the songs to his own computer without the assistance of a centralized server and indexing system. Grokster and StreamCast thus exercised no ongoing control over the software's use, and though they knew that the software would be used on a widespread basis to download copyrighted files they were able to remain unaware of the particular files being transferred and copied by their software. The defendants, in turn, profited from the use of the software by selling advertisements on the website visited by the file sharers.

Faced with the issue of what standard should be applied in determining secondary liability of a technology provider for the direct copyright infringement of others, the Court responded with a test that focuses on inducement of infringement by the defendant. Looking to the distributor's intent for its product to be used for infringing purposes, the Court indicated that one who distributes a device with the object of promoting its use to infringe copyright, as shown by clear expression or other affirmative steps taken to foster infringement, is liable for the resulting acts of infringement by others, regardless of the device's lawful uses. A prime instance of inducement–behavior engaged in by Grokster–is advertisement or solicitation that broadcasts a message designed to stimulate others to commit violations.

The Internet: The Digital Millennium Copyright Act

While the development of appropriate business models in response to the impact of the Internet is in flux, Congress has made a major contribution to the legal framework. The Digital Millennium Copyright Act (DMCA), enacted in 1998, is intended to equip copyright law to meet the challenges of online digital exploitation of music and sound recordings. It aims to prevent digital copyright piracy while at the same time facilitating certain legitimate interests in use of copyright works. A central part of the Act reinforces efforts by producers to employ technical means, for example encryption and watermarking, to limit unauthorized reproduction. That reinforcement of digital rights management takes the form of a prohibition of instruments used to undermine electronic "locks" used by copyright owners to protect their works. Thus, the anti-circumvention provisions of the DMCA prohibit the manufacture and distribution of devices that circumvent technological measures that: (1) control access to copyrighted works: or (2) protect against unauthorized copying of such works.

The DMCA also codifies the key agreement reached between the record industry trade association and a coalition of webcasters and satellite audio delivery services. That provision creates a simplified statutory licensing system for digital performances of sound recordings, such as those on the Internet and through satellite delivery. It provides a statutory license for non-interactive, non-subscription digital audio services with the primary purpose of entertainment. The scheme guarantees webcasters and satellite services access to music without obtaining permission from each sound recording copyright owner individually and assures record companies an efficient means to receive compensation for use of their sound recordings.

The DMCA, in addition, creates limitations on the liability of online service providers (ISPs) for copyright infringement. It includes detailed provisions circumscribing the exposure of service providers in connection with infringing activities on the Internet. In connection with this grant of protection, though, the law also delineates the responsibilities of ISPs in cases of infringement online. For example, the law formalizes a notice and takedown procedure between ISPs and copyright owners. Accordingly, it is now clear that when an ISP is aware it is posting or transmitting infringing content, the ISP must act to remove the infringing works or it may be liable for any resulting damages.

The DMCA is a landmark piece of legislation, and legal disputes in the industry in the coming years are likely to center on its interpretation and application.

Chapter 16

The New Technology

William R. Crowley

INTRODUCTION

In 2000, worldwide music sales declined for the first time since the dawn of the CD era, with many markets experiencing double digit decreases in units shipped. In the USA, only increased list prices for frontline CD's held total dollar volume essentially flat. Though there were undoubtedly many factors at work, including the rapid adoption of CD-Recordable technology on the part of pirates and counterfeiters, the explosive growth in the availability of free, unlicensed music on the Internet has created a crisis for which no answer is in sight.

The music industry, of course, has faced technology driven crises before. As the industry has evolved from the days of Edison's wax cylinders through 78-RPM discs to long-playing vinyl albums to a multitude of tape formats, the total size of the music business has always expanded, to the chagrin of the doomsayers. In the past, new formats have succeeded because they brought significantly improved reproduction quality and ease of use.

By the end of the 20th century, thanks to the evolution in formats, music had become ubiquitous in the marketplace, and could be purchased everywhere from traditional music stores to discount stores, drug stores, convenience and fast food stores and through virtual storefronts on the Internet.

21st century technology will make it easier than ever for consumers to discover, collect and enjoy their music. The challenge faced by the music industry is to develop secure and equitable systems to ensure that artists and repertoire owners are compensated for their work. Just as importantly, such systems must simultaneously support viable business models and be more attractive to consumers than stealing.

THE DIGITAL CRISIS

The roots of this digital crisis can be traced to the industry's introduction, in the early 1980s, of the digital compact disc. For the first time, consumers were promised sound quality equal to that of the original master recording; in fact, the compact disc is a digital clone of the master recording. Despite the music industry's successful fight to mandate use of a primitive form of copy protection (SCMS, or Serial Copy Management System), consumers have never been prevented from making a first generation digital copy of a CD. The consumer's right to make a personal copy was later affirmed by U.S. Copyright Law, though the distribution of personal copies remains illegal.

For nearly twenty years, the security flaw in the compact disc had little practical impact, since digital recording systems were out of reach for the typical consumer. By the late 90's, the advent of the multimedia Personal Computer coupled with the introduction of high fidelity digital file compression software made it feasible for consumers to copy digital music. Advances in magnetic disc storage reduced the cost of digital storage, making it possible for consumers to store vast quantities of music on their PC. But as CD-Recordable technology was embraced by PC Manufacturers, the cost of blank CD's plummeted to less than the cost of a quality blank tape, allowing consumers to easily move music onto, and off of, their PC's.

It has been the advent of reasonably priced high speed Internet access that has liberated the genie from the bottle. Where once consumers might trade unauthorized "personal" cassette copies of their favorite albums with their friends, it now became possible to share their entire collections with other anonymous Internet users. With a high speed Internet connection, the complete recorded works of any artist could be downloaded in minutes (or hours) and burned onto CD in just a few minutes more.

THE INTERNET AND MUSIC DISTRIBUTION

By the mid-90s, the commercialization of the Internet had revolutionized the ways in which consumers could experience music. The World Wide Web's interactive multimedia capabilities made it possible for labels, artists and merchants to provide consumers free and easy access to information about practically any artist, complete with pictures, audio and video. The development of powerful web directories and search tools like Yahoo and Excite made it possible to locate any desired information with just a few keystrokes.

Even some 20 years after the Internet was first created, its original functions—email and file exchange—remain its most widely used features. The introduction of Internet Relay Chat (IRC) and Instant Messaging (IM), basically improvements in email messaging, allowed computer users to instantaneously share files and information with wide groups of like-minded people. Beyond the cost of basic Internet access, users bore no expense, fostering the widely held belief that everything on the Internet is, and should remain, free.

The creation of advertiser-supported music portals like the Ultimate Band List, Rollingstone.com and Sonicnet further expanded the means by which information about both new and established artists' works could be discovered. Real Network's development of the RealAudio player made it possible for any Internet user to listen to 30 second samples of millions of individual songs.

Building upon these capabilities, pioneers like CDNow and Music Boulevard transformed retail music distribution by opening online stores. These virtual storefronts combined a graphical user interface, multidimensional search engine, streaming audio samples and credit card processing capabilities to offer for sale every album currently in active distribution. Whereas a typical mail-based specialty music retailer might stock 20,000 music titles, the online stores offered a selection five to ten times as large, and at a competitive price. For the online retailers, it was not necessary to actually stock any inventory, due to the development of sophisticated pick-and-pack services by the same distributors who service retail record stores. Since online retailers sold the same products as regular stores, no licenses were required; labels received their regular wholesale price and artists and music publishers received the same contractual royalties regardless of whether it was triggered by a retail or online sale.

Though these virtual storefronts leveraged many unique strengths of the Internet, visionaries realized that digital technology was capable of a much more profound transformation of the traditional music value chain. In 1997, Musicmaker.com introduced a service that allowed Internet users to assemble their own custom CD by selecting individual songs of their choice which were recorded on demand by Musicmaker and mailed out just hours later. No longer were consumers' choices limited to retail-packaged albums. Eventually, Musicmaker licensed a catalog of nearly 200,000 songs directly from labels and artists. In doing so, they created the industry's first digital licensing model and developed a sophisticated system ensuring that labels and publishers received timely and accurate royalty statements. Companies including CustomDisc and Cductive eventually launched competitive services. Yet despite enthusiastic support from the independent label community, the major labels did not enthusiastically support the custom CD concept.

TECHNOLOGY AND MUSIC-ON-DEMAND

In 1993, the Motion Pictures Expert Group (MPEG) published the final specifications for a computer program which would allow for digital video or audio content to be compressed to a fraction of its original size for storage and transmission, and to be decompressed for playback while preserving most of its original resolution. This codec, as the program is called, came into widespread use in the late 90's, and is commonly known as the MP3 format. One of several well-known compression/decompression schemes (others include EPAC, ATRAC and Windows Media), the MP3 format is typically used to compress digital music by a factor of 10 to 20 times, allowing music files to be transmitted and stored much more efficiently.

Almost immediately upon its release, the MP3 format was adopted by university students to encode and store their music collections via their high speed connections to their campus servers. As large-scale disc storage and high speed Internet access became available first to business users, then to home users, an underground community of online music traders developed. To these early adopters, the future of the music industry was obvious: some day, music would be liberated from its physical shackles and be delivered and played digitally, and on demand.

By 1998, companies including Liquid Audio, Musicmaker, Music Boulevard, and GoodNoise took the next step in online music sales by offering individual songs for sale as direct digital downloads. For the first time, the entire transaction occurred in the digital realm, products were merchandised, sampled, purchased, paid for, delivered and consumed without any physical world intervention. Once again, the major labels refused to issue licenses to any of the third party aggregators; the majors continued to dabble in free promotional downloads of selected titles and launched their own experimental services in which they made limited catalogs available to online retailers on a wholesale basis. None of these experiments garnered much consumer support, and the cost structures made it impractical for online retailers to aggressively market these downloads.

At the same time, a startup company in San Diego cleverly secured the internet domain name MP3.com, and launched a free service offering a directory and links to many of the underground websites on which unlicensed, unauthorized MP3 music files were hosted. MP3.com quickly became one of the most visited sites on the web, as users began to build large collections of free music. After attracting the attention of the music industry, MP3.com eventually removed the links to questionable material, and evolved into a free, ad-supported repository for music by unsigned artists.

In 1999, a young music swapper named Shawn Fanning developed Napster, a software program that greatly simplified the process of searching for music files on the Internet. In the process, he set off a firestorm that engulfed the entire music industry. Napster users are able to log onto a central server and "publish" a listing of all of the music files available for sharing on their PCs. Other simultaneous users on the Napster server are able to search the combined directory of all users' music collections for songs or artists. Once a user finds a file they want, the central server arranges a Peer-to-Peer (P2P) connection between the two users' computers, and users download files directly from each other. By the end of 2000, Napster boasted some 40 million members and had facilitated the trade of over a billion music files.

The Record Industry Association of America and the major labels eventually filed a suit against Napster, citing massive copyright infringement. Though the lawsuit dragged on for over a year, eventually the federal courts sided with the RIAA and issued an order calling for Napster to remove material for which the labels could prove ownership. This kicked off a cat and mouse game on the part of Napster and its users to mitigate the impact of the order. Along the way, Bertelsmann made a significant investment in Napster with the stated intention of relaunching the service in late 2001 as a legitimate subscription service.

Though Napster continues today as a legal $5/month licensed service, the P2P revolution is launched and will continue to foster unauthorized Internet music swapping. On March 14, 2000, AOL's Nullsoft division released an "open-source Napster clone" named Gnutella, capable of searching for and downloading any kind of computer file.

Within hours, Nullsoft's distribution of the file-sharing software tool which could be even more potent than Napster had closed down, under pressure from parent company AOL, then in the process of merging with Time Warner. However, in the time that the software was available from the Nullsoft site, several thousand downloads took place, and various third parties soon set to work cloning the Nullsoft version of the Gnutella program. These clones were all written to be compatible with the Gnutella protocol established by the Nullsoft program, and could therefore communicate with each other and with the original Nullsoft client. The Gnutella network does not rely on a central server and has no corporate parent, so efforts to control or eliminate unauthorized Gnutella music sharing will pose a more difficult challenge. Other P2P services like Freenet and Aimster incorporate elements of security, encryption and/or instant messaging that will be even more difficult to police.

Because P2P technology does not require service providers to actually store terabytes of files on their servers, and users provide the necessary bandwidth for file trading, these systems are very efficient for providers. For all of its technological virtues, P2P file sharing poses significant risks to consumers, however. By its very nature, P2P file sharing requires users to provide open access to their computer hard disc to millions of unknown parties, posing serious security risks. Attracted by music file swapping's large user base, hackers and vandals have unleashed computer viruses, worms and Trojan horses on the file sharing networks, exposing users to the threat of loss of data and personal information.

THE SECURE DIGITAL MUSIC INITIATIVE

Early in 1999, the RIAA joined with some 200 companies in the computer and consumer electronics industries to address the explosion in unauthorized music trading. The Secure Digital Music Initiative ("SDMI") is a forum that brings together the worldwide recording, consumer electronics and information technology industries to develop open technology specifications for protected digital music distribution. The specifications released by SDMI will ultimately provide consumers with convenient access to music both online and in new emerging digital distribution systems, enable copyright protection for artists' work, and promote the development of new music-related businesses and technologies.

SDMI's goal is to eventually correct the fatal security flaws in the Audio CD standard. By incorporating encryption and watermarking technology in both commercially released CD's and in future generations of computers and audio devices, SDMI will develop Digital Rights Management (DRM) standards that will allow repertoire owners to embed security features that can be used to control the digital use of music.

Digital Rights Management (DRM) is the secure exchange of intellectual property, such as copyright-protected music or text, in digital form over the Internet or other electronic media, such as CDs and removable disks. DRM allows content owners to distribute digital products quickly, safely, and securely to authorized recipients, while setting rules for how the content may be used—for instance, the number of times a song may be played, how long it may be played, whether it may be copied, and if so, how many times and to what devices.

As of mid-2001, SDMI had completed only the first phase of its specifications. However, member companies continue to roll out experimental implementations of Secure Digital Music, most notably the Universal Music Group's Bluematter project.

In May of 2001, the United States Congress convened hearings aimed at determining whether the major music companies should be forced to issue compulsory licenses allowing third parties to digitally distribute their repertoire, much as music publishers had previously been required to do under U.S. Copyright Law. In response to this challenge, all five of the major labels announced future plans to make their catalogs available digitally as part of a secure subscription service.

DIGITAL MUSIC LOCKERS

In January 2000, MP3.com unveiled a new service designed to allow consumers to store, customize and to access music they already owned in physical form from any web-enabled device. The company's My.MP3.com service allowed consumers to purchase CD's from affiliated online retailers and listen to the tracks instantly in streaming audio before they received the physical CD. Users could also use My.MP3.com to copy their CD's and access those tracks through audio streaming. MP3.com believed that since users could not download the tracks or transmit them to other computer users, the service was legal under U.S. Copyright Law. Prior to the launch of the service, MP3.com purchased copies of as many as 80,000 commercially released CD's for encoding and creation of a huge online library.

Because MP3.com was responsible for encoding music tracks off CD's, and hosting that content, the legality of the service was challenged in the courts by all of the major labels. Eventually, all but one of the majors settled their copyright infringement claims out of court, and issued limited streaming licenses to MP3.com for the service. Each label was reported to have received a 20 million dollar settlement. Because the licenses were negotiated to avoid the possibility of a billion-dollar judgment against MP3.com, the licensing rates were viewed as onerous by many competitors in the digital music space. Compounding MP3.com's problems was a judgment in the amount of 53 million dollars granted in favor of Universal Music Group, which was the only major not to settle out of court.

To the competitors' dismay, these rates created a precedent for similar licenses. Another digital locker service, MyPlay.com, avoided the whole issue of licenses by requiring consumers to go to the trouble of actually encoding and uploading their own music to their locker. Under this model, the consumer merely uses MyPlay's free service as a substitute for their own PC disk drive. Because of the need to upload their collection, the MyPlay service appealed mostly to consumers with T1 or Cable Modem Internet access, which allows for high speed uploads as well as downloads. As of 2001, it was estimated that less than 15% of all Internet users had access to such services.

A third competitor, Musicbank.com, was eventually able to secure digital locker streaming licenses from all of the major labels under rate structures similar to those imposed in the MP3.com settlement. However, citing these high costs and unfavorable business conditions, the company shut down before the service was officially launched.

DIGITAL MUSIC SUBSCRIPTIONS

Because of the payment and accounting burden created by the single song digital download model, and consumers' cool reception to early single song/single album download services, many labels and marketers believe that music subscription services will become the most viable commercial model for digital music distribution. Planned subscription services enable a consumer to create a licensed digital music library residing either on a service provider's central server or on a user's PC or other audio device.

The first significant music subscription service was launched in 2000 by Emusic.com, under which subscribers could download an unlimited number of unencrypted MP3 files from a library of about 150,000 songs from independent labels. Subscription fees ranged from ten to twenty dollars a month, depending on the length of the subscription, and users were not limited by any DRM rules in use of their music. Under this service, labels were to be paid royalties based on their pro-rata share of the total number of songs downloaded by subscribers. Consumer response to the service was not overwhelming, with only 10,000 active subscribers at the time that the Universal Music Group announced plans to acquire Emusic in April of 2001.

In April of 2001, through a new venture with three of the five major label groups, streaming service provider RealNetworks announced that it would develop an online music subscription platform called MusicNet, for launch in the second half of 2001. Warner Music, EMI and BMG all committed to providing repertoire to the venture; each label group received a 20% stake in the venture. Terms of the repertoire licensing agreements, as well as details of the consumer offering, were not publicly disclosed, though it is believed that rate structures were based on

MP3.com's infringement rates. Under the plan, Musicnet would license its platform to third parties including AOL and Real.com, which had previously launched a streaming subscription service offering access to broadcasts of sporting events and limited music content.

Previously, Sony and Universal Music had announced formation of a similar music subscription service called Duet, also for launch some time in 2001, in conjunction with Yahoo.com. Both services appeared to be focusing initially on a streaming music-on-demand concept which limits subscribers' use of music to their PC, while exploring the addition of secure digital downloads to create a multi-tiered subscription service.

CONCLUSION

As consumers continue to embrace digital technology in all of its forms, music distribution will face crucial challenges. Not only have consumers become accustomed through the use of P2P file sharing services to expect access to huge libraries of digital music; they have come to believe that all digital music is, or should be, free. Unless the music industry can quickly implement secure digital music technologies and simultaneously make substantial amounts of hit music available through legitimate channels, the decline in the total music market will accelerate. For too long the music industry has fought against consumer adoption of digital music. It will take bold action to fully harness the power of digital technology to develop successful new business models for the 21st century.

The Music Business in Action:

Merging Music and The Cell Phone

South Korea is regarded as the most digitally connected market on the planet. Thus, the Warner Music Group has chosen to mount an experiment there that will smooth the path for music to be available on cell phones. This will be done via a joint venture between Warner Music and SK Telecom of South Korea.

In an unprecedented move a communications network and a music company will employ the cell phone as a platform for buying, storing, and listening to music.

The Warner Group regards the cell phone as the heart of the music business of the future. Ultimately the cell phone will be the device to store, listen, pay for, and free file share, wirelessly, for most or all music. Korea will be the model for this cell phone/music merger. Sixty-two percent of Korea households receive broadband Internet service and can play MP3 music files via mobile phones.

Mobile phones are more tightly controlled than the Internet and thus less prone to file sharing. The Warner/SK merger is a significant moment in this process.

While the music and cell phone industries are drawing closer together, now the announcement has been made that movies and television shows will also be able to be delivered directly to cell phones. Despite the potential limitations of sound quality for music and the diminution of the visual image when watching a film on a tiny screen, the once humble cell phone is making a strong claim as the most convenient delivery device for all media.

Chapter 17

The Technology Manager at a Record Company

Justin G. Sinkovich

Justin Sinkovich is the former manager of New Media Department at Touch and Go Records. He currently teaches at Columbia College Chicago.

CURRENT IMPACT OF TECHNOLOGY MANAGEMENT ON THE MUSIC INDUSTRY

Technology is literally at the root of every department of a record company. Production, sales, marketing, publicity, A&R, legal affairs, shipping, accounting, and more all rely on today's latest technological innovations to be successful. The technology manager is responsible for equipping these departments with the tools that will help them to operate in the most efficient and inexpensive way. As these tools evolve and develop, the tech manager's responsibility is also to educate company employees about departmental advancements and to manage their implementation. The ultimate goals are to stay at the forefront of the industry and to be competitive with other labels.

Despite ongoing reports of mergers, downsizing, and layoffs during the recent decline of record sales, technology roles of all types are in high demand. Responsibilities are increasing for information technology (IT), online marketing, digital retailing like iTunes and its competitors, ring tones, other mobile marketing, and other facets of the industry's new media. CD sales are largely marketed online. And while the industry's CD sales overall are declining, MP3-type sales, ring tones, other newly adopted formats like video sales wallpapers, and on demand content through cable television are partially offsetting that decrease. With this recent and rapid shift in how music is monetized at record companies and how fans want to enjoy music, technology's vital role in the music business has never been clearer. The managers of technology at all influential major and independent labels are largely leading a complete redefinition of how these new medias will ebb and flow to create new standards.

FUTURE IMPACT OF TECHNOLOGY ON THE RECORDING INDUSTRY

The managers of technology at all of the larger labels are leading a complete redefinition of how these new media will ebb and flow to create new standards. What will be the role of a technology manager in the future? The answer: "no one knows." We conclude that technology continues to grow in importance. As the music industry evolves, it twists and turns in ways that no one can fully predict. Record companies and all of their resources can attempt to control the market, but it is the market itself that dictates the future. Innovative, unknown entrepreneurs and new companies are constantly working on ideas that will steer the industry in unbridled new directions.

No one in the industry was prepared for a kid named Shawn Fanning to turn listening habits upside down with his peer-to-peer phenomenon, Napster. Nor was anyone ready for the sudden mass adoption of the iPod and iTunes after so many previous companies failed with similar products. The power and influence of Myspace.com and Facebook.com has made social network marketing a force so powerful in the record industry that some companies devote entire departments to promoting their artists and mining profiles for unsigned talent. Interestingly, none of these aforementioned companies is really introducing technologies that are particularly groundbreaking. More impressive ideas have come and gone without notice. It is the music fans that ultimately decide when to adopt these new avenues of music enjoyment, but a record company has to be ready to capitalize on these shifts.

SKILLS EMPLOYED BY A TECHNOLOGY MANAGER

The more skills a person has, the more versatile and valuable the individual will be to a record company. Within the various components of a technology department, expertise is required in a broad range of computer and other information systems. A keen knowledge of the systems used throughout the company is often necessary. Thus, the eagerness and flexibility to learn and maintain a number of systems is vital. Hardware, software, networking, database engineering, and systems and network maintenance are important and are the backbone of the company. Graphic design and web design along with the creation of compelling content like e-cards and animated pieces are all valuable in giving an artist a visual online identity.

Audio mixing, encoding, and mastering are used constantly and not just inside the studio, but in day-to-day operations as well. The more often expensive studio time can be avoided by completing simple tasks in the office, thus better for the label. With the reemerging importance of video, production and encoding, DVD authoring is once again an important area. Video content is still used on television, but now online is of equal importance. Thus, an array of TV and online formats need to be created, maintained, and distributed.

Lastly, a thorough knowledge is extremely valuable in the most basic business programs like Excel, Word, and PowerPoint along with printing, scanning, and basic computer maintenance. When other departments have a problem, they immediately turn to the technology department. A solution has to be immediately available or the company may miss a crucial deadline or opportunity because of a software problem or an employee error. Obviously, every person in the technology department does not need to be an expert in every department of the company and every application used in the building. Specialization within certain tech areas is important; however, to the technology manager, an overall view of how these tools fit together is vital. The manager delegates to other areas like online marketing and digital retail, and those employees will specialize and be innovative while the manager assures that all projects are completed correctly and in conjunction with the overall goals of the company.

ROLE OF THE TECHNOLOGY DEPARTMENT IN A RECORD COMPANY

The role of a technology manager spans the entire company. All areas, such as information technology (IT), online promotion, digital retailing, the company's website and web store, production of audio graphics and video directly contribute uniquely to the bottom line of the record company and enhance the performance of the more traditional departments.

1. Information Technology
Information Technology (IT) Management is at the core of any company. Although this topic is not discussed in great detail in this chapter, it is important to acknowledge that businesses of all types rely on IT support to keep networks and systems operating smoothly and efficiently. This department is typically responsible for all of the business's software, networks, and hardware. Not only should these systems work individually, but they also have to integrate with each other across the entire company. Sales and shipping systems need to be able to work together seamlessly as do A&R, accounting, and publicity. Real-time access to information such as budgets, sales

figures, radio tracking, publicity reports, and inventory numbers have to be available cross-departmentally and it is the tech department's job to provide a network to allow that to happen. IT is a company's backbone. A malfunction can literally grind a day's operation to a halt, while a powerful and properly maintained IT infrastructure can give a company a major advantage over its competitors.

2. Online Promotion

There are a number of technology-related titles that one individual can hold at today's record company related to technology. One of the newest and most important roles is that of online promotion. The most powerful and cost effective way to reach an audience throughout the world has been proven to be the Internet. Consumers are fifty percent more likely to be influenced by email blasts and blogs than by television and radio advertising. User generated content and social networking are lifestyle forces that continue to gain importance in our society. The methods used to effectively promote both new and established artists are virtually endless, and new opportunities present themselves every single day. This vastness in itself can pose a problem. The challenges of determining where to start, and where to focus can make a huge online marketing effort utterly worthless. Industry professionals that understand the promotion avenues on the web and can carry them out successfully are in high demand.

ELEMENTS OF A PROMOTIONAL ONLINE COMPAIGN

First: Building Artist Identity

The initial obstacle in marketing any new artist is building a compelling identity in such a vast global music market. In the midst of tens of thousands of albums being released every year, new artists and their music need to have a unique and appealing identity for music fans to pay any attention. Big tours, magazine exposure, television appearances, and radio play can be extremely hard to get for fledgling artists, so this identity is often first introduced online. An artist's name, personality, and most importantly their sound can be showcased to millions with comparatively little expense and resistance. The elements to build a proper online identity include: artist's name, logo, photos, cover art, other graphics, biographical information, videos, and free audio via streams and/or downloads. All of which should first and foremost reside on the band's and the label's website in a compelling way that is consistent with the band's aesthetic. These assets can be posted on a number of highly trafficked websites for free. Websites like Myspace.com, Facebook.com, Lastfm.com, Imeem.com, Blogger.com, Purevolume.com, Download.com, Wikipedia.org, and countless others offer free pages targeting a giant cross-section of music fans.

Second: Launching Online Promotional Campaigns

Once the online identity of the artist has been established, the label launches a promotional campaign to introduce this identity to as many potential fans as possible. The label's director of digital marketing can utilize literally thousands of legitimate avenues depending on the resources and budget at the label's disposal for this campaign. Timing, prioritization, and execution are the three critical factors to ensure these efforts are successful. All of the money and employees in the world cannot fix a poorly planned campaign. Conversely, a successful online PR plan by a small label can be successful, if shrewdly planned, even with very limited resources. The timing of a campaign revolves around large events in the artist's career such as the release of a new album, or a single, or the start of a tour.

TARGETING THE RIGHT WEBSITES

Prioritization means targeting the online media sources that speak to the largest and most relevant audiences. Building and maintaining relationships with the editors of influential online destinations is extremely important.

These alliances will get the artist seen and heard by millions of web users. Websites, large and small, depend on traffic to earn revenue through advertising, e-commerce, affiliate marketing, and other revenue streams. This traffic is built by compelling content, and the record company can provide this content in exchange for artist exposure.

Larger sites can be contacted one-on-one to set promotions, contests, interviews, and features. Some of these major sites include Salon.com, Yahoo!, Download.com, MP3.com, MTV.com, Rollingstone.com, Pitchforkmedia.com, and AOL.com. Smaller trafficked sites such as smaller niche online magazines, or e-zines, can be contacted to also set up artist promotion features. However, the label may not be able to contact these many thousands of outlets individually. Maintaining an up-to-date database in order to send email blasts featuring content for them to post, and sometimes including promotional review copies of CD's, can result in an artist being featured or listed on thousands of sites across the globe with little time and expense. And there is also the emergence of web-logs, or blogs and their importance in shaping culture and the acceptance of new artists. When you add downloadable webcasts, or podcasts, to these, there are now literally millions of promotional opportunities available for artists. But the ability to manage this vast network is an enormous challenge for an online campaign. Again, relevance is important because since no one benefits by forcing an artist on the wrong audience. A country singer will not be received well by an online magazine that solely covers hip-hop. So, identifying where not to focus a campaign's resources is very important as well. Fortunately there is no shortage of promotional outlets for any music genre.

ONLINE PROMOTIONAL CAMPAIGN METHODS

Publicity campaigns have been an important facet of marketing long before the Internet. Reaching the public through product reviews, interviews, and live appearances is a critical tactic offline and now used on the Web. Online publicity is similar in many ways to more traditional PR initiatives, where trusted media sources can showcase an artist and her or his work. Unfortunately for online publicists, web destinations do not quite have the overall legitimacy that the more traditional media like television and radio do. However, one unique advantage that online PR gives music fans is an on-demand, multimedia experience with quick links to purchase. Unlike a print magazine, an online magazine can offer audio and video. Listeners can tune into traditional radio, or they can customize their own radio stations online suitable to their taste and then click to buy the song on CD or MP3 instantly. Customization, interactivity, multimedia, and a vast array of choices are all features that makes online publicity possibilities virtually endless. There are a number of tools utilized in online campaigns; the following is a list of some of the more important, but by no means all of the methods used.

Free Promotional Audio Streams and Downloads for Consumers

Downloadable and streamable audio is a controversial subject. The question of how much free music should be given to consumers to provoke them in turn to buy this artist's music has never been agreed upon industry wide and is sure to be debated for years to come. Labels have seen a vast decline in their industry due to the free sharing, distribution, and copying of their music. But providing one or two free tracks to the public can cause music fans to become interested in an artist within a highly competitive market filled with thousands of other artists.

If a record company does allow music to be given away, it must first be cleared for promotional royalty-free use by the rest of the company as well as the artist, manager, and publisher. Then the label has to decide whether to offer the track as a download that a user can save, or provide only a temporary stream. Whether to host all of these files only on their own servers or let others host the files is an important decision as well. The bandwidth cost of hosting audio downloads and streams can be significant. However, hosting the file can assure that it is being used according to the label's wishes, and the label can track keep track of important usage statistics.

Recently some artists both world-famous and unknown have embraced the concept of free music to the point of giving away entire albums. The most notable case is Radiohead and their album *In Rainbows*. One of the world's most popular bands, their previous albums released by EMI were plagued by early leaks and rampant piracy by adoring fans. Finished with their EMI contract, the band surprised the world by releasing *In Rainbows* on their website immediately on MP3 for a price selected by the user, and yes, free was a valid price. They also offered a limited edition box set including additional music, a vinyl LP version, CD's, and extensive booklet of photos and liner notes. By eliminating any distributors or labels, the reported average price paid of $6 per album proved to be far more profitable to Radiohead than any previous album. The press coverage alone proved infinitely valuable for other merchandise, back catalog, and touring revenues. Radiohead later announced a license of *In Rainbows* to independent label XL Recordings to provide the CD and LP to stores, a relationship also proving to be extremely profitable.

Many other artists have taken advantage of this emerging music "freeconomy" including The Cool Kids who initially became popular by giving away their music while being sponsored by select brands, Nine Inch Nails who similar to Radiohead gave away an album but then sold out of a limited edition 2500 copies of a $300 box set in two days to gross $750,000, and Clipse who released a free mixtape entitled *Road To Till The Casket Drops* which announced their new clothing line. Not all have been successful with this strategy. Trent Reznor from Nine Inch Nails released an album on his label by Saul Williams where fans could choose their price. A vast majority of those who downloaded did so for free, thus logging disappointing results for Reznor and Williams.

Promotional Video

Videos lost much of their importance as MTV and similar television stations vastly reduced their music video programming. Now, with the spread of broadband connections, videos are again becoming a vital marketing tool and are one of the most valuable kinds of content for websites. The label can host the video while sites deep link to the video; however, the bandwidth for serving video can be even more expensive than audio. Most of the largest portals featuring video host their own files.

Once the new media department has received a marketable video in time to be used with the release of an album or single, the video must be properly delivered to websites that require physical copies. Duplicate copies are mailed in the various requested formats including DVD's, Beta SP, DV's, and even VHS. If they do not require a physical copy, the tech department has to electronically transfer a video encoded into the required file format and specification. Video premieres are a popular promotional technique online with sites like MTV.com and Yahoo.com offering home-page placement in exchange for exclusive rights to the video for a day or two.

E-Cards

Many labels, including TVT and WEA, have even provided a limited time for full album stream in the form of an "E-card" to any visitor to their site. Their theory is quite simple. If the person grows to like the album, they will want to own the album. Whether the entire full album is available or not, an E-card, which is basically a miniature website, with perhaps a stream of the single, photos, a biography, the video, tour dates, clips from other songs, and more info that can be an exciting find for a music fan. The beauty of the E-card is that fans will actively pass these mini-sites around the Internet on their own. Basic e-cards are relatively inexpensive to develop and virtually spread an artist and their latest work throughout the Web. More elaborate mini-sites can include video games with the artist and their music in the game, and contests to encourage the spread of the site.

Internet Radio

With the mass consolidation and increasing barriers to entry in commercial radio promotion, labels are in dire need of alternate sources of exposure for their artists. Internet radio provides a perfect alternative to commercial radio. In some ways it can have an even greater impact in reaching potential fans. Internet radio can have a far greater reach than those transmitted over local airwaves. Internet radio can reach the global marketplace, and many online providers reach millions of listeners per day. In addition, Internet radio stations can be customized to such a degree that the listener can hear exactly what genre of music interests them, thus finding more new music that they truly like. Radio stations like Pandora, Lastfm, and Slacker push the boundaries of streaming radio. By staying just within the rules of maintaining "non-interactive" status, the service can license all music with a compulsory license from ASCAP, BMI, SESAC, and Sound Exchange. Then the service can provide customized radios streams based on the likes and dislikes of the individual user. Then the listener can conveniently click through to buy the song or album. That is why Internet radio is such a valuable complementary service and partner for digital retailers like iTunes, MSN, and Rhapsody. Other Internet radio stations like 3wk, Live365, and Spinner maintain loyal listeners who rely on the programming to discover new music while they are sitting at work or at home.

Another interesting difference between traditional radio and online radio is that traditional radio does not usually have a direct financial impact on the label. It is the publisher and/or composer who earn performance royalties. Internet radio play actually requires royalty payments to master copyright holders through a collection agency called Sound Exchange, and this typically means a payment to both the artist and the label. Regardless of the royalty recipient, it is the exposure of online radio play that is of the greatest value.

Online Advertising

Online advertising is vital to a smaller record company because the CPM (cost per thousand) of impressions online is a fraction of the cost as compared to print, radio, and television. Impressions have been devalued online because of the failure of online businesses over the past few years who initially concentrated on branding and market share instead of profitability by negotiating higher advertising prices. Advertisers are identifying these opportunities as bargains, and online CPMs are becoming more comparable to other media sources. Online advertising is effective for a label because traffic can be directed to a point of online purchase. The referrals from the ad can be tracked precisely which is impossible in other kinds of advertising. They also offer a great opportunity for a smaller label to reach a highly targeted audience while obtaining direct feedback on the effectiveness of the insertion by how many people click on the ad.

Ads can also be purchased on a CPC (cost per click) basis through services that provide ad opportunities based on key words. Online destinations like Google, Myspace, and Facebook offer advertising that is only seen when a user searches for or shows interest in key words specified by the advertiser. The advertiser then only pays when an ad is clicked, and can automate a capped maximum amount of monthly expenditure based on these clicks.

Publicity Extranets and PR Assets

Web technologies have created a new paradigm in music business publicity campaigns. Writers and editors at music publications, whether they are online or in print, need content that is of high quality and easily obtained. What many readers do not realize is that critics' selection of what they wish to feature often depends not only on whether they like it or not, but whether the album, art work, photos, etc. are available before of their often rushed deadlines. An online extranet or "press section" that is viewable at non-public and/or password protected locations allows on demand access to the assets demanded by the music editorial community. Labels that offer this content have an advantage because, whether they realize it or not, critics are often hurried, rushed, and overworked and in need of as many conveniences and shortcuts as possible. With the vast adaptation of blogging and other fan-generated editorial, many labels provide this special press content publicly. With millions of music fans now posting photos, making playlists, and writing their opinion of music on blogs and social network pages, labels are now facing editorial assets outward to the public in a 360-degree marketing strategy.

A press section can be extremely easy to design and maintain, and often takes the standardized look and feel of the public website. A header denotes the basic information on the release at the top of the page including the artist's name, release name and format, release date, catalogue number, UPC number, link to artist's website, performance credits, and production credits. A biography giving the history of the artist leading up to the release, information surrounding the making of the release, and then information about the artist's plans to support the release would be available on the page as text and also available as a downloadable file.

These files probably would be available in Microsoft Word and/or included in a PDF press kit. Glossy photos have historically always been included in press kits, but they are expensive and publications prefer not to have to scan the image. A press extranet can host an artist's promotional photos without the cost, and almost all publications prefer them already in digital format so they do not have to scan them from the glossy. Print publications need pictures at a high resolution of 300 DPI, while online publications use the standard 72 DPI for online viewing. Both resolutions should be provided for download in the press section with thumbnails to preview the pictures so writers can select which photo they wish to from reviews and features often are provided in press sections feature. Quotes and articles and the downloadable press kit as well. They often assist in validating the coverage of an artist to a critic who was previously unfamiliar with the artist.

Maintaining a good looking and easy to use press portal allows publishers of articles and media to quickly access everything they need to cover an artist. A press section can even provide a full album stream to writers for them to write about the album. This process and this can greatly reduce the costs of mailing and express mailing copies of the album to the press.

Third: Maintaining fans and creating a community that will continue to support the Artist and grow largely on its own.

Once the label has established the band's identity and introduced this identity through online promotional campaigns, hopefully a large audience has been attracted. This audience should be managed and developed into a long-term online community of fans revolving around the artist. The artist's website, the label's website, and then online groups on sites like Myspace, Friendster, and Yahoo! can maintain a long-standing relationship between the artists and fans. Publicity such as tour dates with ticket giveaways, contests, message boards, a steady stream of news items, interviews, new merchandise, radio and in-store appearances and more should be ongoing to maintain and grow this online community. Opt-in email lists can help push information out to fans. Respectfully collecting user data can help target fans. Particularly if a company maintains the zip code of the fan, geographically specific information regarding tour dates and other local events can better serve the music fan and drive revenue.

Marketing a New Artist vs. Marketing an Existing Artist

A new artist's marketing plan and a more established artist's plan can be drastically different. Establishing an identity and breaking into major media portals can be a time intensive goal for a new artist. Both online editors and music listeners are very hesitant to adopt a new artist. The number of new artists introduced to the media and to music fans can easily be hundreds per day, so it is very difficult to get fans, critics, and others interested in new artists. Therefore, the principal goal in marketing a new artist online is building the sound first, and then providing the story and personality behind this sound thus successfully introducing the artist to as many of the right people as possible.

An existing artist may already have a large fan base, but maintaining that fan base in a world full of new trends and choices can be just as difficult as breaking a new artist.

An existing artist's fan base needs to be cultivated into a long-term relationship where the fan will continue to buy music, concert tickets, and merchandise throughout the artist's career. Creating places online for a community to reside and flourish is an older artist's best asset. Often an artist's current audience will diminish over time. Focusing on the remaining market for the artist and often exploring completely new online markets in other countries or in difference demographics can help maintain a lifelong career.

DIGITAL DISTRIBUTION AND RETAIL

What is digital distribution and retail?

Digital retailers of music began to launch in the huge Internet growth era of 1999 -2000. However, labels were largely unwilling to sell music in this way, and consumers were largely unwilling to buy music in this format. The launch of iTunes on January 9, 2001 for Macintosh, a program converting CD's into digital files, organizing music collections, and playing Internet radio changed everything. On October 23, 2001, Apple announced the first iPod, a small, easy to use $399 digital audio player that relies on a hard disk instead of flash memory or CD-ROM's. By the end of 2001, Apple had sold 125,000 iPods. On July 17, 2002, PC versions of iPods were released and prices for the devices dropped. On April 28, 2003, Apple announced the availability of the third generation of iPod that works on either Macs or PC's and along with the launch of the iTunes Music Store that offers 99-cent tracks and $9.99 albums for over 200,000 songs. In October of 2003, iTunes launched their store compatible with PC's.; and before the first PC could connect, iTunes had already sold 10 million songs through their music store. Meanwhile they announced their one-millionth iPod sold. The iTunes Music Store sold its one hundred millionth song on July 11, 2004; and digital music retail had finally come to be a viable and quickly emerging source of revenue for music companies. Major competitors to iTunes currently include Napster, Rhapsody, Zune, Amazon, and the long-standing independent subscription service, Emusic. Digital retail has proven to be a difficult medium in which to make a profit. Big brands have spent millions and have failed to be successful due to small profit margins and increasing competition. Large digital retailers like Wal-Mart, Sony Connect, Musicnow, MTV.com, and Virgin have closed in recent years.

By 2005, five percent of music was being sold digitally, and arguably much more for independent labels that have less saturating physical distribution. Estimates of 23 percent of all music sold in 2008 was from digital revenue. Music formats have come and gone from the LP, to the cassette. Now we are seeing a very slow decline of the CD due to a recent adaptation by the music buying public to buy from iTunes and similar services. Digital retail offers exciting new selection and service for music fans, now able to purchase music more carefully by selecting individual track downloads. In 2008, album sales were down 14% from the previous year, with digital track sales increasing 27%. The bad news for labels is that this ability to select by track decreased overall sales revenue by 7%.

Types of Digital Retailers

1. Traditional Permanent Downloads
Digital retailers earn money with a number of different business models. While there are dozens of new models emerging, there are several different types that are currently driving the market. If you can call anything in digital retailing traditional, a traditional service sells permanent a la carte downloads by album or by track, like iTunes. Amazon.com has been the only other service to make significant headway in the a la carte digital download market. No other permanent download service has made more than a slight dent in Apple's market share. However niche stores like Other Music, Insound, Beatport, and Bleep provide a la carte download purchase capabilities, complimenting their other products, and offering an editorialized product selection. As competitors continue to emerge, the market is destined to become even more competitive; and music fans will have hundreds of options 0f where to buy their downloads online.

2. Subscription Services
Subscription services are different from retailers selling permanent downloads because subscription services allow users to listen to any of the millions of tracks on their service for a monthly fee, but the user does not permanently own any of these tracks. Users can even download all of the audio files on the service for no additional cost if they wish, but the files will only work if the user is still paying a subscription fee. If the subscription lapses, the files become inoperable. A label gets paid by the amount of listens its catalog accrues. However, the major subscription services like Napster, Rhapsody, and Zune are luring users away from purchasing permanent versions of albums. Many predict them to be the future of the music industry; but so far, they have yet to earn any substantial

monetary market share as compared to selling permanent downloads due to the lower per track listen royalty rate. These subscription services, like iTunes, do also offer permanent downloads on a per album and per track basis, making them a multi-faceted user experience.

There are dozens of new business models offering music to consumers, and paying labels in new and creative ways. The following are brief explanations of the typical models, but this is by no means a comprehensive list of how digital services operate.

3. Advertising Supported Services

Some digital services offer entire catalogs to their users for unlimited on demand streaming, and pay labels for this usage by ad revenue in lieu of subscription money. Royalties are paid to content owners like subscription services, based on a pro rata share of advertising revenue. Myspace Music is the most popular ad supported service. In 2008 they began offering most major label and some independent catalogs for free, with plans to offer a more comprehensive selection in 2009. Previously streams on Myspace were free, so the introduction of a royalty was unanimously seen as a step in the right direction for labels. The downside of Myspace and similar services is their royalty rate typically equates to a fraction of a penny per track streamed. This rate can never provide the revenue that physical and digital a la carte sales have historically, and this ad-based streaming has proven to cannibalize these more profitable revenue sources.

4. Cellular Ring Tones

Ring tones have been considered a component of digital retail and a saving grace of the music industry over the past few years, making up for the decline in CD sales at major labels. Independent labels have far less of a market in ring tones because mobile companies concentrate on offering the most popular songs on phone screens that are small and difficult to navigate. While mobile companies are making an effort to offer a broader and deeper range of content, there is a question as to whether ring tones will really exist in the near future on their own. Most smart phones for example offer the capability to simply use an MP3 as a ring tone.

Ring tones for cellular phones had already reached three billion dollars in revenue for 2004, and which was an estimated 10 percent of the total music sales market. This growth has continued to increase into 2006 as the launch of ring back tones reach the market. Ring back tones are songs that dialers hear when they are waiting for the receiver of the call and transmitter of the ring back to take the call. There are two types of ring tones. The first type that was introduced is the polyphonic ring tone, which is the karaoke reproduction of a song. There is no original recording used in these ring tones, only the composition. Master tones actually play the original recording of the composition. Both types of tones are usually available for anywhere from $1.50 to $2.95 and are usually available for a 90-day license although some are permanent. Buying multiple ring tones at one time provides a discount.

Ring tones are generally between 20 and 40 seconds in length. One of the most attractive things about ring tones features is that they not only are a good revenue generator, but they encourage the phone owner and people around them to buy the actual song or album. Third party companies gain licenses from copyright holding record and publishing companies and then encode them for the various cellular phone carriers. Third party companies like Zingy, Dwango, and Moviso provide ring tones to most all of the carriers and have well-maintained relationships with these cellular providers that are otherwise largely unapproachable by smaller labels. As phone technologies progress and increase in their acceptance in the marketplace, revenue opportunities through cellular phone providers like full song downloads, on demand song streaming, and music video downloading and streaming will continue to emerge.

4. Download Kiosks

Download kiosks in stores like Best Buy, Hot Topic, and Starbucks, and many more, allow customers to download music right in the store. A user can download this music to their laptop or other storage device, or they can burn their own CD or customized a CD. These kiosks' long-term longevity are in question. Nevertheless, these music stations have been a substantial revenue source; therefore, it is important for labels to embrace this technology and partner with these companies.

5. Selling Videos

The recent emergence of a market for video sales has created a limited revenue source for something that has typically been only an expensive marketing tool. Historically, music videos have only been given away by record companies to promote album sales. These videos can cost millions, and now videos can be sold to watch on iPods, cell phones and other portable devices. Also, now record companies are negotiating a royalty per view from the major websites like Yahoo's Launch and MP3.com to be paid for each time a video is watched on their site.

MANAGING DIGITAL DISTRIBUTION AND RETAIL AT A LABEL

Determining Digital Rights

Many record contracts between the record label and the artist from years past do not acknowledge digital retail. The first step in managing the label's digital catalog is to confirm the digital rights for all albums. Contracts and relationships with current and past artists need to be revisited. The digital catalog and what can be legally sold can differ greatly from the physical rights. If the label has sublicensed their masters to labels in different countries, the digital rights of these licenses need to be determined as well. Also, once these rights are determined, a constant "policing" of the catalog is necessary to assure ensure that others are not illegally selling catalog.

Creating and maintaining the digital catalog library

Creating a digital library of music that includes master audio files, usually in uncompressed .wav's, cover art, and the information to include with all tracks and albums. The information that accompanies each track and album is called metadata and is attached to every single album and every single track. Since every track is sold individually, it has to have its unique information and identification. An album is identified by its UPC number, which is the numbers on the bar code from the back of the CD. A track is identified by it's International Standard Recording Code, or ISRC number. The Recording Industry Association of America (RIAA) assigns the ISRC prefix for a label's catalog and the label can then assign its own ISRC numbers to each track. Once a song has an ISRC, that is its identifier everywhere. Even if it appears on numerous releases including compilations, soundtracks, etc, the ISRC should remain the same for that master recording. If there were a different version of the track, the ISRC would be different.

A database manages all of this information and allows the record label to view and manage this data along with the files. Then they and then send these files and their accompanying data to digital retailers to their specification. All of these retailers ask or request that the catalog to be sent to them slightly differently. Therefore the database and other systems need to be flexible enough to accommodate their needs for delivery.

Once an agreement with a digital retailer is in place, the process of getting this retailer a copy of the digital catalog and the information attributed to it can be extremely complicated. Even small independent labels can have hundreds of albums in the catalog, which means thousands of individual tracks that will be sold. Each track requires dozens of fields of information to accompany the transfer of the music to the retailer, and each retailer's needs are slightly different. Not to mention that retailers sell their catalogs in different audio formats including AAC, ATRAC, MP3, and WMA. The technology department is responsible for maintaining this catalog. They then work with the retailers to deliver this canon of music to their servers in the cheapest and most effective way possible whether it be electronically via FTP, XML, spreadsheets, hard drive, or simply by shipping physical CDs.

Negotiation of Agreements with Digital Retailers

When selling through a digital retailer, the label's share of revenue and the general terms of selling the catalog are always negotiable. Understanding the industry standards and the possibilities in negotiating these retailer deals can add millions to the bottom line without having to increase sales. A digital retailer will typically initially offer record companies inferior deals to the ones that are made with the larger more savvy companies; however, with the right information and skill, a record company of modest size can negotiate the best deals for its catalog.

DELIVERY OF CATALOG TO DIGITAL RETAILERS

Promotion and Placement on Digital Retail Sites

When the label's catalog of music is placed on a digital music service, positioning within the store on the most prominent pages is extremely important in order to maximize sales, just as the use of listening posts, displays, and rack placement in physical stores. Working with retailers to feature important releases, both new and old, is a science that has recently become a major marketing focus at labels. As with online marketing, establishing relationships with the editors of these pages and delivering them the right information at the right time can help increase sales dramatically.

Accounting, Auditing, and Royalty Payments from Digital Retailing

While the digital catalog and its delivery are complicated by individual track sales, so is its accounting. Accounting statements from digital retailers to the label is a huge obstacle that most labels did not expect, and systems to manage this data at major record companies are still being developed with varying amounts of success. Instead of getting sales figures for each album, the amount of information is multiplied by the number of tracks per album. Then, many tracks on the same album require different royalty payments determined by who wrote the song, and whether the song was downloaded or streamed. The digital retailers often provide wrong and poorly organized accounting data, and all retailers report their sales differently. Therefore, the accounting, auditing, and then payment of royalties to artists, publishers and other parties are new and largely unexpected challenges for record companies.

Online Physical Retailers

Online sales officially exceeded brick and mortar sales on the day after Thanksgiving 2004. This statistic, along with the ongoing reports of huge jumps in online buying in the fourth quarter of 2004, showed that consumers were finally starting to become accustomed to the idea of buying online only a few of years ago. Music retail is no exception to the increase in the practice of buying online. As of 2006, Amazon.com often accounts for as much as ten percent of a record company's total sales. Thus, obviously, it is imperative to maximize sales on this site and its major competitors. Many users of online physical retailers like Amazon or Insound.com go to the site trying to find new music, and this is where the savvy music company can use marketing programs to attain a more premium placement.

Building a relationship with the staff at these stores, buying the appropriate marketing packages, and encouraging editors to listen to the label's music for a possible feature are important factors in online retail promotion. Amazon.com editors, for example, compile their favorite 100 albums of the year; and albums ranking high on this list are certain to see a spike in sales. The independent music retailer, Insound.com, offers paid-in promotional placement for their online store starting at $200 per month. They will trade "clean" retail copies in exchange for the promotion. For $250, Insound offers independent labels a homepage feature (at least one day), four-week banner campaign (468x60), one streaming radio player track with link to buy, a free MP3 featured track, and one email newsletter mention. Their newsletter is read by over 150,000 users per week making this package a fraction of the cost of a print ad with arguably more impressions. In addition, their newsletter adds the ability to immediately click to buy, which is something missing from print, radio, and other advertising.

RECORD COMPANY'S WEBSITE AND WEB STORE

The website is the first priority to a new media department in representing the company to the world. This URL is the epicenter of all other online marketing and commerce for a record company. The website needs to not only draw the attention of the user initially, but must be creative and also compel the visitor to be interested in the artists on the roster and return regularly to the site. The content has to be imaginative and useful while also providing the capability of browsing with easy to understand navigation and functionality. Keeping the site current with the latest releases, tour dates, and news along with multimedia of videos and audio is the key to a satisfied user who will return to the site.

WebSite Design and Flexibility

Many managers are attracted to the development of eye-catching flash sites, and they do have their aesthetic advantages. However, they load slowly and can crash web browsers and not work with older systems or a slow connection. Even now, much of the world's population still surfs the web with dial-up instead of broadband. Flash sites also can often be disorienting to navigation and discourage users with short attention spans. Therefore, a flash site needs to have an alternative html site or only use an html-based site. A label's website can easily be compelling on the homepage or on the navigation bar by having dynamic rotating content images featuring different images of new artists and current news scripted to rotate automatically. Another important theory in web design is to lure users with the homepage by having images and "headlines" of text that encourage the users to go deeper into the site instead of leaving after the initial home page impression. These additional page views distribute more information and foster a closer relationship with the potential fan and buyer.

A great number of label websites have been hard coded over the years. This type of coding means that with any changes in text, images, or the addition of new features or pages have to be changed within the site's code. These sites are easy to identify because the content often is awkwardly placed and outdated. Alternatively, a data-driven website with a fast and easy-to-use back end content management system (CMS) is inexpensive and easy to develop. A CMS gives the website the flexibility to be changed easily and the ability to grow. A data system of this kind has tools to create new standardized pages to add a new template of releases and artists. Once the page is created, a series of fields are presented on the screen to fill out the text. Pull down menus are available to select features, and browsers are included to upload images and other local or remote files. With these CMS tools, new pages can be created and existing pages can be updated and robustly maintained.

Traffic Evaluation

All major website hosting companies provide statistics regarding site usage, and this information is vital for evaluating the site's effectiveness. Numbers and graphs are available regarding the number of visitors, page, which pages on the site are viewed most often, and which outside URL's are referring traffic to the site. All of these statistics are important to design and content decisions. For example, the home page will always have the most traffic, but redesigning or adding more links that flow deeper into the website can increase traffic into the site and result in more page views. Typically, these statistics will show that the most traffic for a music website occurs later in the workweek as individual schedules become more flexible, and they are able to surf the Internet more. Tracking the visitors' countries of origin is available with many reporting tools, and this information can be used to identify spikes in traffic related to emerging markets.

Statistics on traffic numbers are viewed using these statistic-reporting tools, and the traffic itself can also be directly affected by savvy web marketing campaigns by the company. Campaigns can be undertaken to attain mentions and links on other websites, and the result can be tracked by the hosting facility's referral tracking application. A mention on one of the larger sites can easily double another site's traffic. For example, *Salon.com's* weekly download featured every Wednesday reportedly can increase a site's traffic by several thousand visitors in one day. An employee of the label can post links without relying on the publishers of other URL's to link to them by targeting blogs and message boards. Chat rooms can also be targeted, and scripts or 'bots' can be developed to systematically enter chat rooms and post a link. However, these scripts are often identified as bogus by users and hosts

Another basic way to build traffic is by targeting returning users through building an opt-in mailing list. A field on the main page of the site where visitors can receive weekly or monthly news regarding the label develops a closer relationship with users and will encourage them to use the site more often. Enticing visitors to sign up is easy by providing giveaways of related items like CDs, concert tickets, and posters. Separating the subscribers by zip code or country and sending appropriate regional tour dates can better target the user and assist in the identification of markets interested in the label or particular promotions.

Physical Web Store

A web store provides an easy to maintain retail outlet where the label receives 100 percent of the revenue and builds a direct relationship with the customer. Most web store applications can be customized and implemented at the time of the site's design. There are also web stores with templates are also available with installation for as low as a couple of hundred dollars. The major factors to consider when building a web store are functionality, ease of use, transaction reliability, speed, and security.

Another important decision when building a store is the payment method. Credit card transaction services usually cost a small business as little as $30 per month to maintain. However, the variable cost of running a transaction, which is generally a percentage of the purchase price, lessens as the amount of purchase increases. These variable costs have a minimum payment. Until recently this minimum payment has deterred the per track purchase of music. Micropayment services and services that bundle small payments into a few transaction charges per day are emerging as a solution for low cost online purchases. Another solution is using a payment system that externally interfaces with the user and where the user signs up for payment offsite like Paypal. There is no fixed cost, although the cost to the label per sale is higher.

Building a Digital Web Store

Record companies building their own digital stores are quickly becoming a reality. Now that the framework of building a digital store has already been developed and has become cheaper to build and maintain, record companies are creating their own. Labels like Touch and Go, Merge, Thrill Jockey, Warp, Sub Pop and Beggars Group were some of the first to build a digital store because many record companies do not want to rely on retailers like iTunes, because they do not agree with many of the terms of sale. Labels want the flexibility and control to sell digitally on their own terms and to cut out a third party's revenue on their catalog. The same basic concerns like functionality, payment method, and security apply to a digital store as they do to a physical one. The technology behind the delivery of the digital music to the consumer reliably and securely is a major hurdle. However, there are companies in the marketplace that can help implement tools to establish a well running digital store. Undoubtedly the music industry will see many of the larger labels launching their own digital retail stores in the near future.

Providing Technology Support to Other Departments
While the technology department is responsible for the aforementioned roles within the company, it can also provide much needed support and enhancement to other departments. The following are some examples of how new media works with other departments.

Radio. The radio department's role is simply to get recorded product played on radio. The New Media Department can assist in this effort by helping deliver singles electronically to radio stations. Technology can complement the list of traditional radio stations with emerging satellite and online radio stations, while also providing content for radio stations, blogs, and podcasts.

Video. As mentioned earlier in the chapter, video is more important than ever for large and small music companies. The tech department can help not only promote, but now also sell videos.

Publicity. Publicity is now as important online as it is in magazines, newspapers, and other traditional media. Not only can the technology department manage the Internet component of a publicity campaign, it can also provide traditional publicists with tools like e-Cards, video, streaming audio, and digital photos so that they have what they need to better approach their contacts.

Sales. Like with the publicity department, new media can add its own contribution to sales with digital and other online avenues, but it can also help to increase physical sales in stores by providing assets to store buyers like e-Cards, videos, audio, to encourage them to sell the artist. Meanwhile, successful online promotional campaigns create a larger demand for releases in stores.

Combating Piracy, P2P, etc.

The major topic in technology and music over the past ten years has been the piracy of music. The music industry's actions against pirates so far have been largely futile. The pirates range from the large peer-to-peer file trading companies like Limewire, to the Russian pirate download stores like Allofmp3.com, to the torrent trackers like Pirate Bay and Mininova, and to individual CD copiers, file traders, and bootleggers. Innovations like copy-protected CD's generally either do not work, are not effective, or do not work in a manner appealing to consumers. As the record industry accomplishes one thing to combat piracy, another major threat presents itself. There are many methods that exist to fight piracy, but not to stop it. Monitoring P2P and other services and implementing a number of tactics including swarming files on a server until they can no longer be accessed, inserting "dummy" inoperable tracks to frustrate users, legal action including cease and desist letter and lawsuits, and even lobbying Congress can help. It is the tech department's job to identify these potential threats and to act accordingly.

TECHNOLOGICAL HIGHWAY/GETTING IT ALL DONE

Outsourcing Technology vs. In-house Technology

With the industry changing so rapidly, it is often difficult to stay informed of new developments and emerging trends, even for the most tech savvy record label. While many labels choose to develop and maintain their own technology, many choose to outsource their needs for new media promotion and distribution. This concept is not new. Many labels, especially the smaller ones, outsource to publicists, radio promotion companies, and exclusive distributors. Toolshed Media (www.toolshed.biz) has represented some of the most successful independent labels in the world. Toolshed manages online promotional campaigns for labels, such as Matador, Rough Trade, Touch and Go, Mute, and Rykodisc. They maintain their own online press extranet and push the releases they are representing to hundreds of websites. Toolshed can also help labels negotiate the agreement between digital retailers and the label.

Beyond publicity, there are a number of areas where outsourcing to a third party can be more effective. Digital distributors with the storage, databases, content management systems, and contract negotiation experience can facilitate distribution batched in the various proprietary format and metadata specifications. This expense is considerably less than building an infrastructure within the walls of the record label. Also, the digital retailers are more and more resistant to signing direct deals with independent labels because they do not have the staff to maintain so many relationships. Reputable companies that manage the needs of a number of the larger independent companies in this arena include Consolidated Independent (www.consolidatedindependent.com), IRIS Distribution (www.irisdistribution.com), The Orchard (www.theorchard.com) and Independent Online Distribution Alliance (www.iodalliance.com). A label signs a termed agreement with one of these agencies, and they represent the digital catalogue. They can usually do this better than the label can internally. Many exclusive physical distributors like ADA and RedEye have developed their own digital distribution representation departments as well and operate much like the physical distribution does in putting the music in the digital stores and then collecting a percentage of the revenue.

Piracy protection can be outsourced as well. Companies like Media Defender and Web Sheriff identify piracy threats throughout the world and combat them on behalf of the label according to priority and budget. They also specialize in using these same feared services to virally promote artists by intentionally "leaking" audio and video.

With any project, the choice of whether to outsource technology versus doing everything within the company hinges on two factors. First, will it be less expensive to use another company's technology? If that exact technology already exists, using theirs may be a far better idea than building from scratch. Second, who will do a better job? Will another company do a better job because that is their specialty, or will it be done best in house? Answering these two questions with the proper research and analysis should lead any technology manager to the correct answer.

Technology Manager's Role in Small Labels vs. Large Labels

We've explored the major areas of technology management at today's record company in this chapter. These areas do not differ all that greatly from the smallest one person operation to a major record company employing thousands. The goal for all of these companies is to identify the technologies that contribute to the buying habits of music fans. The next step is to utilize these technologies to generate as much profit as possible from the label's catalog whether it is from an artist's exposure or from sales.

Major record labels may have an advantage because of their size, resources, and influence within the industry. These labels often have entire departments devoted to the online marketing of one album and another department solely concentrating on digital retail. Massive marketing campaigns by a major label promotes a new album to hundreds of millions of potential buyers.

Meanwhile, a small label has its employees to do a little of everything. The technology department may also be the person in charge of sales or publicity or both. Too little time and too few resources always challenge small labels. However, one advantage that small labels have over the larger ones is the their ability to react quickly. Technology is constantly changing the competitive marketplace of music, and large companies are usually hesitant and slow to shift its resources into emerging areas. Conversely, a small company can move into a new area of promotion and sales almost instantly. This is why smaller companies are typically the most innovative and creative. The owner of a small company, who is also on the front lines of selling their music, sees an opportunity or has an idea and then has the ability to react quickly.

CONCLUSION

Technology management at today's record labels is important regardless of the size of the company, the number of employees, or the number of releases in the catalog. The way fans enjoy their music is changing faster than the music industry has ever seen. Having someone who understands these changes in promotion, retail, distribution, and other avenues, and who can manage them effectively is someone that no music company can afford to be without. There are arguably more employment, leadership, and entrepreneurial opportunities in the technology side of the music industry currently than any other area. While major record companies continue to merge and downsize, they are clamoring to embrace the new ways in which their music is being discovered, purchased, and enjoyed. While all labels find it more difficult to consistently get commercial airplay, land on magazine covers, and sell CDs, the music industry is increasingly, placing the controls more in the hands of technology managers. These are the individuals who will be steering the industry's future.

INDEX

Want to keep up with news about the music industry?

Now that you've read this book and understand something about the music business, you know how fast things change in this ever-changing, ever-evolving industry. The authors think it would be great if we could provide you with a way to stay current. So we have devised *Understanding the Music Business Updates.* Your purchase of this book entitles you to receive up-to-the-minute updates as we publish them, and enables you to keep current in the field. Go to: **unopress.uno.edu** and give them this information:

Name _____

Email Address _____

College, school, or work _____

How you purchased this book _____

That's all you need to do to receive our updates. So register now while you are thinking about it.

Enjoy!

Harmon Greenblatt and Irwin Steinberg

_____